THE SUFI BOOK OF LIFE

Neil Douglas-Klotz, Ph.D. (Saadi Shakur Chishti), is a world-renowned scholar in religious studies, spirituality, and psychology, and a leader in the International Association of Sufism. An American living in Edinburgh, Scotland, he is codirector of the Edinburgh Institute for Advanced Learning and cochair of the Mysticism Group of the American Academy of Religion. He is also a founder of the worldwide network of the Dances of Universal Peace. A frequent speaker and workshop leader, he is the author of several books, including *The Genesis Meditations* and *Prayers of the Cosmos*.

The *Sufi* Book of *Life*

99 Pathways of the Heart
for the Modern Dervish

Neil Douglas-Klotz

PENGUIN
COMPASS

PENGUIN COMPASS
Published by the Penguin Group
Penguin Group (USA) Inc., 375 Hudson Street, New York, New York 10014, U.S.A.
Penguin Group (Canada), 90 Eglinton Avenue East, Suite 700, Toronto,
Ontario, Canada M4P 2Y3 (a division of Pearson Penguin Canada Inc.)
Penguin Books Ltd, 80 Strand, London WC2R 0RL, England
Penguin Ireland, 25 St Stephen's Green, Dublin 2, Ireland
(a division of Penguin Books Ltd)
Penguin Group (Australia), 250 Camberwell Road, Camberwell,
Victoria 3124, Australia (a division of Pearson Australia Group Pty Ltd)
Penguin Books India Pvt Ltd, 11 Community Centre, Panchsheel Park,
New Delhi – 110 017, India
Penguin Group (NZ), 67 Apollo Drive, Rosedale, North Shore 0632,
New Zealand (a division of Pearson New Zealand Ltd)
Penguin Books (South Africa) (Pty) Ltd, 24 Sturdee Avenue,
Rosebank, Johannesburg 2196, South Africa

Penguin Books Ltd, Registered Offices:
80 Strand, London WC2R 0RL, England

First published in Penguin Compass 2005

ScoutAutomatedPrintCode

Copyright © Neil Douglas-Klotz, 2005
All rights reserved

Pages 290–291 constitute an extension to this copyright page.

LIBRARY OF CONGRESS CATALOGING IN PUBLICATION DATA
Douglas-Klotz, Neil.
The Sufi book of life : 99 pathways of the heart for the modern dervish /
Douglas-Klotz Neil.
p.   cm.
Includes bibliographical references.
ISBN 978-0-14-219635-9
1. Sufism.   I. Title.
BP189.6.D68 2005
297.4'4—dc22   2004053402

Printed in the United States of America
Set in Guardi Roman
Designed by Sabrina Bowers

For
Hazrat Pir Moineddin Jablonski (1942–2001), friend and teacher—
a "comrade of the tulip and the rose"

Contents

Quick-Start Guide   xiii
Introduction   xvii

Setting Out on the Journey   1
0. The Yes and No of Existence   4
1. The Sun of Love   7
2. The Moon of Love   9
3. The "I Can" Power of the Cosmos   12
4. Sacred Space   14
5. Peace at the Beginning   17
6. Support   19
7. Protection   21
8. The Strength of Form   24
9. Repair and Restoration   27
10. Concentration   29
11. Carving and Forming   32

Bathing in Unity   34

12. Radiating Creativity   35
13. Designing and Training   37
14. Burning Away Tension and Hurt   39
15. Natural Power   42
16. Flowing Blessings   45
17. Sustenance   47
18. Opening to Unity's Breath   49
19. Understanding Names and Forms   51
20. Contracting Boundaries   34

21. Expanding Boundaries   56
22. Diminishment   58

Bathing in Unity   61

23. Exaltation   63
24. High "Self" Esteem   65
25. Low "Self" Esteem   67
26. Awakened Hearing   70
27. Awakened Sight   72
28. The Sacred Sixth Sense   74
29. Putting Things in Order   77
30. Subtle Mystery   80
31. The Seed of Potential   82
32. Dissolving Chains   84
33. Flexible Strength   87

Bathing in Unity   89

34. The Forgiveness of Light   92
35. Gratitude, Giving Back   95
36. Experiencing Life at Its Peak   97
37. Outward Creative Power   100
38. Remembrance and Preservation   103
39. Embodying a Steady State   106
40. Feeling Divinity in the Details   108
41. Pooling Strength   110
42. Abundant Expression   113
43. Watching with Presence   116
44. Reflective Listening   119

Bathing in Unity   121

45. The Heart Has No Limits   122
46. Discriminating Wisdom   125
47. Love Is a Give and Take   128
48. Dazzling Energy   131
49. The Return of What Passes Away   134
50. Experiencing a Universe of Unity   137
51. The Truth in Each Moment   140
52. Meeting Challenges   142
53. Winds of Change   145

54. Step-by-Step Persistence 147
55. Friendship 150

Bathing in Unity 152

56. The Gift of Purpose 154
57. Assessing What Is 156
58. Individuated Creation 158
59. Reviving What Is Worn Down 160
60. Personal Life Energy 163
61. Transition 166
62. Universal Life Energy 168
63. Rebounding 172
64. Extraordinary Sensing 174
65. Channeling Extraordinary Power 177
66. Counting to One 180

Bathing in Unity 183

67. Uniquely One 184
68. Refuge for Every Need 186
69. Holding the Center 189
70. Embodying Power in Action 192
71. Preparing the Way 195
72. Doubling Back on the Path 198
73. Sacred Surprise 201
74. Completion 203
75. The Star 206
76. The Hidden Traveler 208
77. Mastering Life 210

Bathing in Unity 213

78. Inhabiting an Expanded Consciousness 215
79. Burnishing 218
80. Returning to Rhythm 221
81. Sweeping Out 223
82. Blowing Away the Ashes 226
83. Healing Wings 228
84. Passionate Vision 230
85. Overwhelming Power and Beauty 233
86. New Roots, New Foundation 236

87. Gathering Gems   238
88. Tending Your Garden   241

Bathing in Unity   243

89. Life's Larger Garden   244
90. The Gift of Resistance   246
91. Pain and Loss   248
92. Immediately Useful Blessing   250
93. The Light of Intelligence   253
94. Most Direct Guidance   256
95. Unexpected Wonder   259
96. The Real That Remains   261
97. Reclaiming a Forgotten Inheritance   264
98. Illuminating the Path of Growth   267
99. Perseverance   270

Bathing in Unity   273

Biographies of Sufis Cited   275
Contacts for Sufi Teachings   283
Formal Transliterations
    of the Pathways of the Heart   288
Acknowledgments   290
Notes   292
Bibliography   295
Index   301

Quick-Start Guide

NINETY-NINE PATHWAYS OF THE HEART
FOR THE MODERN DERVISH

Don't start by reading this book from the beginning. Instead, open it at random a few times and read what you find. If something strikes you, stay with it. You will likely discover some things you can identify with immediately and others that seem like they are from another planet. If you first try to read the book from start to finish, you may not be able to face so many seemingly paradoxical corners of your heart all at once.

Don't worry about "getting the point." The Sufi teaching stories scattered throughout the book work on many different levels. The obvious meaning or moral shows only the surface level. The rest of the story works "below ground," so to speak, in your subconscious. If you get a chuckle or even a "humph!" from a story, it's probably having its effect.

Browse consciously. Read the preface, "Setting Out on the Journey." Then take some time each day, perhaps before bed, to familiarize yourself with some of the pathways. Each one presents a quality of feeling, sensation, or experience. Some may be familiar to you, some may not. Some pathways seem to contradict others. Some pathways connect to others, as I have indicated in the Roots and Branches section of each chapter (for instance, themes of work, love, power, relationships, and so forth). Do any of the qualities or challenges speak to your situation in life right now?

Forage. When confronted by a situation in life in which you would like some guidance, take a breath or two with your hand placed lightly over your heart to calm yourself, then open the book at random, as you would an oracle. This may be the best way for the new user to experience the pathways. If you use the book this way, you might also want to read the pathways immediately before and after the one to which you've opened. The Sufis have used lists of the pathways of the heart in this way for more than a thousand years. The Meditation section of each pathway suggests ways to contemplate or experience the quality. The default meditation is simply to breathe in your heart with the feeling of what you have read.

Cut up the book. Or you can photocopy and enlarge the table of contents, cut the list of pathways apart, and place the pieces in a bowl. Take a breath and pick one. This is another way to use the pathways as an oracle, as mentioned above. Alternatively, a list of pathways that you can easily cut up is posted at www.sufibookoflife.com. This site will also link you to other sites where you can hear various traditional pronunciations of the practices.

Hunt. Perhaps you are consciously working on an issue in your life or psyche, or supporting other inner work such as counseling or psychotherapy. Check the table of contents or index for a topic that seems relevant and, still breathing in the heart, find what you need.

Read this book. After you have done all of the above for a while, begin to read the book from the beginning to the end. Take a break and put the book aside occasionally, so you don't get indigestion from meeting too many different facets of yourself. Just as wine tasters need to frequently clear their palates, you may need space from tasting the wines of your soul. To help you create this space, you will find several unnumbered chapters titled "Bathing in Unity" interspersed throughout the book. Use these to dive into the pure ocean of the Beloved before looking down another pathway.

A Note About "Bugs." The book's "program" has not been de-bugged. Actually, it has been re-bugged. Paradox and foolishness are built in, as is what is deeply serious. Sufism is a living twenty-first-century tradition with many different approaches. Expressions in the book such as "a Sufi would say . . ." or "the Sufis . . ." should not be taken to imply that there is one unified Sufi way of being or acting. The program is incompatible with any attempts to use it to find a consistent philosophy, metaphysic, or history that can be called "Sufi." The programmers take no responsibility for your rational system crashing under these circumstances.

> *Your heart is the browser.*
> *The pathways are the search engine.*
> *The universe is the real Internet.*
> *And there are many addresses to the Beloved,*
> *whose server is always online.*

Introduction

A CCORDING TO A NUMBER of news sources, the bestselling poet in the English language today is Jelaluddin Rumi, a thirteenth-century Persian Sufi. Is this good news for Sufism, or bad news for the state of English poetry?

Both Rumi and Hafiz (who lived a generation later) have entranced readers because they emphasize passionate love. We are all looking for love, and while we may not know what the word means, we know love when we feel it. Sufi poetry speaks eloquently and passionately about the Beloved, and about intoxication, longing, lust, misunderstanding, and mistaken identity (of both lover and beloved). That is, all the stuff of life and soap opera. What makes Sufi poetry and story different from soap opera, however, is that they take place in a kind of magical universe of long ago and far away, a universe in which some greater, benign Reality encloses everything.

Most contemporary English poets would reject the whole context of Sufi poetry as romantic and idealistic. What matters today is today's world, one in which we construct our own meaning. We can't be anywhere but here, slogging along in the bleak reality of postmodern life.

Try telling that to the millions of people who are reading Sufi poetry. Their response is the good news for Sufism.

The bad news is that most people reading Rumi and Hafiz would like to bridge the gap between reading about divine love and actually experiencing it, but don't know how. They have been led to believe (often by some academic or scholarly source) that Sufis only lived long ago and far away, where they wore robes and turbans and spoke with foreign accents. Nothing could be further from the truth.

Sufism is a living twenty-first-century tradition, with many different approaches and practices. Authentic Sufis speak in all languages, and may wear completely ordinary clothing. The word *dervish* means one who sits in the doorway, or on the threshold of something, ready to move on and transform him- or herself. This book is for modern dervishes, people who want to start living the Sufi poetry of love. It is based on this writer's experience following the Sufi path for the past thirty years and applying it to everyday life.

If Sufism is a living spiritual path today, why isn't it better known?

The twelfth-century Sufi Saadi once said, "You can get ten dervishes under a blanket, but you can't get two kings to share the same continent." However, in the modern era it has seemed more like wherever you have two Sufis together, you have three opinions. Since the Indian Sufi Inayat Khan brought a form of Sufism to the West in 1910, many different groups and teachers have arrived.

Most Sufi books have presented academic, historical, or philosophical information on the tradition, designed to appeal to the intellect. Some contemporary teachers have presented their own work and approaches, which often seem contradictory to the work of others. This has actually been a blessing, since unlike some other traditions, Sufism has not been organized to the extent that its wild character has been tamed.

Historically, diversity has been Sufism's strength. It is ultimately a nomadic tradition, one that has constantly deconstructed and transplanted itself rather than settle and build gigantic shrines, institutions, monolithic rituals, or organizations. There is no Sufi Vatican or Potala. Rumi, for instance, was well positioned to take over his father's business, being the main Sufi preacher of Konya, but along came his spiritual soulmate Shams-i-Tabriz. Rumi gave up his ordered way of life, spent all his time with Shams, and ultimately became a broken-hearted dervish who created the greatest oriental poetry in history. Ibn Arabi could have remained in Spain and built up a large following, but instead he chose to spend most of his life moving from place to place. On the other hand, when the Sufis have been co-opted by the establishment (as in the late Ottoman Empire), they have usually experienced serious problems. We Sufis are itinerant and like our freedom, which is probably also why we usually agree to disagree.

Who (or What) Is a Sufi?

Sufism is, first of all, a series of "not's"—not a religion, not a philosophy, not even a mysticism, as that word is usually conceived. It's best to call Sufism a way of experiencing reality as love itself. The modern Sufi writer Massud Farzan said it well and succinctly:

Sufism is a unique phenomenology of Reality. The psychology of Sufism is Sufism itself; the art and science of Sufism is the very practice of Sufism.[1]

Given such a slippery definition, is it possible to talk about any kind of "pure Sufism" today? A person with common sense would say no, but this has not stopped scholars and Sufis themselves from attempting to answer this question. Even the relationship of Sufism to Islam is fraught and may be another reason why Sufism as a path is not more popular today in the West. Is Sufism, as the more simplistic dictionary definitions maintain, the "mystical side of Islam"? Does Sufism (or its philosophy or practices) predate Islam? Is Sufism "the real Islam" (just as some people would maintain that such Christian mystics as Meister Eckhart or St. Francis of Assisi represent the real teachings of Jesus, more than any form of the institutional church)? Here is a typically Sufi answer, again given by Massud Farzan:

Does Sufism, derived from Koran and Mohammedan tradition, go against the sayings of the Book and the Prophet? The answer is yes and no. Insofar as Sufism strips the dogma from the religion and goes to its heart, insofar as it insists on the reality beyond the ritual, the thing behind the symbol, Sufism is at once Islam par excellence *and distinctly apart from it.*[2]

Inayat Khan had this to say:

[A]ccording to the sacred history which the Sufis have inherited from one another, it is clear that Sufism has never been owned by any race or religion, for differences and distinctions are the very delusions from which Sufis purify themselves. It might appear that Sufism must have been formed of the different elements of various religions which are prominent today, but it is not so, for Sufism itself is the essence of all the religions as well as the spirit of Islam.[3]

There is no doubt that Sufism and Islam have an intimate relationship. What people disagree about is how one defines the words *sufism* and *islam*. Literally, the word *islam* means "surrender" to the one Ground of Reality, not to some thought-form or dogma. The

xx   o—   *Introduction*

word *sufism* derives from a word that simply means "wisdom," and the Qur'an itself advocates "seeking wisdom, even as far as China." Historically, Sufis have not adhered to any one school of Quranic interpretation or jurisprudence, and this has made the fundamentalists of all ages very nervous, even up to the present day, when some Islamic countries outlaw the practice of Sufism.

Whether this is reassuring or disturbing will depend upon your point of view. Does the history matter? To some it will, and to some it will not. It depends upon, in the words of the modern American Sufi Samuel Lewis, whether you want to allow your concepts to get in the way of the solution to your problems. And the main "problem" for most of us is the purpose of life itself.

Purpose and Organization of This Book

This book proposes to take the reader into the living experience of Sufism. It follows a genre that is hundreds of years old, called a "dervish handbook," a companion to life's experience. In one sense, this book presents a series of short essays or contemplations, illustrated by Sufi stories and poetry. Each chapter includes meditations and suggestions for further pathways to explore. In a deeper sense, it illustrates a way of approaching life in order to discover fully who we are, as completely human beings.

As you might guess, the Sufi training is not like going through classes in a school. Although some classical Sufis proposed that seekers progress through certain stages, made up of expanded states of awareness (*ahwal*), which then settle into the more stable ways of living everyday life (*maqamat*), life doesn't organize itself in a linear way. So, all attempts to organize Sufi teachings in this way are inherently artificial, or at least up for revision every generation.

This book conveys the most essential practice shared by Sufis of all historical streams—the meditation on the heart qualities of the sacred (called *al Asma ul Husna,* or "the most beautiful names"). In this book, I am translating the same word (*asma*) as "pathways" in addition to "qualities" or "names" in order to emphasize the dynamic experience of the practice. I have not yet encountered a Sufi tradition, group, or order that does not use these practices. Any of these pathways of the heart can lead you to experience life with deeper feeling and more insight if you approach the practice at the right time. You need only one pathway, if you relentlessly follow it to its source.

In the Sufi tradition, as we move toward becoming fully human, we revive an inner ecology and diversity of spirit. We feel and understand more in life because we can recognize it as a part of our own soul. Both freedom and joy come with being at home in the heart, a heart that we gradually discover to be much wider than we thought. The various pathways may seem to contradict each other (just like life). They are not neatly organized and proportional (just like life). They do work, at least in my experience.

One of the first renditions of these practices in English was Edwin Arnold's *Pearls of the Faith,* published in 1882. Arnold's book took the form of a small volume of Victorian poetry, a format that cultivated English-speaking people of his time could assimilate. We now live in a much different era, one of the Internet and mass media, and a Sufi must be adaptable, if nothing else. On its surface, this book appears to fit into the "how-to," self-improvement genre, a format that mirrors Western culture's desire to receive things quickly and easily. We might bemoan this tendency as counterproductive to a spiritual life: What is easy is not necessarily better, and responding quickly often does not leave much time for reflection or feeling. Most self-help books want only to reconfirm what we already know. They aim for an "uh-huh," not an "aha!" I would call this self-hypnosis rather than self-help.

This book attempts to subvert the simplistic side of the self-help genre by building in various Sufi features, including randomness, paradox, and spiritual practice. As noted in the Quick-Start Guide, one can use this book as an oracle or search within it to find appropriate wisdom for the moment. What the reader finds under these circumstances may be surprising or even disturbing. Hopefully, it will be illuminating.

Viewed through the lens of Sufism, the self-help genre may be perfectly appropriate. For most of its history, Sufism has operated as a kind of do-it-yourself tradition. We have no overall leader, potentate, or pope (which is not to say that some people haven't tried to establish themselves, or someone else, as one). The Sufi guide is more a cross between a companion, therapist, and trickster than an almighty guru, and Rumi once said that ultimately the real *pir* (senior spiritual director) is Love itself.

Updated for the twenty-first century, the pathways of the heart function very much like a search engine to the Internet of life, with our heart acting as the browser through which we view the world, inside and out.

Some Words About the Words

In order to cultivate the proper reverence for the divine, most previous books and lists have translated the Arabic names or qualities in the pathways using only the language of transcendence. These translations can encourage us to see the qualities of the One as always outside of us, which suggests that we need to ingest them, like vitamins. Devotion is an important fuel for the path, but mandatory reverence is not. We have a very different relationship to "religion" today than did our ancestors, who mostly lived in societies where behavior was dictated from above. When we use only the language of transcendence, we receive the impression that these practices are magic formulas by which we can compel the divine to fulfill our wishes. Such language, whatever its intent, encourages us to see prayer and spiritual practice as a type of bargaining. The modern Sufi M. R. Bawa Muhaiyaddeen comments on this tendency:

> For what purpose are we supposed to recite these names? For what purpose do they tell us to shout in the supermarket? It is to buy the market produce that we desire in our minds. . . .
> You may recite His names 1000 times for this, 7000 times for that, and 8000 times for the other, but even if you recite it 50,000 times you will not receive anything. Why? Because God has already given everything to you. You have only to open that treasury within your qalbs (hearts) and take out what has already been given.[4]

The classical Sufi tradition contains a very strong emphasis on the divine unity of all life (called *tawhid*). In this view, shared by Rumi, Ibn Arabi, and many others (and justified by a reading of the Qur'an itself), the whole creation came into existence to express the unlimited, sacred qualities through all beings. In particular, God created the human being as a mirror capable of holding and expressing the totality of the divine reflection, including the whole consciousness of nature and the universe. This is what, in the Sufi view, being fully human means. In this sense, as Bawa Muhaiyad-deen notes, we already have all the pathways of the heart within us.

Despite the emphasis on the unity of being, devotional practice, phrased in an I–Thou manner, is essential on the Sufi path. It teaches us to let go of our own limiting concepts and helps us open our hearts to a wider dimension of feeling. Similarly, modern 12-step programs propose that we do not really feel the impetus to change until life becomes unmanageable, and we decide to let go and try another way.

This development of devotion in what the Sufis call the path of ef-facement (*fana*) presents, however, only one side of the story. We also find a parallel development in the evolution of the self, or *nafs*. The latter word is often mistranslated in versions of Sufi poetry as the "animal self." We can best see the *nafs* (a term consistent with the old Hebrew *nephesh* and Jesus' Aramaic *naphsha*) as a fluid soul-self. This includes what modern psychology calls the "subconscious." Really, the *nafs* is more a way of looking at the whole self from a subcon-scious viewpoint rather than as a separate self inside a self (like Rus-sian *matrushka* dolls). From this view, we have within us an inner community of evolving voices, some of which contradict each other. Similarly, some modern psychologies work with a male and female inner self, or an inner judge or child. Sufi psychology expands this inner community to include a whole ecosystem, including non-human voices such as plants and animals. These "basic selves" are here to be transformed, to realize their unity of "one to the One."

In my experience, the practices of the pathways of the heart, when approached with devotion, can radically transform one's sub-conscious reality. This new translation therefore approaches these pathways as though they are all already within us, waiting to be rec-ognized and reunited in the circle of the heart's unity with the divine Beloved.

Personal Background

I grew up in a multicultural American family, hearing German, Yid-dish, Polish, Russian, and English. Perhaps this made it easier for me to work with foreign languages later. In addition, even though my brothers and I were raised outwardly as protestant Christians, my parents were both interested in spirituality, ecology, and holistic healing. When I went on my own spiritual search in my twenties, I felt I needed to find something that would include everything I had already experienced and allow me to continue to explore the depth of my being. Because Sufism honored all the prophets and messengers who had preceded Muhammad, I found that I could include my deep love for Jesus in my own developing spiritual practice.

I have had the benefit of studying or receiving teaching from a number of Sufis, East and West, over the past thirty years, including Pir Vilayat Inayat Khan, Pir Hidayat Inayat Khan, Pir Shabda Kahn, Murshida Fatima Lassar, Murshid Wali Ali Meyer, Murshida Vera Corda, the Rev. Frida Waterhouse, the Rev. Joe and Guin Miller, Irina Tweedie, Sheikh Suleiman Dede of Konya, Sheikh Muzaffer Ashki al-Jerrahi, Pir Sufi Barkat Ali, Shah Nazar Seyed Ali Kianfar, Nahid Angha, and others.

My primary teacher was Hazrat Pir Moineddin Jablonski, the spiritual successor of Hazrat Murshid Sufi Ahmed Murad Chishti (Samuel L. Lewis, d. 1971), who was himself a student of Hazrat Inayat Khan (d. 1927). My teacher exemplified a complete approach to spiritual practice in his work with students. He realized that an unbalanced emphasis on transcendence in spiritual practice delays spiritual growth. He built upon the work of another of his teachers, Frida Waterhouse, and developed what he called "Soulwork," a new way to do psychospiritual counseling based on the ancient path of Sufism.

Although I have written a number of other books on Middle Eastern spirituality and an Aramaic approach to the words of Jesus over the past fifteen years, I didn't feel that it was appropriate to write a book on Sufism while my own teacher was still around in the body. When Moineddin left his body behind in 2001, my inner life shifted. He had encouraged me in all my translation work, and when he left it seemed time to reap the harvest of the work I had done on the pathways of the heart since 1976. Through his friendship, counseling, and wisdom, Moineddin showed me a way to live an ordinary human life, unaffected by the world of "hype" that today surrounds even spirituality and spiritual teachers. In many ways, he saved my life, and I have dedicated this book to him.

The translation work in this book is also inspired by Hazrat Haji Shemsuddin Ahmed, my Pakistani Qur'an teacher, who passed away about twenty years ago. A friend of Samuel Lewis's, Shemsuddin taught traditional methods of interpreting and translating the Qur'an on various levels of meaning. Because Semitic languages such as Arabic use a root-and-pattern system, one can literally—that is, by the letters—translate various words in a number of different ways. In addition, through these roots, sacred words like those in the pathways of the heart show their affinity to each other through families of meaning.

So this type of translation is not simply a matter of looking a word up in a dictionary. It is both sacred science and art. The translations here result from three decades of practice, and more than fifteen years of conscious work, in which the author has experienced all the pathways many times and worked to refine translations from the roots. The main difference between these translations and previous ones is that they presume that the names describe living spiritual experiences rather than simply metaphysical categories of a thought-form called "God."

Past translations have also used exclusively masculine language, which the Arabic original does not justify. For instance, even though the Arabic word *Allah* is usually gendered masculine, both the words *sifat* (referring to each divine quality of the One) and *dhat* (the divine essence, a sort of homeopathic combination of all possible qualities) receive the feminine gender. A number of classical Sufi writers have commented on this gender play in the Arabic of the Qur'an, which is virtually impossible to translate, given that English tends to make qualities and concepts grammatically neuter and only gender "persons."

All translations of Semitic languages such as Arabic, Hebrew, or Aramaic into English are by nature limited. Likewise, no one translation in any other language can hold all of the meaning of the pathways of the heart in Arabic. These translations are also limited by my own experience. They do offer the benefit of being internally consistent (the same roots are translated in the same way) and linguistically sound (different Arabic words are not translated in using the same English word, as they are in some previous translations).

When you use this book with an attitude of devotion, you benefit from a very strong line of transmission for these practices. In many of these sacred names, we see forms of phrases used for thousands of years in the Middle East, including by the Hebrew Prophets and Jesus. According to one scholar, early Middle Eastern Christians used as a similar practice 130 different names or attributes of Jesus in Syriac Aramaic, a language related to Arabic.

Normally, lists of the pathways of the heart are limited to ninety-nine qualities. Because the Qur'an contains more than ninety-nine such qualities of names of the One, different lists vary. This collection uses one of the most common lists as a basis. In addition, I have added chapters for the Arabic name of unity itself (*Allah*) and for the traditional phrase with which one begins an endeavor (*bismillah*). By one tradition, the names of Reality are countless, but starting with ninety-nine different ways of knowing yourself makes for a good beginning.

Do I Need a Teacher?

This book intends to serve as both a handbook for those on the path and a way to begin for those who are not. The effects of a spiritual practice vary according to whether it is intoned, spoken, sung, chanted, or breathed; whether it is done sitting, standing, walking, or lying; with a definite rhythm or tempo or without. The best way to do a spiritual practice is the way in which one's spiritual guide has given it, and in no way is this book meant to be a substitute for seeking such personal guidance. The relationship with a teacher and the blessing (or *baraka*) created by two people in a spiritual relationship remain the most active forces on the Sufi path. In the form in which we have them, the direct transmission of the Arabic sacred names that appear in the Qur'an is through the Prophet Muhammad. This provides both a blessing and a protection, and some Sufis believe that one can directly receive a transmission from a teacher whom one has never met in the flesh.

Many different Sufi teachers and groups now reside in the West. In one appendix, I have listed brief biographies of all the Sufis mentioned in the book. In another, I have detailed some of the Sufi groups, with which I am personally familiar, that carry on the transmission of these teachers today. In addition, the bibliography mentions a few of the many books on the various viewpoints on the background of Sufism. If this book is your first exposure to Sufi practice and you find some affinity with it, I would recommend going further. If you are already a practitioner, haven't been put off by what I have said so far, and want to renew your practice, you are welcome—*marhaba!* If you come with an eye to criticize, you will no doubt find many deficiencies, all of which are due to my own limitations, and not those of my teachers.

How does one go about looking for a teacher? First, do not imagine that a Sufi teacher will "fix" all your problems. A Sufi teacher does not operate the same way that a psychotherapist would (although many teachers today are also trained in some form of Western therapy). Rumi illustrates the way of the Sufi teacher in the following story:

> A man goes to a barber and says, "I have to go for a job interview. Can you cut all of these white hairs out of my beard?"
> "Certainly," says the barber, and proceeds to cut off the man's whole beard and wrap up the hairs. "Now take this home. You can sort out the white hairs for yourself."

The Sufi teacher does not analyze you; she or he is dedicated to transformation. In this regard, I usually tell people, "Go as far as you can on your own. When you've come to your limit, look for a guide."

Pronunciation of the Words

The question of the correct pronunciations of these names often arises. In Appendix C, the reader will find formal transliterations of each name from the Arabic, which indicate that there are different sorts of *h* and *a* sounds, for instance. Where necessary, the meditation portion of each listing mentions what I feel to be an important aspect of the pronunciation for experiencing the practice in an embodied way. Sometimes, I will suggest that you breathe into and sense your body awareness. Do not worry if this is unfamiliar at first. With experience, it becomes very natural. The "default setting" for each meditation is to breathe a gentle, full breath with one hand placed lightly over the heart to help you center there. I usually recommend preceding each quality with the sound *Ya* (meaning *O* in Arabic). This traditional prefix opens the heart and reminds us to respectfully address the particular quality of the sacred we are seeking within us.

Despite concerns about pronunciation, intoning or breathing sacred names in any of the Semitic language traditions has never been a matter of "correctness," which has to do with linguistics and who defines correctness in what context. Rather, practice has to do with spiritual experience. For this reason, we find that both Kabbalists and Sufis throughout the ages have used various pronunciations (and, some would say, mispronunciations) of sacred sounds in order to receive the richness of feeling-meaning in each letter. One sees this even in the construction in the Qur'an of "twin qualities," like *Ma'jid* and *Ma`jid*, or *Wa'li* and *Wa`li*, which vary in meaning according to their pronunciation. If you first center in the heart with a feeling of devotion, the correct rhythm and pronunciation will reveal themselves to you. If the Arabic seems too confusing, simply breathe in the heart with the feeling of each pathway after you have read it, which you can do while sitting or walking.

Calling a Circle of Your Inner Self

Some of the meditations recommend using a "round table" model of work with one's inner self. When working in this way, one seeks to figuratively invite and gather all aspects of one's inner being together and integrate them in the heart. Presiding over such sessions is your "highest guidance" (or high self), which is called in Sufi terminology the *ruh*. You can see this as the voice of your intuition, which is linked to your unique purpose in life. As mentioned, the "circle of selves" or "inner self" is the *nafs,* with its various voices, in various stages of evolution.

I also use the term "Wisdom's table" in the sense that the book of Proverbs mentions Holy Wisdom inviting all beings to a dinner party to eat and drink together. According to one reading of this, which is consistent with Sufi psychology, this dinner party symbolizes the way that consciousness arises. By gathering and integrating feelings, thoughts, and impressions, Holy Wisdom builds an "I," an awareness of self each moment. This gathering is also the way in which the various inner selves (the *nafs*) are born. All these feelings and impressions are really part of the only "I Am," Sacred Unity, but we can, and do, forget this connection. Learning the "wild and scenic" territory of one's own *nafs* is part of the Sufi path.

Besides Sufi Soulwork, other psychotherapeutic models that work on a similar basis include psychosynthesis (which some have argued is based on Sufism) and voice dialogue. In Sufi work, the divine Beloved is the Reality in which all events take place. Nothing is outside or excluded.

Unlike some other traditions, Sufism cannot be made scientific, rational, or secular to fit modern tastes. In order to discover deep love, the kind that Sufis have expressed in poetry, one must be willing to love. So, paradoxically, Sufism is a devotional tradition with a very ancient lineage, yet devoid of any set dogma or ritual. Perhaps the notion of devotion pushes your buttons because you have been bruised by organized religion in the past. Just because a love affair goes bad does not mean that love is unimportant. As I have mentioned, Sufism as a path is so wild and nomadic that if you find yourself feeling too enclosed or settled, you can strike your dervish campsite and move on.

One final note: When undertaking such work, do not monitor the progress of your inner self obsessively. If your highest guidance leads you to approach your inner self at the right time through one of these pathways, a seemingly small intervention can create large changes over time. Ultimately the most important growth happens in the "darkness" of our being—that is, when we're not looking. An old Hasidic story makes this point:

> One day a Hasid went to his Rebbe for help. "What I am doing wrong, master? I plant seeds in my garden but they never come up."
> "Tell me exactly what you're doing," said the Rebbe.
> "Well, every day I plant and water. Then at night, I go to sleep, but in the middle of the night, I wake up and get worried that the seeds might not be growing. So I go outside, dig them up and, sure enough, they're not growing!"
> "I think I understand your problem," said the Rebbe.

—SAADI SHAKUR CHISHTI (NEIL DOUGLAS-KLOTZ)
April 2004

The Sufi Book
of Life

Setting Out on the Journey

بسم الله

Bismallah

When you are guided to this pathway of the heart,
take a moment to breathe, and begin what you are
about to do wholeheartedly.

WHEN WE BEGIN ANYTHING new, much is unknown. We have plans, but will they work out? Can we be fully ourselves and still connect deeply with others? Is it possible to keep changing and growing, yet still maintain friendships and relationships over time? Each decision to love, to pursue something passionately, means a step into the unknown.

When we take time to meditate, or breathe momentarily in silence at the beginning of each day or year, each new job or relationship, we confront the unknown. This requires courage and heart. The Sufis often begin something new by breathing the Arabic word *bismillah*, which can be translated poetically:

We begin by remembering
the sound and feeling of the One Being,
the wellspring of love.
We affirm that the next thing we experience
shimmers with the light of the whole universe.

If we look at the world this way, then the reason we exist—and the reason to begin any journey—is to bring out our full humanity, the unique flavor that we alone can offer to the universe's still-cooking stew. According to the twelfth-century Sufi poet Saadi:

Every being is born for a certain purpose,
and the light of that purpose is kindled in its soul.

Yet, as physicists now tell us, we are inseparably linked to every-thing in the cosmos. We cannot do without each other. So how do we balance being an individual with being in a relationship?

Our individuality is a unique gift. Yet, the Sufi would say that the origin of this gift lies within the heart of the equally unique, divine "I Am" that fills the whole cosmos. Every blade of grass says, "I am!" as it expresses its selfhood. We can affirm that we can become fully integrated, fully human beings, deeply in contact with other people, with nature, and with the ultimate Source. It is yet another way of saying "bismillah!"

To the Sufi, each of these pathways is really like an e-mail address of the Beloved, which all go to the same in-box. Of course, the feel-ings, names, and qualities of the Sacred are really limitless. But find-ing ourselves capable of a hundred or so different feelings and responses to life is a good start toward self-knowledge and, ulti-mately, greater joy and fulfillment.

Perhaps life is calling you to begin something, an outer or inner quest. This path asks you to begin wholeheartedly, if you want your heart to still be in it at the end.

ᢒ Roots and Branches ᢒ

Traditional translations of bismillah are "in the name of God" or "with the name of Allah." From its roots, the word means, literally, "with, along with, or within (B) the sound, atmosphere, name, or light (SM) of Unity or the One Being (ALLAH)." In the Aramaic ver-sion of the Gospels, Jesus uses a similar expression when he men-tions praying "in my name" (b'sheme), which can also mean "with my sound or atmosphere." He points to a way of prayer native to the Middle East: If I bring myself into the same rhythm of breath or movement as a teacher or guide, that person becomes a door to re-connect me to the remembrance of sacred unity.

Meditation

With one hand lightly on your heart, breathe easily and gently. Feel the awareness of breath and heartbeat creating a clear, spacious place inside. Breathe with the sound of the word *bismillah* (BiS-MiL-LaaH). When we remember to connect our heart to the Heart of the Cosmos, we recall that, as the Sufis say, "God is your lover, not your jailer."

0. The Yes and No of Existence

Allah

When you are guided to this pathway of the heart,
take a moment to reflect on the quality in you that unites all qualities,
that joins the yes and no of your being.

A GOOD PLACE TO BEGIN any journey is to practice the feelings of affirmation and negation, so that when choices arise, we can really feel how each alternative resonates within our innermost being. This is one way we can clarify our own sense of affirmation or resistance. Knowing our own true *yes* and *no* is part of being fully human.

The feelings of *yes* and *no* connect to the most ancient names of the divine in the Middle East. These names use the root word *AL* (or *EL*), meaning the sacred Something, the ultimate Yes, coupled with the root *LA* (or *LO*), meaning the sacred Nothing, the ultimate No. People in the Middle East have used some form of this name for at least four thousand years, from the time of the Old Canaanite *Allat* or *Elat* (a name of the Middle Eastern Goddess), to the Hebrew *Elohim*, the Aramaic *Alaha* (used by Jesus), and the Arabic *Allah*, used by both Muslims and Arabic-speaking Christians today.

The thirteenth-century Sufi poet Jelaluddin Rumi beautifully expresses that the gulf between yes and no, individuality and relationship, diversity and unity, may be no more enduring than the wave that returns to the ocean:

I looked for my self, but my self was gone.
The boundaries of my being
had disappeared in the sea.
Waves broke. Awareness rose again.
And a voice returned me to myself.

It always happens like this.
Sea turns on itself and foams,
and with every foaming bit
another body, another being takes form.
And when the sea sends word,
each foaming body
melts back to ocean-breath.

Yes and no, existence and nonexistence, are built into the cells of our bodies. So if we can dive deeply enough into the heart, we will find the place where the two need not split us in two.

Perhaps life is calling you right now to let go into Unity, to release for a moment everything you think you know about yourself. As you begin to mine the gems you find on the pathways of the heart, remember to return repeatedly to the feeling of bathing in Unity's ocean. The many qualities of the heart can be overwhelming to the inner self. Yet the Qur'an says that the divine created all these qualities, capabilities, and feelings within us before we were born, at the very beginning of the cosmos, when it held us in its heart as part of the divine image reflected in the first human being. We can explore the divine wealth within us for our whole lives and still not exhaust the treasure hidden there.

❧ Roots and Branches ❧

Traditional translations of this name include "God" and "the One and Only." The final H of *Allah* affirms that there is yet a divine secret, something not heard or pronounced, the life behind all life, without name and form and beyond all our ideas of the divine. As one Sufi writer commented, "Allah" is really not "God"; that is, Allah points to a being that is beyond humanly constructed images, ideals, and names. It (not the name) is the ground of Reality, the Only Being. In lists of the "beautiful names," *Allah* is not counted as one of ninety-nine. To show that it is beyond numbering and yet includes all numbers, it is sometimes symbolically numbered zero, indicating both everything and nothing, being and nonbeing, infinity and each moment. Just as zero times any number equals zero, when any other quality is "multiplied" by this Reality, only the Reality remains.

Meditation

With a gentle hand on the heart, feel the breath rising and falling. While affirming "yes!" notice how the heart and breath react. What images arise? Then affirm "no!" and notice the difference. Then breathe with the wordless place that unites both the yes and no of existence. Feel your own breath as part of the breath and air that surround the whole planet.

With one hand lightly over your heart, intone the open sound *AhL* a few times. Feel the sound fill your chest with vibration, affirming your own part in the Sacred yes. The wave rises, a unique gift to the universe. Then intone the sound *LaH* a few times. Feel the sound clearing space in your chest, affirming your own part in the Sacred Void, the no of existence. The wave returns to the ocean, changed yet changeless. Which is easier to feel? Finally, intone both parts of the word and feel them connect, *AhL-LaH.* Be both the wave and the ocean.

1. The Sun of Love

الرَّحْمٰنُ

Ar-Rahman

When you are guided to this pathway of the heart,
take the opportunity to consider your ability to give deep,
wholehearted compassion.

"THE SUN SHINES ON the just and on the unjust," according to a saying of Jesus. The Sufi alchemists cultivated an ability to radiate love wholeheartedly, unconditionally, from the deepest part of themselves. Do not confuse this type of love with what people call "codependency." It is a natural, glowing, "sunny disposition." At times, we shine because we can't help it, because our light comes from a deeper source. This feeling causes a pregnant woman to glow from within, with the warmth of new life.

Like the other pathways of the heart, the Sufi would say that this "sun of love" is already part of one's own inner being. It lies waiting to be discovered. In the Arabic language, this word for love comes from the word for *womb*. This creative love and energy shine naturally from the deepest place inside us. We don't need to try. Each time we feel it, it's like giving birth to a new sense of ourselves.

In order to feel more deeply, and to bring that feeling into our own voices and actions, we may have to give up some ideas of who we think we are. Jesus said, "Seek and ye shall find." But the question here is this: Can we dare to allow ourselves to find, as well as to seek? The thirteenth-century Sufi poet Mahmud Shabistari compares this process to gambling:

The stakes are high for real prayer.
You must gamble your self
and be willing to lose.
When you have done this,
and your self shakes off

what you believed your self to be,
then no prayer remains,
only a sparkle of the eyes.
Knower and known are one.

Perhaps right now life is calling you to reach deeper within yourself for this source of compassion, or to remember it as you begin a new project, relationship, or phase of life. Or the message may be to first direct some of this compassion to your inner self. Even if you feel restricted and unable to shine outwardly, acknowledge and love this limited part of yourself unconditionally. Just as we are held within our mother's womb until the time is right for us to be born, we can think of our own limitations as a new self waiting to be born.

—◦ *Roots and Branches* ◦—

Traditional translations of this quality include "the compassionate" and "the merciful." *Rahman* and the name that follows, *Rahim,* are both derived from the old Middle Eastern Semitic root *RHM,* which points to a raying forth (*Ra*) from a deep, dense interiority (*HM*). As the Hebrew word *rahm,* it expresses the function of *womb.* Consider *Rahman* the so-called positive, active, or solar side of this creative love. The Qur'an uses the phrase *bismillah ar-rahman ar-rahim* at the beginning of all but one *sura* (or chapter) to indicate that the Reality we're talking about is both the "sun" and "moon" of deep love.

Meditation

Take a moment today to breathe in the heart. Then place your hands lightly over your belly as you expand the heart to include it, and breathe more and more deeply there. Feel a sun there, radiating warmth and positivity in all directions.

2. The Moon of Love

الرَّحِيمُ

Ar-Rahim

When you are guided to this pathway,
take the opportunity to consider your capacity to receive deep love
and compassion on all levels of your being.

*I*T'S EASY TO LOOK at how much love we're giving. Many self-help books venture to tell us how much is "too much." It's less often that we look at our own capacity to receive love. No matter how much is coming our way, if our cup is too small, it will overflow before the deepest part of our being feels anything. The Sufis have practices for developing a spacious container inside for thoughts, feelings, and sensations. What we can truly hold, we can also release. As the fourteenth-century Sufi Hafiz says:

The sun is the wine, the moon is the cup.
Pour the sun into the moon if you want to be filled.
Drinking such wine could be good or bad—
why not drink anyway!

When the sun is poured into the moon, deep joy happens. No one outside of ourselves can give us this joy. They can only remind us that we are already the wine, the cup, and the ecstasy.

Here's a story about how we sometimes receive love:

One day, a student of the legendary wise fool Mullah Nasruddin went to visit him at his home. Already expecting some crazy behavior on Mullah's part, he steeled himself to "not react." Another spiritual teacher once advised him, "If you react unconsciously, you push the lesson of the moment away."

When Mullah opened the door, he was overjoyed to see his student.

"My friend! Just in time . . . you can help me draw water from the well! Here, take this bucket and follow me!"

The student followed Mullah to the well and watched while he began to pull water from the well and splash it into the bucket the student was holding. "No problem," he thought to himself.

After a few moments, he began to notice that the level of the water in the bucket was not rising very quickly. Where was all the water going? Then he chanced to look underneath the bucket. It was leaking almost as much as Mullah put in each time. This went on for a while, and then, finally, the student couldn't take any more and cried out in exasperation:

"Mullah, you idiot! Can't you see that the bucket is leaking!"

"My friend," Mullah responded, "I was only looking at the top of the bucket. What does the bottom have to do with it?"

As frequently happens in Sufi stories, Mullah acts out and exaggerates a certain habit of mind in which many of us engage. We are so busy looking at how much we're getting right now that we don't notice how we've used what we've already received. In such a frame of mind, more is never enough—whether it's love, knowledge, or wealth—because our bucket has no bottom.

Perhaps life is calling you right now to ask these questions: How do I receive love, friendship, or any gift offered? Do I look at the top of the bucket or at the bottom? Do I estimate how much more I could receive, or do I consider the part of me that always feels unsatisfied? Is there a bottom to my bucket? This pathway reminds us that all new birth, including the birth of deep love, includes giving and receiving, pushing and letting go, radiating and reflecting.

﹋ Roots and Branches ﹋

Traditional translations of this quality include "the merciful" and "the compassionate." The roots of *Rahim* show the receptive side of the same womb-like compassion elicited by the previous pathway *Rahman*. The ending *-im* indicates that this raying-forth of warmth and creativity is received in an abundance of ways by an abundance of beings. Through this, it is related indirectly to pathways we encounter later, like *Karim* (42) and *Halim* (32). According to the Prophet Muhammad, *Rahman* expresses the divine love we see in the constant creation and re-creation of the universe. *Rahim* expresses the promise that divine love will respond to each and every individual need in the future.

Meditation

Breathe and center again in the heart. Feel its surface like a mirror, becoming clearer and clearer with each breath. Like the mirror of a telescope, this heart-mirror can receive and magnify light. Receiving love is not a matter of passivity. It calls for a different kind of concentration, focus, and strength than acting like the radiant sun. When you truly receive friendship or love, its effect grows. As the "moon of love," you can reflect almost as much light as when you are being the sun, and this love transforms the whole atmosphere around you.

3. The "I Can" Power of the Cosmos

المَلِك

Al-Malik

When you are guided to this pathway of the heart,
take the opportunity to focus on the "I Can!"—the vision-power—
of the cosmos coming through you.

NO COMPROMISE. NO NONSENSE. Sometimes in life you must decide to go for your own full realization as a human being, no matter what it takes. Usually it takes some great crisis to bring us to this point. Pain is often the greatest motivator when it comes to envisioning an entirely new life. Boredom and a habitual sense of "playing safe" keep this vision-power bottled up within us.

In many Sufi stories, a dervish shocks those around him into looking at life completely differently. The Sufis tell many stories like this about Jesus, whom they call "the breath of God" and revere as a great dervish:

> *One day Jesus was walking with his disciples when they saw a dead dog up ahead. The disciples wanted to pass on the other side, since the dog was considered unclean. But Jesus made them stop in front of it and look. Then he commented: "Look how beautifully white its teeth are!"*

Here Jesus forces his students to ignore meaningless superstition and find something totally unexpected—the reflection of divine light—in what they would otherwise have avoided. One of Jesus' famous sayings from the Gospel of Thomas could easily express the theme of this pathway:

> *If you give birth to what is within you*
> *the voices you redeem will redeem you.*
> *If you fail to find and give birth to them,*
> *they become part of what is destroying you.*[5]

Perhaps right now life is calling you to reconnect to your own sense of sacred vision-power, or to help others rediscover their own. This vision is not a fixed image or form. It is a dynamic, radiant quality that helps redefine and clarify what is important in life right now. According to the Sufi tradition, this pathway is the part of our being that bolsters our courage and power to be. A clear vision can empower us to go forward. Seeing, feeling power, and taking responsibility are not separate.

─✑ *Roots and Branches* ✑─

Traditional translations of this quality include "master" or "king." The ancient Semitic roots of *Malik* (*MLK*) go back to a time before there were either queens or kings in the Middle East, a time when the power to envision, decide, and take responsibility could mean life or death to a wandering people. The root of this word formed the name for the old clan and community leaders in the ancient Semitic languages (for instance, *malkatu* in Old Canaanite). The roots of *Malik* (*MLK*) point to empowerment, reign, counsel, and vision. Jesus frequently used the Aramaic form of this word (*malkuta,* which is gendered feminine) in sayings in which it is usually translated "kingdom." For instance, in the third line of his prayer (Matthew 6:10), he affirms, *teete malkutakh,* "Let your vision power, the 'I Can' of the cosmos, really come!" (usually translated as "thy kingdom come").

Meditation

Center again in the heart. Breathe with as much courage as you can muster—courage not to do, but to be. Only you have control over this. No one outside can stop or hinder you.

Walk and breathe with the words YA MALeeK in a definite rhythm of four (the last beat is a rest: ya-Ma-Leek-rest). Notice how the rhythm of your breath can become synchronized with that of your heartbeat, giving you more energy. Try walking down the street with this rhythm, and begin to feel your own heartbeat included in this divine quality of vision and empowerment.

✑──────✑

4. *Sacred Space*

القُدُّوس

Al-Quddus

When you are guided to this pathway,
take the opportunity to clear a sacred space inside to remember
what's really important in life.

A T TIMES, LIFE SEEMS like a perpetual series of appointments or a never-ending "to-do" list. Under these circumstances, how can we discover the "I Can" power and what we really want in life, as mentioned in the previous pathway?

The next pathway of the heart tells us that we need to undertake one of the most difficult spiritual practices of modern life: creating space for ourselves simply to be. This is not the same as stopping and dissolving into exhaustion (although this may be the first step). Creating sacred space demands that we bring some energy to the process. This means developing our feeling of staying within ourselves and being "at home." Here's what Rumi says about it:

> *When dust clouds your heart-glass,*
> *how can the mirror clear?*
> *Remove the dust and*
> *rays reveal your real face.*
> *Grape juice doesn't ferment overnight,*
> *that's why wine ages in a bottle.*
> *So if you want your heart to brighten,*
> *expect to exert yourself a bit!*

So it's another one of those good news/bad news situations. The good news is that, for the Sufi, there is much more to life than the surface of things—more love to give and to receive, more vision and energy. The bad news is that there is no easy way to get there. Yes, we may catch glimpses at any moment that alert us to what we're missing. But that's a far cry from saying that there is any easy way or "dummies' guide" to opening your heart. Anyone who tells you that is more interested in entertaining than guiding you (and probably more interested in what they can get from you than give to you).

In this pathway of the heart, creating space and learning to focus are linked. We create space for that which interests us most in life. Interest is a kind of love. And we'd prefer to choose our interest from our deepest heart, rather than have it imposed on us from the outside. For thousands of years, many people have found space to focus within by being in nature. Those of us who live in the city, therefore, have to work a bit harder. In addition, modern life draws our attention much more to the surface of things and to making fast decisions than did the life our ancestors faced. To engage our interest, we have unconsciously conspired with each other to create the subtle seductions of advertising, mass media, and shopping. The power of these tools, which can be seen as both blessings and curses, show how much energy and creativity lie waiting inside us. They demonstrate how powerful we could be if we took back our time and space from the plague of being busy.

Perhaps life is calling you right now to step out of the flow for a moment, to consider what you make space for in your life. Creating sacred space, inside or outside, takes time. This pathway allows us to turn within, to unburden ourselves of repetitive thoughts and feelings, and to find a mirror of the holy re-created within.

～ Roots and Branches ～

The traditional translation of this quality is "the holy." The roots of *Quddus* show both focus (*QD*) and emptiness (*US*). Symbolically, this is a point surrounded by a circle, creating separate space. Jesus used an Aramaic form of this word in the second line of his prayer when he said *nitkaddash shmakh*: "Let holy space be created for the name and vibration of Unity." When we become spacious enough, we find room to remember what is truly important in our lives. This remembrance creates a still point around which our life can turn. So, paradoxically, when you let go into divine Unity, what remains is divine Focus. The Qur'an often pairs this word with the previous

pathway, *Malik* (3). Vision-power and the space to receive it go together. Together, they open doors to a process that can lead through
the following six pathways, which the Qur'an includes in one verse
(59:23).

Meditation

Center again in the heart. Allow the breath to come into rhythm
with the heartbeat. Gradually add to the breathing the sound *Ya
QuDoos*. Feel your heart as a mirror, waiting expectantly for the divine reflection.

At another time: Enter the silence with the name on your breath
and allow it to lead you. Call a circle of your inner self by imagining
a round table at which all your inner voices can gather. Allow your
sense of your highest guidance (the "high self," which the Sufis call
ruh) to send out an invitation to all the exiled parts of your being to
come to a dinner party, where there is enough for all. All the relative
selves are welcome to join the circle of unity.

5. Peace at the Beginning

السَّلاَمُ

As-Salaam

When you are guided to this pathway,
take the opportunity to meditate on the beginnings of the universe and the
potential present before creation, and to remember the source
of the deepest peace.

AS THE NEWEST TELESCOPES penetrate deeper and deeper into space, we look back further and further toward the origins of the universe. We have now seen stars being born within galactic clouds, and even the creation of space itself in the form of dark matter.

Our ancestors in the Middle Eastern traditions, who created sacred space and time for themselves, took the opportunity to look deeply into the night sky and into nature, wondering what existed before the beginning. In the Middle East, those who spoke Semitic languages imagined the beginning of the universe as a caravan, with the past ahead and the future behind. Some beings have gone before us, some will follow later. Everything is moving: the divine, nature, humans, time, and space. The mysterious moment of beginning is full of that quality that is called in Arabic *salaam*, similar to the old Hebrew *shalom* and the Aramaic *shlama*.

Most Westerners know that these words mean "peace." But it is not the "peace" that is the opposite of "war." Instead, "peace" here refers to the peace and creative potential that were present at the beginning of all, and which are still present within the whole caravan of ancestors ahead of us. In this context, saying *"salaam"* or *"shalom"* to another person should mean more than saying "hello." To a Sufi, it's a way of saying, "Remember, there was a time when none of us was here. In the greater scheme of things, what do our problems, conflicts, and offenses given and received really matter? Peace!"

Perhaps life is calling you right now to offer another person, or a part of your own inner being, this greeting of peace. This pathway reminds us of the preciousness of the life we have been given, and of the blessings of the moment. It also reconnects us with those who have gone before us, as well as those who are coming along behind.

～ Roots and Branches ～

Traditional translations of this quality include "source of peace" and "author of safety." The roots of *Salaam* point to an unfolding reality of potential (*SA-*), which continually creates possibility, health, and wholeness (*LaM*). From the same root comes the word *islam,* which means the way of peace, to resign oneself to the greater reality of unity. The tradition of remembrance and greeting is very old in the Middle East. In the old Hebrew tradition, *shalom* points to the seventh day (or illuminated period) of creation, during which the Holy One remembers and restores to itself the awareness of all that went before. During the day of rest, the Divine says, "Peace be with you!" every moment to what has been created. In a famous story told by Muhammad, Allah asks Adam to greet the angels using the words *salaam alaykum*—peace to you. The angels respond, "Peace to you, Adam, and also the radiant compassion [*rahman*] and creative blessings [*baraka*] of the One to you!" Allah then asks Adam to pass along this greeting to all the human beings after him. Jesus enjoined his followers to offer a similar Aramaic greeting (*shalama bayta*) to every household they visited.

Meditation

Center again in the heart. Count to four with each breath in and out, feeling your breath in the heart. Use this opportunity to bring the feeling of your whole inner self into the circle of sacred space within you. Breathe YA SaLaaM to each feeling, thought, or sensation that arises. Then, or at another time, do the same for every person in your outer life. Upon completion, include everyone who has ever helped you—teachers, healers, friends, family—and, finally, all beings.

6. *Support*

الْمُؤْمِنُ

Al-Mu'min

When you are guided to this pathway,
take the opportunity to feel the support of the universe just as surely as you
feel the earth under your feet.

THE TWO PREVIOUS PATHWAYS (*Quddus* and *Salaam*) have invited us to create space to be and to contemplate the far reaches of the cosmic beginning. The next two call us back from this expanded state to one that is fully embodied. Life is not only space and waves, it is also particle. Divine support surrounds and holds us, like a mother holding her children.

This is where the Sufi gets tested as to how much she or he really believes that the Divine Unity is all there is. The twelfth-century Sufi Hakim Sanai says:

> *On rubbish pick-up day,*
> *bring everything you own and think you are*
> *down to Trust-in-the-One Avenue.*
> *When you get to the curb,*
> *your real fortune will meet you*
> *unveiled in your own face.*
> *The head of doubt has two ears,*
> *the heart only one.*
> *The ears of the head listen to*
> *a million voices here and there.*
> *The heart only has an ear for*
> *the song of the Beloved.*

Perhaps life is calling you right now to renew your sense of confidence, or to help others renew theirs. It may be time to breathe into the depths of your being and find the ground of being that can support all your inner selves. *Mumin* directs us to feel not only that the Divine Beloved carries us, but also that the whole universe is expressing the trust and confidence of Sacred Unity.

ᚥ *Roots and Branches* ᚥ

Traditional translations of this quality include "the faithful" and "guardian of the faith." The Semitic root *MN* means trust or faith, the confidence that the support of the One is beneath us at all times. A form of this word completes prayers in Judaism, Christianity, and Islam: *ameyn, amen, amin*. This is to say, "We affirm that what we have just said will be the ground of our actions, the earth from which our new growth will spring." The word *amin* is also used as a personal name in Arabic (and was a name of the Prophet Muhammad earlier in life). The prefix *MU-* adds to this root the sense of an action fully embodied (as it does in other pathways of the heart). So divine support is not only around us, but within us as well.

Meditation

Center again in the heart. Take this time to feel your whole self as the universe's body becoming conscious that only the One exists. Review the situations of your life. Breathe and feel: Where do you feel supported, where unsupported?

7. *Protection*

Al-Muhaimin

When you are guided to this pathway,
take the opportunity to contact your highest guidance and your connection
with your teachers. Feel divine support combining with life energy to create
a blanket of protection surrounding you.

IF, AS THE SUFIS believe, Sacred Unity includes everything, do we actually need protection? Doesn't everything come from the divine? On one level, this is true. On another, there is still a part of our being that feels separate and in need of protection. On yet another level, even if everything comes from the divine, we still have the responsibility to act, because our actions affect and change the fabric of divine reality. To the Sufis, "God" is not a puppeteer, moving things around at his or her whim. In the words of St. Paul, "We live and move and have our beings in the divine." None of us can rest on our laurels or afford to stand back from life in studied indifference. The twelfth-century Sufi Saadi says:

> *Kings forget they should serve the poor,*
> *not the poor them.*
> *Sheep don't pasture shepherds—*
> *it's the other way around.*
> *Likewise, just wait a bit if you think*
> *you're destined for greatness,*
> *and someone else for the trash heap.*
> *The earth turns.*
> *One day's success gives way to another's cares,*
> *and if you dig up the ashes of a grave,*
> *who can distinguish rich from poor?*

Perhaps life is calling you right now to develop a sense of care and protection for your own spiritual life, or for the life of your family or community. We can never determine what is right or true for another person, but we sometimes must make a decision about what is right and true for us at a particular moment. It may seem that you are called upon to act in a dualistic way, but if you remember that "Allah is on all sides," the question to ask in meditation becomes, "How am I called upon to serve divine compassion in this moment? What is really mine to do in this situation?"

—✑ Roots and Branches ✑—

Traditional translations of this quality include "the protector" and "the one who determines what is true and false." In *Muhaimin*, we find the root of the previous pathway (*Mumin*), combining with the root of *Hayy* (62)—the divine life energy. In this sense, support plus life energy equals protection. The roots depict a hen spreading her wings to protect her chicks. This protection also offers the ability to distinguish true from false right now—that which furthers one's purpose in life or not. In addition, the Qur'an uses this word to refer to itself as the protector of all previous messages. As it says, "Tell everyone: 'We believe in the One Being, and what has been revealed to you, and what was revealed to Abraham, Ishmael, Isaac, and Jacob, and to the tribes, and what was given to Moses, Jesus, and all the prophets from their Source. We will make no distinction between any of them, and we resign ourselves to the same Source of All'" (Sura 3:84). In Aramaic, Jesus uses a similar word when speaking about the source of his active healing power. As he says to those whom he has healed, "Your embodied trust in the One Life [*haimanuta*] has made you whole."

Meditation

Center again in the heart. Breathe the sound *MU-* into the belly, and as it changes to the sound *HaaY*, bring it to the heart. Then breathe out the sound *MeeN* and allow it to radiate in all directions, with the feeling of protection. After some minutes, release the sound and pattern of breathing and breathe naturally. Feel the power of Unity protecting your whole inner self.

Breathe the feeling of *Muhaimin* to the places within you where you feel unsafe and unprotected. You can also direct this breath outward, to friends, family, and communities in need.

8. The Strength of Form

العَزِيزُ

Al-`Aziz

When you are guided to this pathway,
take the opportunity to feel the embodied strength of the One moving
through you, at the same time that it also moves through everything
that has material form.

THE TWO PREVIOUS PATHWAYS (*Mumin* and *Muhaimin*) reminded us that we are not only linked to the ineffable, the spacious, and the ancient caravan of ancestors, but also to embodiment and here-and-now practicality. This pathway takes us further in this direction by reminding us that our physical form itself, and the form of every being in the universe, is also part of Sacred Unity. In the old Semitic creation stories, *earth* means our unique, material form; *heaven* means our communal relationship to the rest of the universe. Just as scientists view the nature of light as particle or wave, our "earthiness" shows us our individual nature as particle; our "heavenliness" reveals our connection to everything else as wave. So in this view, earth is not less than heaven, and the Sufi theory of relativity would be: matter=energy=us. If we primarily look to spiritual practice for techniques to escape from the here and now, we are missing part of the opportunity of human life.

Rumi says:

Listen to this story:
When the soul left the body
it was stopped by God at heaven's gate:
"Alas! You have returned just as you left.
Life is a blessing of opportunity.
Where are the bumps and scratches
left by the journey?"

Most of us have quite a few bumps and scratches from our life's journey so far. Some of the injuries to our heart, whether they occurred in childhood or adulthood, may feel too painful to even remember. We tend to create emotional scar tissue over our ability to feel because of this. Part of the message of this path is that we can never avoid life's abrasions completely. We can redeem the bumps and scratches of the past by feeling the blessing and strength of having physical form to work through.

Perhaps life is calling you right now to manifest a focused, concentrated energy in your life, in order to bring things out of the realm of the possible into the actual. What is the challenge that life is presenting you now? Or you may be feeling inwardly weak. Is there a way to reach deep inside yourself, feeling the firmness of earth supporting your bones, in order to bring this strength to the situation at hand?

⌒ *Roots and Branches* ⌒

Traditional translations of this quality include "exalted in power" and "almighty." The roots of *Aziz* point to a compression of life-breath into form (*'AZ*), which leads to embodied strength (*-Z*). All of this strength belongs to sacred Unity—the ground of reality in the universe. We can see this compressed strength in the dark matter within all form, which upholds and supports it, from the smallest subatomic particle to the largest galaxy. We find a more embodied or internalized form of this pathway in *Mu'izz* (24). In Arabic, when the sound *'A* is intensified, indicating that the life-breath has become too locked into form and egocentric, *'Aziz* becomes *'Izza,* personal pride or arrogance. The message here is this: When feeling the strength of the earth working through you, keep breathing and feel your relationship to those around you. You are not the ultimate source of this strength.

Meditation

Center again in the heart. Sit for a moment on your hands and feel the solid connection between your pelvis and what is underneath you. Sense this firm support rising through you, and feel it as the power of the earth and form. Breathing in the heart, call a circle of your inner self and invite the various voices within you to the table: Who is there? Who feels strong? Who feels weak? What resources in my life could allow the strength of earth to work through me?

9. *Repair and Restoration*

Al-Jabbar

When you are guided to this pathway,
it is an opportunity to feel the restorative power of the One
and to take action to heal what has been broken.

JUST AS THE LAST pathway (*Aziz*) reminded us of the gift of embodying strength in form, so this one tells us that sometimes we need to act with strength to repair what has been damaged in order to heal ill health or misfortune. No doubt, life contains many moments when the wise thing to do is surrender to circumstances. Now is not that time, this pathway tells us.

According to the twelfth-century Sufi Abdul Qadir Jilani:

> *Faced with trial, I first exhausted my own efforts, then those of my family, community, connections, and acquaintances. Only then did I try God. But the One Being did not answer until I had exhausted all other means, and only when I had given up everything else. I was in the hands of the One, like a baby in the arms of its mother, like a polo ball before the mallet. At that point, deliverance arrived. Then I saw that Allah always acted through all circumstances of life—the actions of me, my family, friends, everything. I just didn't recognize it before, and so thought "I" was doing it "myself." Now this person sees nothing but the work of the One. I have vanished from my self.*

Perhaps something in your life, inner or outer, needs repair or restoration. Life is calling you now to take action and take yourself in hand. Instead of being afraid that you can't do it, allow yourself to feel the One Being acting through you. This pathway of the heart asks for concentrated, creative energy.

∽ Roots and Branches ∾

Traditional translations of this quality include "the compeller" and "the irresistible." The root *JB* indicates the creative power of the One, enclosed and working within the organic limits of nature and of creation itself. This power heals wounds, repairs bridges, and closes circles that want to come full, all in the right time. The same root appears in the Arabic word *jabara,* meaning to restore (or set) a broken bone. The second half of the word, *-BAR,* shows that this restorative and creative power gives birth through the divine light and intelligence. We naturally bow to this power. In this sense, *Jabbar* is also what compels us to wonder at Allah's creation and to surrender to the power behind it. The equivalent root is used in the Hebrew word *Gabri-el,* the angelic expression of divine power (who is called *Jibril* in the Qur'an and credited with bearing the Quranic revelation to Muhammad).

Meditation

Center again in the heart. Breathe the sound *Ya JaBaaR* rhythmically, bending slightly forward as you breathe out, and back as you breathe in. Allow the sound to rock you into action, like the feeling of riding a camel in the caravan of life. Allow the sound to spread first to the periphery, and feel healthy boundaries restored. Then gently invite all voices of your inner self to gather, and allow the arms of the Beloved to enfold you in healing.

10. Concentration

الْمُتَكَبِّرُ

Al-Mutakabbir

*When you are guided to this pathway,
take the opportunity to find the divine focus in your own ability
to concentrate.*

THE FAMOUS SUFI OF Baghdad, Abdul Qadir Jilani, represents the way of concentration in classical Sufism. His writings emphasize being in right relationship with the divine, and present powerful practices of the heart that lead to mastery through accomplishment. His message essentially is: What the heart can hold, the being can accomplish. And it is not worth the heart holding anything unless it comes from the One. One of Jilani's practices for developing concentration was this: Don't begin something without completing it.

If following through is a problem for you, try beginning with anything: getting up for a glass of water, or following through with your intention to stop work at a particular time for lunch. Even though these things may be ultimately irrelevant, take up each for a while as a sacred practice; that is, intend to do the action, and then do it. Don't let your concentration unconsciously waver to something else.

A practice like this doesn't aim to make you obsessed with the minor occupations of life (it's only "practicing," after all). Instead, it intends to build your inner strength and concentration for when life really requires them. The practice is like a dress rehearsal before the performance. Another benefit is that when you find yourself becoming obsessed by a thought or feeling, you can use the powers of concentration and focus developed through spiritual practice to release it.

Concentration doesn't mean thinking a lot. As the modern Sufi Idries Shah once said:

A great deal of thought is only a substitute for the thoughts that the in-
dividual would really find useful at the time.[6]

Instead, concentration means developing the energy of the heart,
which is planted with interest, sprouts into affection, and then blossoms into something for which the word *love* is only a shadow. As
Rumi once said:

Whether you love God or love a human being,
If you love enough you will come into the presence
of Love itself.

Perhaps life is calling you right now to concentrate on what is important in your life, or to refocus on your next steps. Embodied focus also allows us to expand our awareness and notice more closely
the opportunities around us. This is one of the keys to finding our
purpose in life.

～ Roots and Branches ～

Traditional translations of this quality include "the majestic" and
"the supreme." The word root *KB* indicates a central point, or the
process of something settling, really the image of concentration itself. It is like the keynote in a piece of music; the melody constantly
moves around and returns to it. *Ya Mutakabbir* opens a door to the
part of our being that is waiting to express itself. The prefix *MU-*
again reveals the full embodiment of the quality. This pathway
branches to two others: *Mutakabbir* fully embodies the outward creative power of *Kabir* (37) and fully externalizes the inward creative
power of *Khabir* (31). That is, there is in this quality of our being no
outer or inner. There is only focus: All aspects of us are involved and
unified in the heart. Such a great outpouring of love is both stunning and majestic. As Jesus says in one of the Beatitudes from the
Aramaic language, "Ripe are those who wholeheartedly follow their
passion, by being unified, they see Unity everywhere."

Meditation

This practice also comes from Abdul Qadir Jilani: Center again in the heart. If you have difficulty doing this, place one hand lightly over the middle of your chest and feel how it slightly rises and falls. Then breathe rhythmically with the feeling of *Ya Moo-ta-kab-beer.* Notice how the breath and feeling in the heart changes. Allow yourself to become more present in your own holy of holies with each breath. After a while, bring into the feeling of your breathing and heart any choice in life that you are contemplating. Breathe with each alternative in turn for a minute or so, feeling how the breath and feeling in the heart change. Do you feel expanded or contracted, light or heavy, spacious or dense? Don't expect any particular response, but simply notice if you feel a difference, and what that difference is. Then release all alternatives and return to breathing with a feeling of *Ya Mutakabbir.* Do this practice at least three times for a particular decision. Then follow the direction that the One Being points out to you through the response of your own heart and breath. If you wish, begin with a decision that means less to you, in order to build up your ability to bypass thought and strengthen the intuition being revealed to you by the One.

11. *Carving and Forming*

الخَالِقُ

Al-Khaliq

When you are guided to this pathway,
take the opportunity to feel the hands of the Holy One as your hands,
carving out a new life and shaping it creatively.

THE PREVIOUS PATHWAY—divine focus—leads us to the next: taking a hands-on approach. The time to visualize is over; the time to act is now. There are various words for *create* in the Semitic languages, and the one associated with this pathway shows us the image of someone carving a piece of wood or stone to fit a certain measure and proportion. Each movement must be definite yet patient, with an intuitive sense of harmony and the overall goal in mind.

Whether we have used it or not, this quality is already within us, waiting to be used. How do we know? Because this is the way that the universe was created, and we carry a reflection of the universe within us. It was not a once-and-for-all project that was over and done at a certain time. The universe continues to evolve and change over time, and *Khaliq* describes this action of the divine Beloved.

Perhaps life is calling you right now to shape a beautiful work or composition that will serve others as well as yourself. Visualize it, and then take definite action, without any half-measures. As Rumi says: "When in doubt, start a large foolish project like Noah!"

─◌ *Roots and Branches* ◌─

Traditional translations of this quality include "creator" and "maker." The word roots *Kh* and *Q* show the energy of definition and shape, carving out reality. In the middle of the word is *AL*, the sign of *Allah*, which is the creator. *Khaliq* creates definition through distinct shapes and forms that are simultaneously full of divine life and vibrancy. This is one of the miracles of creation: An extravagant diversity of unique forms and beings each carries within it its own sense of interiority and each expresses a facet of divine Unity. In the Qur'an, *Khaliq* is used to describe the creation of things both abstract and material. It uses the word *Badi`* (95) for the original creative act from which the universe began.

Meditation

Center again in the heart. First breathe with the quality, and then use the name itself to walk in a rhythmic way in a count of four: *Ya Khaa-Leeq*-rest. Feel the definition of the sound *Q* at the end, and allow it to help you feel definition, focus, and applied determination. Each action strikes the right note, hits the nail on the head.

Then, or at another time, breathe in the heart and focus more inwardly. Call a circle of your inner self, and welcome all your inner voices. Acknowledge each for the distinct gift it can offer to your becoming a more whole and complete human being. Each already possesses the essence of *Khaliq*, which is waiting to be awakened.

BATHING IN UNITY

When we follow the many pathways of the heart, it is easy to get lost or overwhelmed. We are not intended to map out our whole inner landscape in one day, one year, or (perhaps) even one lifetime. Indeed, the path is not about mapping at all, but about experiencing.

Just as when we taste too many different wines in a row, we may need to clear our palate. The Sufi clears his or her palate by returning to Allah, the feeling of Unity. Now might be a good time to do this.

The Prophet Muhammad once told a story about Moses and Allah, which goes like this:

> Moses came to God and said, "O Holy One, teach me a way that I can remember you constantly."
>
> "Just repeat la ilaha ilallah—there is no Reality but the One Reality."
>
> "But, O Holy One," said Moses, "all of your servants already say this, during each cycle of prayer."
>
> "Just repeat la ilaha ilallah."
>
> "Yes," said Moses, "there really is no reality except you . . . but still, I long for some prayer or practice you could give that is especially for me."
>
> "Beloved Moses, if I would bring the seven levels of heaven and the seven levels of earth and place them on one side of a scale, la ilaha ilallah would still outweigh them."[7]

Meditation

With a gentle breath in the heart, breathe the sound *Allah* and feel each breath bringing you back into unity with the present moment. On the breath out, breathe away every impression you've received that is not yours to work with. On the breath in, breathe inspiration from the heart of the divine Beloved.

12. *Radiating Creativity*

الْبَارِئُ

Al-Bari'

When you are guided to this pathway,
take the opportunity to feel the potential to create something completely new
and different—something from what seems like nothing.

D ID CREATION ARISE FROM something, or from nothing? Perhaps we can't answer that question, but it doesn't stop scientists—or all the traditional storytellers of all time—from having a go at it. The Arabic of the Qur'an implies that after the first mysterious moment of origination, a defining process continued creation, followed by a radiant energy that enlivened it and kept it going.

Some of us are better at starting processes, others at keeping them going, still others at finishing. We could just play it safe and say that we're better at one than the other, and leave it at that. However, if we want to fully experience our humanity, we may need to go outside the envelope that circumscribes who we think we are.

The human expression of this pathway is a reflection of the divine, which was created in us at the beginning of time. That's when, both the Bible and Qur'an report, we were created in the divine image. But the word for *image* (in either Hebrew or Arabic) does not mean a fixed picture. Rather, it's like a moving shadow of a living, breathing Being, one that encompasses all beings. If, as some scientists feel, the earth itself expresses its being as Gaia, why couldn't the whole universe also express a unified, evolving, living being? In a saying of Allah through Muhammad (a "sacred tradition," in Islamic terms), the One Being speaks to the question: "Why bother with creation, anyway?"

I was a Hidden treasure and I loved to be known, so I created the world
that I might be known.

A Sufi feels that the reason for the entire universe was love. Without love, it would have remained a universe only in potential, not in action.

Perhaps life is calling you right now to breathe, feel, and radiate possibility and creativity, rather than to act outwardly. Sometimes a person enters a room and you feel possibilities open up. That person could be you. Or perhaps the atmosphere you bring to a situation reveals a blocked process in a new light. This may also be an opportunity to feel restored after being depleted by life's challenges. We can connect with the power of Allah at the very beginning of the cosmos, before there was anything to create from or with.

～ *Roots and Branches* ～

Traditional translations of this quality include "maker" and "evolver." This pathway shows the action of the One as it brings something from unmanifest to manifest with power (*BA-*), emanating like a ray of light (*-RI'*). Whereas *Khaliq* (11) is "particle" creation, *Bari* is "wave" creation. Similarly, according to Genesis 1:1, God creates (the Hebrew *bara*) both heaven (*shemayim,* wave) and earth (*aretz,* particle) as the first realities. In the Qur'an, *Bari* is used to express the sense of the creation that departs from preexisting circumstances, that frees or liberates.

Meditation

Center again in the heart. Imagine at the center of your being a living fountain, or a spring bubbling from deep within. You are the water; the source is Allah. Breathe out the sound *Ya BaaR-* and breathe in the sound *-ee,'* feeling the final *ee* sound as though it were falling backward inside you. Feel the spring flowing out in all directions as you breathe out. As you breathe in, touch the source deep within.

13. Designing and Training

المُصَوِّر

Al-Musawwir

When you are guided to this pathway,
it is an opportunity to feel the One's power to design a new existence for
you, and to gradually guide and train you to experience it in the most
loving, blessed way possible.

SOMETIMES OUR WHOLE LIFE needs a redesign. This doesn't usually happen overnight. In the same way that the universe continues to evolve, we need to trust that we can shape our lives in a creative way, like a potter raising a lump of clay on a moving wheel. The feeling for what it will become is in her hands.

Rumi compares our whole lives to this process of kneading, shaping, and fashioning. Sometimes we act in concert with the Beloved, sometimes not:

Love flies without limits.
Cuts through all veils.
Rejects the life you knew with looking back.
Gives up on feet entirely—much too slow!
Sees right through appearances.
Ignores obsession and addiction.
My soul remembers its source:
I was in the potter's hands while
he mixed clay and water—
a new home for me, I think.
The kiln is hot. I'm trying to escape!
Willing, unwilling—what does it matter?
No longer resisting, I get kneaded and molded,
just like every other lump of clay.

Perhaps life is calling you right now to remember that the design of your life is a continual process, and that Reality's hands knead and mold through yours. Or maybe you face a long project with many steps. Start with a feeling for the design, even if each individual step is not yet clear. Or, in relation to a part of your inner community, some voices need taking in hand with gentle but definite training, a program of love and discipline. The One Being brings a full bag of tools, everything you might need to design and redesign your life.

Roots and Branches

Traditional translations of this quality include "fashioner" and "bestower of forms." The roots of *Musawwir* carry the sense of gradually forming a design, like a river gradually shapes a riverbed (*SW*). If the previous two paths of creation were the beginning and the middle, this one shows us that there is a definite end in sight, in full color, dimension, and detail. The path differs from the creativity of *Khaliq* (11) in that the latter engraves or carves a clear image or shape with one stroke. Here we contain a process for a while—we hold it in our hands—so that it takes shape gradually. The Qur'an uses this word to describe the type of creation that brings things to completeness or perfection.

Meditation

Center again in the heart. Breathe with a feeling of patience: You can learn what you need to know as you go along. Breathe with the sound *Ya Mu-Saa-Weer* and feel it containing and shaping the creative possibilities within you, waiting for the right time to complete itself.

14. Burning Away Tension and Hurt

الغَفَّارُ

Al-Ghaffar

When you are guided to this pathway,
take the opportunity to release any restriction or constriction you feel, with
regard to your self or another, into the heat and fire of Unity.

W E OFTEN FEEL WOUNDED by what we feel to be the unfair-
ness or ignorance of others. In response, we could toughen
our skin in order not to feel things so deeply, and become more cyn-
ical about life. Or, we might just give up asserting ourselves and become a doormat for others. Or, we could become hypersensitive and
react against every perceived slight. All these options essentially
make us the passive victims of life, and there is no greater block to
harmony and peace than obsessive victimhood. As the fourteenth-
century Indian Sufi Nizamuddin Auliya once said:

> *If someone places a thorn in your way and you place another thorn in*
> *his way, there will be thorns everywhere.*

In 1993, while on a citizen diplomacy trip with a group to the
Middle East, I had the opportunity to spend time with the Palestin-
ian Melkite priest Fr. Elias Chacour, who lives near Nazareth, Israel.
Fr. Chacour, who has been engaged in peacemaking his whole life
and who has suffered tremendously for his work, told us very forcefully, "There is no greater obstacle to peace than people emphasizing that they are victims." When I saw him again a few years later, he
was even more emphatic, telling his audience, "If supporting me
means that you learn to hate anyone else, I don't want your support!"

What, then, is the solution to the pain we feel from our relationships with others? The twentieth-century Sufi Inayat Khan had two
answers: First, there is no solution. Second, develop your heart,

which means to the Sufi not merely the emotions, but a combination of feeling and intelligence that can illuminate life more clearly. A few of his sayings follow:

> *The heart sleeps until it is awakened to life by a blow. It is as a rock, and the hidden fire flashes out when struck by another rock.*

> *You can have all good things—wealth, friends, kindness, love to give, and love to receive—once you have learned not to be blinded by them; learned to escape from disappointment and from repugnance at the idea that things are not as you want them to be.*

> *The quality of forgiveness that burns up all things except beauty is the quality of love.*[8]

The final saying returns us to the Sufi emphasis on love, not as a decoration to our lives, but as the most powerful creative force in the universe. We may spend our whole lives distinguishing real love from passion, romanticism, lust, sentimentality, and all of the other ways that our culture tries to sell us counterfeit forms of love.

Perhaps life is calling you right now to use the burning power of love to heal and erase the impressions that have lodged on your heart. We know that if we suppress our anger, it just goes into other channels of our lives and resurfaces later. According to this pathway of the heart, we should use the heat of the anger to burn away the impressions of tension and hurt that have lodged on the mirror of our hearts. Another practice the pathway suggests we use is to imagine our heart like a pressure cooker that is softening and cooking something in order to assimilate and release it. Sometimes this process can take a while, and can be painful. The energy tied up in the compacted hurt returns to join the universal energy; that is, it is healed. We then find the face of offense transformed into another manifestation of the face of Allah.

～ Roots and Branches ～

Traditional translations of this quality include "forgiver" and "absolver." The roots of *Ghaffar* show a constriction (*GhF*) that is released through heat and fire (*AR*). This form of the word also shows an action that happens repeatedly. The Qur'an says that the One Being forgives again and again, and that even a whole life of error can be forgiven in an instant. This is the inspiration behind Rumi's famous saying, "Come, come whoever you are, even though you've broken your vow a hundred times, come again." Another face of forgiveness appears at the address of a similar pathway, *Ghafur* (34), which works with light and intelligence rather than heat. Both arise from the same word root, as does the Arabic prayer *istaghfar Allah* (or *estaferallah,* in a form often heard in Turkish Sufi circles). The latter phrase adds a devotional quality by including the name of Unity.

Meditation

Center in the heart and imagine a mirror there. If you're conscious of a particular hurt or offense, hold it in the mirror. Or, hold the aspect of your inner self that has given or received offense. Imagine burning away any impression so that the other person—or the part of your self that feels separate—can be seen in the clear light of Unity.

Breathe the feeling of the sound *Ya GhaF-FaaR* and allow it to resonate through you, like bringing heat to "cook" and soften something that has been tense and compact. The first part of the sound constricts the throat; the second opens it. Sometimes *Ghaffar* acts like a steam cabinet, softening the wound so that it can heal. Sometimes it acts like cauterization, stopping the bleeding and closing the raw surface so that healing takes place inside.

15. Natural Power

القَهَّارُ

Al-Qahhar

When you are drawn toward this pathway,
take the opportunity to feel the overwhelming, primordial power of nature
as part of your own being, spreading through your life.

*I*N THE PREVIOUS PATHWAY, we saw how fire could be used as a force for healing. This pathway introduces us to the larger face of that radiant force as the action of Sacred Unity working through the power of nature.

When people ordinarily speak of "the blind force of nature," a Sufi wonders what force they're talking about. To speak of blind nature presumes some separation between the natural world and the divine one, usually along the lines that the natural world is sinful, or at best unintelligent. For the Sufi, the whole universe is an expression of the power and intelligence of the One, as the twentieth-century Sufi Shah Maghsoud says when he compares human life to a drop of water:

If the raindrop knew its fate,
And could see the vastness of the ocean,
It would not remain an empty
Bubble caught between two worlds.[9]

This pathway is not the power to *do* something, but the power that has and will accomplish anything. This original power not only works through all the "laws" of nature, but it also expresses itself in ways for which human beings have found no law or explanation. When we stand in awe of this power, and feel it as part of our own being, our small self feels that it disappears for an instant and is transformed. The seventeenth-century Indian Sufi Fatima Jahanara describes the experience this way in her spiritual diary:

That person has become
a drop in the ocean,
a mote in the rays of the sun,
a part of the whole,
raised above death and the fear of punishment,
above any regard for Paradise or Hell.
Whether woman or man,
a complete human being
by the grace of the One Being.

Perhaps life is telling you that your own "personal" power is not enough. If so, you're walking close to this pathway. This original power has the ability to steer and guide events in any direction, to create what human beings call miracles, which are simply more living signs that we exist in a sacred universe contained in the divine heart.

ᴐ Roots and Branches ᴐ

Traditional translations of this quality include "dominant" and "irresistible." The root *QH* expresses the power of Reality, welling up from before the primordial beginning, into the present. In the Qur'an, this word is often associated with both the beginning and end of time, both of which can be experienced in this moment: one as boundless potential, the other as the moment of reckoning. From these depths, the sound of the word spreads like a wave or spiral into existence with life energy (the *H* sound) and continues to radiate (*AR*) through all the worlds. Related to the primordial fire, it burns through what we no longer need in our lives. Related pathways in this family of the One Being's "natural" power are *Qawi* (53), *Qayyum* (63), *Qadir* (69), and *Muqtadir* (70).

Meditation

Center again in the heart. Imagine the moment of the beginning of the universe, when everything, including the "laws of the universe," unfolded from a single point, which some scientists have called the "big bang." Feel this fireball of power clarifying and purifying your heart, connecting you with the power that began the universe.

16. Flowing Blessings

الوَهَّابُ

Al-Wahhab

When you are guided to this pathway,
you have the opportunity to enter the flow of Allah's love-filled grace.

SOMETIMES THE FORCES OF nature overwhelm us; sometimes we feel that we can bask in their healing presence. The previous pathway invited us into the first experience; this pathway invites us into the second. There are times when we can simply float downstream on the flow of love until we reach the ocean.

This particular face of love grows slowly, like friendship, or like a fire kindled slowly from tinder. It can eventually blaze and burn for a long time, but only if we don't rush it. The ancient Hebrew Song of Songs uses a similar word when it reminds us that "Love is as strong as death." That is, a love that opens and befriends, that considers the Beloved first, is stronger than the pathway between the worlds.

In this pathway, life is good. As Saadi says:

It's the first breath of spring
But do I smell a garden or
the aroma of two friends meeting?

Why on earth would we ever want to leave this pathway? Because the river does lead to the ocean, and along the way there are many twists and turns. Identify with the water, the riverbed, the stones, or the flow itself. There are this many possibilities of being, and more.

Perhaps life is calling you right now to feel the divine flow of blessing in which you find yourself and to refrain from any unnecessary action. Celebrate Sacred Unity as the river, the source, and the ocean of life. This name also shows us the process by which change can happen in the inner self: Once a slight ripple happens, the whole is affected, so it is not necessary to continually "stir the soup."

～⟡ *Roots and Branches* ⟡～

Traditional translations of this quality include "bestower" and "the one who grants bounties." With the word root *WaH-*, we open to divine connection. Allah is the eternal "and" of existence (the literal meaning of *wa*). There is always more in the depths of the One Being. Read another way, the root *WaH* indicates a transformation, a process of being carried from one reality to another. The root sound *-HAB* shows us the bestowing of blessing that flows from the heart, setting us free. This river never dries up.

Meditation

Center again in the heart. Breathe the sound of *Ya Waa-* into the heart, and feel it coming to the top of your head. Then, as you exhale, feel the sound *-Haab* showering over you like a fountain. Which part of your being is waiting to bathe in this waterfall of blessing?

17. *Sustenance*

الرَّزَّاقُ

Ar-Razzaq

When you are guided toward this pathway,
take the opportunity to receive the nourishing sustenance of the One Being,
and to explore your relationship to feeding and being fed.

ARLIER, WE EXPLORED THE ability to contain what we receive, symbolized by Nasruddin's leaky bucket. No matter how
much we receive, it may never be enough if we do not create a conscious, embodied container for it. In this pathway of our heart, we
work further on developing the container. When we realize that all
nutrition comes from the One, in whatever form, then what we con-
sume becomes less important than the way in which we unite with
the life energy that it provides. We are always surrounded by this life
energy, but as Rumi notes, we often don't recognize it, ignoring the
flow of blessing around us:

> *Even the hills and fields are flowing,*
> *so why do you feel you're all alone,*
> *tears hugging you to yourself?*
> *The world is a tree bowed down with fruit,*
> *while you bend over stealing rotten apples.*

The recognition of the earth's bounty also lays on us the responsibility to share it. In fact, sharing it seems to be the key to discovering this quality within us. The following saying of Muhammad
invokes an ancient tradition of hospitality and sharing similar to one
expressed by Jesus in the Gospels:

> *On the day of resurrection, Allah will proclaim:*
>   *"Children of Adam, I asked you for food and you didn't feed me."*
>   *The souls will respond:*

"Sustaining One, how could we feed you, who already command all levels of existence?"

"Weren't you aware of my servants who asked for food, and you didn't feed them? Don't you know that if you had fed them you would have discovered Me through this gift?"[10]

Perhaps life is calling you right now to feel a more grounded way of containing life energy, a way that secures the bottom of your bucket. In working with our inner selves, we can use this pathway to explore how we receive, and who is really asking for sustenance.

⁓ᴐ *Roots and Branches* ᴐ⁓

Traditional translations of this quality include "provider" and "bestower of sustenance." The root sound *RA-* shows us a raying-forth of unlimited power and light from the Holy One. The root *-ZAQ* shows us the conscious container created for this power, as well as a chain linking to the divine source.

Meditation

Center again in the heart. Breathe the sound *Ya RaZaaq* and use this feeling to help direct you to the right food for you at this moment. This could be food for the body, emotions, or psyche.

Call a circle of your inner self. Which part of your being shows up to join the communal meal? Which voice within you feels hungry? What nourishment can your higher self provide?

18. *Opening to Unity's Breath*

Al-Fattah

When you are guided to this pathway,
take the opportunity to experience the Sacred Unity opening you
to your destiny.

IN RELATION TO THIS pathway, the Sufi often says, "God opens doors." There are many sayings, in both the Qur'an and the sayings of Muhammad (called *hadith*), in which Allah says that if seekers take one step on the path, Sacred Unity will take ten steps toward them:

> *If they remember me in their heart,*
> *I remember them within my heart.*
> *If they come toward me walking,*
> *I come toward them running.*[11]

We may, however, find it unsettling to be more open than we normally are. How complete an image of our real self can we bear right now? With regard to our inner community of voices, which Sufis call the *nafs,* it is important to recognize that some parts of our self will not experience forceful opening in a harmonious way. So when you begin to follow a pathway with strong energy like this one, invite the different known aspects of your being to a "common area" first (for instance, the image of the round table of Holy Wisdom), and inquire who is willing to participate. Practices of both power and subtlety proceed together in one's evolution. Devotion, love, and respect help in all aspects of inner work.

When we find ourselves confronted with a totally new view of ourselves and our purpose in life, we may have to take a leap of faith into the unknown, which can feel like annihilation. As Rumi says, what is there to be afraid of?

Don't be afraid of nonbeing.
If you want to be afraid,
fear the existence you have now.
Your hopes for the future,
your memories of the past,
what you call your self,
are nothing.
So nothing is being taken from nothing, and
a nothing is being absorbed by a Nothing.

Perhaps life's circumstances have opened you to a totally new view of yourself, your relationships, or your occupation. Usually this is the result of either great love or great pain. Rather than fearing the opening, use the opportunity to find the key to the door that leads to your purpose in life.

ᲘᲬ Roots and Branches ᲘᲬ

Traditional translations of this quality include "opener of truth" and "judge." The roots show us the mouth or face of something opening (*FT-*) to give and receive breath (*-AH*). Probably one of the oldest sacred sounds in the Middle East, *Fattah* carries resonances at least back to the name of the ancient Egyptian god *Ptah*, who created the universe through space. Old Hebrew also contains a form of the same word. In addition, the Gospel of Mark, even in the Greek version, records Jesus using the Aramaic equivalent in healing a deaf man: *eth-phatah*—"Be opened!"

Meditation

Center again in the heart. While breathing and feeling the sound *Ya FaTaah*, look through the eyes of your heart at the various situations in your life. Which situations call for more spaciousness, more opening? Which are encouraging you to open to a larger view of yourself? With love and respect, invite to Wisdom's table all members of your inner community who would like to feel a door opening to their purpose in life.

19. Understanding Names and Forms

Al-'Alim

When you are guided to this pathway,
you have the opportunity to allow the depth of Unity to penetrate your
learning and knowing.

DO WE WITHDRAW FROM life, or attempt to master it? If we withdraw, we don't get caught up in life's busy-ness and superficiality. But we may also miss the opportunity to complete ourselves through experiencing life fully. Very few of us are called to be hermits, at least permanently. On the other hand, if we attempt to fully engage in life, we may get lost in the outer details and forget about discovering who we really are. The twelfth-century Sufi Fariduddin Attar noted this in one of his stories, perhaps based on his own experience:

> *A dervish came into a new town and was accosted by an unfriendly and presumptuous person:*
> *"Go away! No one knows you here!"*
> *"Yes, but I know myself, and it would be much worse if it were the other way around."*

One of the most attractive seductions of this pathway is the one where I believe I have everything figured out, or that God manifests only one particular way (and usually just to me). A saying of Muhammad addresses this danger, which seems to be a pitfall that the fundamentalists of most religions fall into:

> *Muhammad once clarified the nature of judgment day:*
> *"In the future, there will be a certain community composed of immature believers. Allah will manifest itself to them in an aspect*

other than what they are used to and will say to them, 'I am your Sustainer—follow me.'

" 'No, we take refuge in Allah from you,' they will answer. 'We will not move from here until our Sustainer comes to meet us, and we will know our Sustainer instantly.'

"Allah will then return in the form they are used to and say 'Here I am: your Sustainer.' Then they will rejoice—'You are really our Sustainer!'—and will follow.

"When they have reached the other side of the bridge over the fire of time and judgment, then Allah will tell them: 'Whoever worships me in any one of my infinite qualities should follow me confidently from their understanding of that quality.' "[12]

Perhaps life is calling you now to use your mind in a complex or rigorous way. This pathway will help center that knowing in the heart of Allah. It relaxes the grasp of the self-conscious aspect of your inner self, which can jump to the false conclusion that manipulating an outer name and form is the highest wisdom. The greatest learning and knowing is knowledge of the self. As the companion of Muhammad, Imam Ali, said, "Whosoever knows him-/herself, knows the One."

ᔍ Roots and Branches ᔍ

The traditional translation of this quality is "all-knowing." The root ALM really means, in the Semitic languages, "world" or "a gathering of substance" (similar to the Buddhist term skandha). It can refer to levels, times, or anything that has name and form. Jesus uses the Aramaic form of this word in several of his sayings, for instance in Matthew 16:26: "What does it benefit a person to know about and acquire the worlds of form, if she or he loses touch with their own naphsha, the inner self." Alim refers to the ability to know and understand all the worlds of form. The classical Sufis refer to two essentials of the spiritual path as Ilm (divine intelligence, related to Alim) and Ishk (divine passion). Head and heart balance each other in the way of transformation.

Meditation

Center again in the heart. Breathe in the sound `AL and feel the initial *A* as though it were falling backward into you, to the level of your solar plexus. Then, as you breathe out the sound -*IM*, feel the sound rise from the solar plexus and purify both heart and head. Feel the breath become a fountain of blessing showering over and through the rest of the body, as well as your inner self. At the completion of practice, take a moment to allow for the possibility that the One Being can know itself through you.

20. *Contracting Boundaries*

القَابِضُ

Al-Qabid

When you are guided to this pathway,
you have the opportunity to realize your self more fully by closing
boundaries of your being that may have opened too far.

*I*NAYAT KHAN ONCE OBSERVED:

All things existing have their opposite, except God; it is for this reason
that God cannot be made intelligible.[13]

Just two pathways ago, we were invited to a profound opening of our beings. Why would we ever want to close? For one thing, life requires it. Our physical, mental, psychic, or emotional boundaries may become too open due to various circumstances in life, including intoxication, illness, over-receptivity, or a codependent empathy—that is, an attachment that does not further either our own purpose in life or that of another. In these cases, the unprocessed impressions and subconscious material of others can flood our inner being. We may lose a healthy sense of personal unity (that is, an integral "I am") or our connection to Sacred Unity (the only "I Am").

Like the breath, the heart not only expands but also contracts. With opening must come closing, as the Hebrew version of the Genesis creation story describes: "And the evening [closing] and the morning [opening] made one day [one period of the Holy One's illuminated activity]." Rumi notes:

Just look at your hand.
Closing the fist always precedes opening it.
A hand that's always closed or open
is a crippled hand.
So your heart also contracts and expands,

just like a bird needs to close and open
its wings to fly.

Perhaps life is calling you now to "pull in your horns," or maybe you have found that you opened yourself to something that has knocked you off-center. Or, you are experiencing a compression around your heart that seems to have no cause; now is a good time to take a breath and see what it might be. This pathway can also help us explore a constricted or contracted relationship with a particular person, or with a particular part of our self. As in exercising a muscle that we've ignored, the first step to capacity is consciousness. Feeling a muscle (or capability of emotion or mind) precedes using it properly. Not-feeling ties up energy that could be used in service to the Real.

⌒ *Roots and Branches* ⌒

Traditional translations of this quality include "restrainer" and "closer." The roots of *Qabid* show the enclosure of the divine creativity (*QAB*) as a living presence (*-iD*). So the purpose of this period of contraction is to allow something new to incubate within us, like a chick getting ready to hatch from an egg. The roots of *Qabid* also show a bird drawing in its wings while flying. This pathway is not like shutting a door; it is more like gradually folding the wings of love around us. These wings unfold again in the next pathway, *Basit.*

Meditation

Center again in the heart. Place your hands lightly together over your heart. Gradually open your hands and arms as you breathe in the sound *Ya-,* and bring them slowly back to enfold you as you breathe out *Qaa-bid.* The final sound (with the *d* buzzed or pronounced halfway toward a *z*) closes the boundaries of all bodies that may be too open. Feel your own arms as the wings of the divine love enfolding you.

⌒ ⌒

21. Expanding Boundaries

البَاسِطُ

Al-Basit

When you are guided to this pathway,
take the opportunity to allow Allah to gradually expand your
boundaries—physical, mental, emotional, and psychic.

SOMETIMES FEAR INDUCED BY being hurt in the past causes some part of us to close, like a clenched fist. We may have been hurt in a relationship or experienced ourselves "failing" in some other situation. Or, as we explored in the previous pathway, *Qabid*, the effects of various illnesses or intoxication can create very dense boundaries, a sort of emotional-somatic scar tissue.

Typically, Sufi poets have pointed out that what we call "self" and "other" are very relative when every being is already contained in the heart of the One Being. Shabistari expressed it this way:

"I" and "you" focus light
like decorative holes cut
in a lampshade.
But there is only One Light.

"I" and "you" throw a
thin veil between
heaven and earth.
Lift the veil and all
creeds and theologies disappear.

When "I" and "you" vanish,
how can I tell whether I am
in a mosque, a synagogue,
a church, or an observatory?

Perhaps life is calling you right now to expand your boundaries again, to be as porous as you need to be for this moment of your life. This does not mean eliminating all boundaries between yourself and others. We need some enclosure and container as long as our community of inner voices, the *nafs,* is still "cooking"; that is, still finding its way to a complete sense of self. The Qur'an advocates:

Spend your life in the cause of Unity—
consider it a loan to Allah.
Your life will double, at least, in interest.
Only the One expands and contracts you—
no other source of need or bounty.
And only to the One do you return.[14]

❧ Roots and Branches ❧

Traditional translations of this quality include "spreader" and "uncloser." In *Basit,* the sound of *BA-* opens from the inside and reverses the direction of the *QAB* in *Qabid.* It expresses the same radiating, creating energy that we saw in *Bari* (12). This is not the sudden opening of a door, as in *Fattah* (18). Rather, *Basit* gradually expands from a center in all directions. From a still centerpoint, we unfold into a larger circle with definite boundaries; this begins by our rediscovering sacred space inside, as in *Quddus* (4).

Meditation

Center again in the heart. Place your hands gently over your heart, then breathe and open them as you feel the sound *Baa-* opening outward. As you reach the end of the word, the sound *-sit,* feel your boundaries more porous and expanding to the right place for this moment. They are only as thick or thin, as closed or open, as is helpful to you right now. If so guided, you may also experience *Basit* and *Qabid* alternately, opening and closing, until the rhythm of your heart returns to that found in the heart of the Holy One.

22. Diminishment

Al-Khafid

When you are guided to this pathway,
take the opportunity to honor the part of your being that may feel
small, immature, depressed, or diminished.

SOMETIMES LIFE JUST MAKES us want to hide. You may find it surprising that "divine depression" is one of the names of the Beloved, yet there are moments when honoring what seems like the "least" in us may be the most important thing to do. As my own Sufi guide Moineddin Jablonski once told me, "Sometimes your worst is good enough."

What feels small in us may resist the light of consciousness and want to remain hidden in the shadow. When we find the love of the One in our own love for this aspect of our self, the part of us that feels diminished can be integrated into the soul as the awareness of another divine potential reborn. And yet, to accomplish this, we have to overcome our tendency to shy away from looking into the unknown corners of our being. The following famous story about Mullah Nasruddin illustrates this:

Once upon a time. . . . It was late at night, and Mullah Nasruddin was crawling on his hands and knees under a corner streetlight. A close friend discovered him and, thinking that Mullah may be drunk, tried to help:

"Mullah! Do you need help to find your way home?"

"No, no, my friend . . . I've lost the key to my house. Here . . . get down on your hands and knees and help me look."

Groaning, Mullah's friend lowered himself onto the hard street and began to crawl around. He made a thorough search, peering into all the crevices in the cobblestones, gradually widening his search. After what seemed like hours, his knees were aching. No luck.

"Mullah, I've looked everywhere within thirty feet. Are you sure you lost your keys here?"

"Noo . . . actually, I think I lost them about a block away, over there."

"Mullah, Mullah—you idiot! Why are we wasting our time here, then?"

"Well, the light was better here . . ."

Looking in the dark means a journey into our depths. Where is the place that we find least lovable? It may prove to be the key to our greatest power and joy.

Perhaps life is calling you right now to find the voice inside you that feels diminished through such events as illness, pain, or loss. The One may be hiding in the smallest faces of our inner nature, like a homeopathic medicine that can have great effects even though slight in substance. Hold this part of yourself in your heart, and feel your own heart within the heart of the One. One way you can do this is by calling a circle of your inner self and imagining a table prepared for all the voices within you. Use *Khafid* to gently invite whoever feels an inclination to show up.

⌁ Roots and Branches ⌁

A traditional translation of this quality is "the abaser." The root *KhF* indicates a covering or protection over something. Or, it can indicate the one needing protection. The ending *-iD* reveals that a part of our being is hidden and growing under this protection. The roots of *Khafid* also show a camel walking gently and slowly, but gradually getting to where it needs to go. Indirectly related to this pathway is the Arabic word *Kafi*, meaning "just enough," which is often used as a sacred phrase in healing. When we find healing and growth for the part of us that feels diminished, *Khafid* becomes *Khabir* (31), the seed of great creativity. The Qur'an uses *Khafid* to indicate "those of the left hand," who will feel diminished at the *maliki yaumiddin*, usually translated as "day of judgment." This "day" (literally, an illuminated moment) can be any instant in which we can honestly and lovingly look at all the parts of our being, and allow the love of the One to penetrate them with purifying light.

Meditation

Center again in the heart. Breathe with as much compassion as you can feel at this moment as a benediction to your inner self, a call of recognition and acknowledgment to those voices feeling diminished by the stress of life. Consider the circumstances of your life, and look through the lens of your heart at what seem to be the outer causes of your feeling diminished. Allah is in and with the small as much as with the large. As Jesus said, "Except you become as little children, you will not enter the empowering vision, vibrating through the cosmos" (Matt. 18:3).

BATHING IN UNITY

Sometimes we may work very hard in one area of life without success. Later we discover that what we have learned by "failing" is more important than anything we could have learned by "succeeding." This is why Sufis teach using methods that others consider insignificant. Instead of conveying abstruse philosophies and bundles of facts, the Sufi works through story, silence, dreams, the arts, and music. Some have called this way of working "unlearning."

Once upon a time, Mullah came up with a successful way of making a living: smuggling. Each week, he crossed the border between Persia and Greece with two donkeys, each loaded with a large bale of straw. As he crossed the border in each direction, the customs officials went through everything, but could find only straw. And yet Mullah was getting richer and richer, and everyone knew it. Week by week, the customs officials became more desperate to find something, but always failed.

Many years later, Mullah retired to Egypt. One of the former customs officials looked him up and asked, "Mullah, we know that you were smuggling something all those years ago, between Persia and Greece. Now that you are safely out of harm's way, can't you tell me what it was?"

"Yes, my friend," said Mullah, "now that you are also free of your responsibilities, I can tell you. I was smuggling donkeys."

In reviewing the many books on Sufism, scholars look for consistent historical or theological trends, philosophers look for an overriding metaphysical framework, and scientists look for methods that always work under all circumstances. The actual Sufis, however, concern themselves with the transformation of each person who comes to them. That means smuggling the teaching to the soul while the conscious mind is looking the other way.

Meditation

Take this opportunity to release all preconceptions about your self or your inner selves, including those you have found so far in this work, and simply breathe with the sound and feeling of *Allah* in the heart.

23. Exaltation

الرَّافِعُ

Ar-Rafi`

When you are guided to this pathway,
take the opportunity to contact the part of your being that feels like
jumping for joy, honored and exalted.

SOME PEOPLE WOULD ARGUE that the board game of "swings and roundabouts" (or chutes and ladders), in which one can rise and fall instantly at the throw of the dice, was originally a Sufi game. When we're down, we're really down, and when we're up, we're really up. Rather than swing emotionally between the two extremes, which really means holding on to one or the other as the false identification of our soul, the Sufi would ask, "Can I allow them both to find their places in the heart, in balance?"

When he was young, Mullah Nasruddin's father wanted to train him to take over the family business, which in this story was minding the burial shrine of a Sufi saint. Pilgrims usually tipped the guardian of the shrine, and this could slowly amount to a living. For one reason or another, Mullah was not catching on very well, so his father gave him some time off to go on a journey to the East with his favorite donkey.

Far from home, Mullah's donkey suddenly died, and he was so distraught that he buried the donkey, then sat down and began to cry. And cry. Soon other people began to pass by, and asked Mullah what had happened. But he could only cry.

"This must be the grave of some really great saint!" said one to another, and they sat down and began to pray and meditate. A few weeks later, there was a crowd. One very enterprising and pious person organized to collect money to build a shrine around the grave, where more people could gather.

At this point, Mullah's father became worried about what had happened to him. After months of searching, he finally found him. Mullah explained to his father what had happened, and his father whispered in his ear, "Don't worry, my son, the same thing happened to me. That's how I got into the shrine business."

Perhaps right now, life is calling you to feel refreshed, redeemed, exalted, and high. As with the previous pathway, *Khafid*, this could change tomorrow. Enjoy the experience, but don't hold on. The full-grown plant sheds its leaves and returns to the earth in its season.

⌒ *Roots and Branches* ⌒

A traditional translation of this quality is "the exalter." The root *RF* indicates a recovery or a redemption, an experience or situation that refreshes. Adding the *I'* sound at the end creates the energy of lifting something up or carrying it away. In this sense, *Rafi* expresses the experience of "being carried away." Through its initial root it is related to *Ra'uf* (83), the divine wings of healing. The Qur'an uses this name in a way similar to that of the previous quality, *Khafid* (22), to indicate those who will be "of the right hand" at the "day of judgment." We can view this as the place in our being that, when standing in the honest light of the One, fully reflects the Beloved's dignity and honor.

Meditation

Center in the heart and breathe this sound gently toward the belly. Call a circle of the inner self and use this name as a greeting. See who shows up. Who feels exalted or honored? On the breath, the sound can become both an invitation and a blessing, which allows our small self to feel carried away by its connection to the greater Self of the divine.

24. High "Self" Esteem

المُعِزُّ

Al-Mu`izz

When you are guided to this pathway,
take the opportunity to contact the place in your soul where you
find stability and feel evidence of the One's beauty, grace, and richness in
your soul, the place of sacred high self-esteem.

MANY OF US FIND it much easier to deal with failure than with success. Outward success can be so seductive that we know subconsciously we can easily be pulled off-center and do something foolish. The fear of doing this almost always causes us to do something foolish. So we'd just as soon not try, and keep to ourselves instead.

You may find it difficult to reconcile the notion of high self-esteem with the Sufi idea that ultimately the ego we think of as ourselves isn't real. What "self" are we trying to improve? And why build a self in order to tear it down?

Rumi, however, compares the situation to chickpeas cooking in a pot. They keep trying to jump out, and the cook keeps batting them back in with his spoon. Life is cooking us, and we resist because we don't know our purpose in life, the "meal" that is being prepared. The cook says to the chickpeas, "You were once drinking fresh dew in the garden. That was so you could be a nice meal for the Guest. Don't dwell on the self you think you are. Let yourself be transformed into something even better—a meal for the Beloved." In Rumi's view, the whole universe is involved in transformation, in eating and being eaten for the sake of an evolution driven by love.

Perhaps life is showing you right now a face of the Beloved reflected somewhere within, which feels greater than your small self or any part of it, and you cannot deny it. Or, you are calling to the place deep within you that is ready to manifest this face in yourself. This is not your spirit of guidance, which is always connected to the One, but the most confident and faithful part of your *nafs,* or inner self, the reflection of "saving grace." This place in you also honors others—it doesn't have a messiah-complex—because it feels the source of its own honor in the certainty of the One.

⌒ *Roots and Branches* ⌒

Traditional translations of this quality include "the honorer" and "the exalter." The roots of this name indicate the embodiment or internalization (*MU-*) of the persistence and strength of a rock (*-`IZZ*), a deep sense of certainty. The outer aspect of the name shows a strength that others prize or honor, because it reflects their own divine certainty back to them. Since, however, the real source is Allah, the outward honor passes away in time. In this sense, while you are either experiencing this quality inwardly or are being seen in this capacity, *Muizz* can help to anchor the experience in the Holy One. Its parent is the pathway of *Aziz* (8). The Qur'an uses both this name and the next, *Mudhill,* to indicate that both high and low self-esteem can change from day to day, and have no ultimate reality except in the being of the One.

Meditation

Center again in the heart. Breathe rhythmically the sound *Ya Moo-eez.* Try bowing the upper body forward slowly as you do this, with the final sound resonating into the heart, and then down into the belly as a blessing. Isn't the certainty and esteem of the One already in every particle of existence? If so, why not in you as well? What others see in you really belongs to the Beloved, which everyone is chasing in various forms.

25. Low "Self" Esteem

المُذِلُّ

Al-Mudhill

When you are guided to this pathway,
take the opportunity to acknowledge and include in your heart the place in
you that feels weak, exhausted, divided, and overextended, low in
self-esteem because you feel that "you" have to do it all.

THE LAST THREE PATHWAYS have seesawed us between some frightful extremes in our being. How could "low self-esteem," under any definition of "self," be sacred? Our culture is relentlessly focused on making us feel "up," good, and together, or at least to appear that way. The subliminal message is this: If you don't feel (or look) good, stay at home. Or go to therapy. Or both.

The Sufis, however, take another point of view. Just as the pathway *Khafid* (22) showed us, the part of our being that we avoid can hold great treasures. For instance, the "undeveloped" side of our personality, which is not cultured and socially acceptable, can provide protection for our inner work. People ignore us and leave us to get on with our lives. Because real learning means unlearning everything we falsely believe we know about ourselves, excessive praise from the outside can reinforce who we think we are. For this reason, some Sufis actively took the "path of blame." That is, they deliberately acted in a way that guaranteed they would be ignored, dishonored, or marginalized. Throughout the tradition, we find stories about hearing wisdom from those whom we ignore, because their manners don't fit our stereotypes. For instance, here's one that Rumi told about Muhammad:

One day during prayer time, a simple peasant came into the mosque while Muhammad was leading community prayers. As part of one of the prayer cycles, Muhammad recited the portion of the Qur'an in which Moses comes before Pharaoh, but Pharaoh refuses to listen.

"That goddamn son of a bitch!" exclaimed the peasant. After everyone had held their breath, some began to shush him, and the prayers continued.

Afterward, several of the Prophet's companions began to lay into the peasant, telling him that not only was his interruption rude, it had invalidated his prayer.

While they were still haranguing him, the angel Gabriel came to Muhammad and said to him, "Allah has two messages for you. First, peace to you. Second, would you please tell your friends to stop harassing this poor peasant? His sincere cursing pleased me more than the others' prayers."

Perhaps right now, life is offering you the opportunity to hear wisdom from the part of your being that feels unacceptable, like the peasant in the story. Perhaps this voice is telling you that you've been following other people's agendas and ignoring your own inner needs. This can lead to you feeling divided and weakened, as if you were wandering in a desert. Here is an opportunity to discover your low self-esteem as part of the divine low self-esteem. As one of the late Jewish Wisdom texts, *Thunder, Perfect Mind*, says, speaking in the voice of Holy Wisdom:

Advance together to childhood:
the small, the simple, the poor
can live with
the great, the complex, the rich.
Don't isolate great from small,
rich from poor within you.
By one you know the other
and none can live in health divided.[15]

~ Roots and Branches ~

Traditional translations of this quality include "the reducer" and "the leader astray." Both *Mudhill* and *Muizz*, the previous pathway, embody or internalize (*MU-*) certain feelings, qualities, and processes of the One in you. The root *`IZZ* of *Muizz* shows the divine strength expressing itself in a multitude of ways. In a manner of speaking, the direction is from Sacred Unity to Sacred Diversity. The root *-DhLL* of *Mudhill* shows the starting point as diversity and division (*Dh*, pronounced similar to a *z*), which then becomes magnified (*LL*) without a connection to the divine life force of the One. In its extreme, the word symbolizes isolation. Yet by recognizing this feeling, we have already taken a step toward reconnecting our diversity with Unity. When this happens, *Mudhill* transforms itself into *Dhul* (85), the mastery of a particular quality, one to One.

Meditation

Center again in the heart. As the medieval German Christian mystic Meister Eckhart once said, "God is at home. We are the ones who have gone out for a walk." Breathe *Ya Moo-zill* down into the belly. Find where division and forgetfulness reconnect to the circle of the Holy One. Call a circle of the inner self and invite everyone to return home to the table of Holy Wisdom. Breathe with the feeling of love and respect toward all the exiled parts of your being.

26. *Awakened Hearing*

As-Sami`

When you are guided to this pathway,
take the opportunity to stop and listen to the sounds of Sacred Unity all
around you. In each, there is a drop of the One, and in that drop is the
ocean of all divine qualities.

CERTAIN SAYINGS OF MUHAMMAD contain what are called "sacred traditions" (*hadith qudsi*), which are the voice of Allah coming through Muhammad, but not contained within the Qur'an. One of these sayings, loved by Sufis, follows:

> *My intimate servants never cease to come nearer and nearer to me*
> *through performing acts of loving worship beyond what I have com-*
> *manded until I embrace them entirely in My Love. When I embrace*
> *them, I am the hearing by which they hear, the seeing by which they*
> *see, the hands with which they grasp, and the feet with which they*
> *walk. If they supplicate Me for all humanity, certainly I will respond.*
> *If they seek refuge with Me for all humanity, surely I will grant it.*[16]

This tradition reminds us of the purpose of any spiritual practice, or of life itself, according to the creation stories shared by Judaism, Christianity, and Islam. We are here to hold within us the consciousness of all the beings that have traveled before us in the caravan of life, and to include the view of the whole cosmos in our vision. This is what it means to live up to our divine image, to be essence-beings, or *a-dam* in the Hebrew language (*dam* meaning "essence," "juice," or "blood").

Perhaps life is asking you to receive something beyond what you're hearing—an energy, atmosphere, light, or texture behind the words. Or you may need to open your hearing to the divine voice and resonance coming through your own voice. This usually requires clearing out the voices of others who have told you that your voice (or creativity) must sound or appear a certain way. This pathway opens a door to allow us to hear with our own ears, which, at the deepest level, are the ears of the One.

⟶ Roots and Branches ⟵

A traditional translation of this quality is "the all-hearing." This and the next few pathways take us into the world of sensation, body awareness, and vibration. Like the Semitic word root *ShM* of the Hebrew and Aramaic languages, *Sami* indicates the name, sound, and wave reality of the cosmos. The ending sound *-I`* connects each sound to the Source of sound. When we are able to hear Unity's sound everywhere (or at least somewhere), we are reconnected to the source of all life. The Qur'an often uses this quality in tandem with *Alim* (19), the understanding of forms. One notable instance is in Sura 2:256, which forbids "compulsion or coercion" in any matter of faith, belief, religion, or moral law.

Meditation

Center again in the heart. Breathe the sound *Ya Sa-Mee* and bathe in the center of all sound, without focusing on any particular sound. Follow the sense of hearing inward instead of outward, back to its source: Where within you does hearing begin?

27. *Awakened Sight*

البَصِيرُ

Al-Basir

When you are guided to this pathway,
take the opportunity to open your sense of sight to the light of
Unity everywhere.

LIKE THE PREVIOUS PATHWAY, *Sami*, this one also asks us to let go of the rigid ways in which we sometimes grasp and hold on to things with our senses. Most of us find this more difficult to do with sight than with hearing, because Western culture bombards us with many quick, visual images, in advertising, television, and the Internet. This pathway recommends: Don't close your eyes, just allow Allah to use them.

> *Once upon a time, a shopkeeper had an assistant who looked at everything cross-eyed, so he always saw double. One day the shopkeeper asked the assistant to go into the storeroom and fetch a large jar of oil to bring to the front.*
>
> *The assistant returned a moment later and asked, "There are two there. Which one should I bring?"*
>
> *The shopkeeper sighed, since she was used to these questions. So she decided to try a new tack.*
>
> *"Just break one of the jars and bring the other!"*
>
> *So the assistant did it, but when one jar broke, so did the other.*

This story suggests that what we perceive as duality or "two-ness" may have no more ultimate reality than the two jars seen by the cross-eyed assistant.

Perhaps life is calling you right now to look beyond the appearances of things; not to find just a deeper meaning, but a whole new way of looking. Is what you're seeing in any way a mirror of your life, or of your inner self? Can you see the "other" as a part of yourself, and view him or her with as much compassion as you can bring to this moment?

❧ Roots and Branches ❧

A traditional translation of this quality is "the all-seeing." We can read the roots of *Basir* in a number of different ways. In one sense, the word is the illumination (*-IR*) of embodied growth (*BaS-*). By another reading (*BA+ SIR*), it depicts sight as that which stops the gaze from seeing straight through a thing back to Unity, and causes it to circle around the outer appearance. Related words in Aramaic (*besra*) and Arabic (*bashar*) indicate our flesh—that is, our substance—which can either express our purpose in life or not, depending upon our awareness of the divine in the moment.

Meditation

Center again in the heart. Breathe the sound *Ya BaSeer*, radiating outward, directing it to and through the eyes. Release the jaw and let the eyes relax, becoming windows of the soul through which the One can look. Then, or at another time, internalize the sound, breathe the name, and continue to gaze, not fixing on any particular form but seeing through all forms to the light of the One that permeates them. Feel this light as the divine intelligence seeing through you. Or, as in the previous pathway, breathe the sound, close the eyes, and follow the sense of seeing back to the Source.

28. The Sacred Sixth Sense

الحَكَم

Al-Hakam

When you are guided to this pathway,
take the opportunity to contact the place in you from which sensing
arises—the Sacred Sense behind the outer senses of seeing, hearing,
smelling, touching, and tasting. Remain in the middle of the swirl of
impressions surrounding you, as a witness.

OUT OF A CHAOS of impressions, we somehow discriminate between what our senses take in and what we consciously experience. Even though we might call this the brain, the nervous system, or the self, there is really no scientific name for this organizing "sixth sense." It prevents us from being overwhelmed by the flood of impressions to which we are constantly subjected and enables us to say "*I* smell, *I* hear, *I* taste, *I* touch, *I* see." We know that something in us must do this because there are people whose sense of "I-ness" has splintered into multiple selves and who are unable to act as unified beings. Modern psychology has found that this often happens when a person does not receive enough healthy touch early in life.

For the Sufi, our individual "I," as well as the various impressions and feelings within us, find a home in the heart of the divine, the only "I Am." Likewise, our individual senses are empowered by a Sacred Sense, which can connect us directly to the Source. Because this sense does its work without the need for us to consciously focus on it, we might ask, why even think about it? In one sense, this part of our being represents our more primitive human intelligence, the animal part of our nature. Driven by the need to achieve, we often ignore and overwork this part of our being. If we listened to it, it would tell us that we need to respect certain limits if we want our bodies to stay healthy and so help us fulfill our heart's desire. Many Sufi stories talk about animals to show the way we treat these more instinctive parts of our inner self:

Mullah Nasruddin decided that he would like to get into a new line of work: raising donkeys. He consulted with all the best minds and found that the main expense in the business was food. So he decided that the way to increase his profit margin would simply be to feed the donkey less. He began to train his first donkey by starting with a normal meal, then slowly, day by day, cutting down on the donkey's ration. At first, it seemed to work. The donkey actually looked better after a few days and Mullah was encouraged, so he gradually reduced the donkey's food more. However, just as gradually the donkey started to look more and more unhappy, weaker and weaker. Finally, it couldn't even stand. And then it died.

"Too bad," said Mullah, "If it had just held out a bit longer I would have trained it to live on nothing."

Perhaps right now life is calling you to sense what is behind your senses. What is feeding you in your food? What breathes through your breath? What makes love when you do? Pull back the senses from always reaching outward, and try directing them inward by taking a few gentle breaths. Take this time to clear the senses, which may be overstimulated or exhausted. Fall back into the dark arms of Sacred Sense. Remain in the middle of things.

☜— *Roots and Branches* ☜—

Traditional translations of this quality include "judge" and "arbitrator." The roots of this pathway point to breath fully embodied (*H*) within a dense, yet-to-be-explored territory (*KM*). It is from the latter root that we have the Arabic *al-khemia*, the origin of the English word *alchemy*. Both roots also appear in the Hebrew word *Hokhmah*, the Holy Wisdom (or Sacred Sense) mentioned in Proverbs 8–9. As the creation story in Genesis 1:2–3 says, when divine darkness and divine breath make love, light-intelligence or consciousness is born. *Hakam* is directly related to another pathway, *Hakim* (46), discriminating wisdom, as well as indirectly related to *Haqq* (51), the embodiment of life energy.

Meditation

Center again in the heart. Like the previous two pathways, this one can take us to the place inside where darkness turns into light, unknowing into knowing. We can begin to feel this place in the pause between two breaths. Gently withdraw from the pull of outer sensation and experience for a moment. Breathe the sound *Ya HaKam* (with the *H* lightly aspirated) into the belly. Breathe into a hidden place where you can experience life as one.

29. *Putting Things in Order*

العَدلُ

Al-`Adl

When you are guided to this pathway,
take the opportunity to contact the place in your being that can put things in
order in your life. This is the face of the One Being in us that establishes
material, mental, and emotional justice.

USING THE WORD *justice* in relation to our own feelings and thoughts may raise questions. Some of us have an overactive interior voice that judges us constantly. We know the downside of being overcritical of ourselves—in a nutshell, being afraid to do anything.

This pathway introduces us to the potential "Solomon" of our inner self, a place that analyzes experience with loving wisdom. This voice in us tries to accurately reckon and reconcile time and space, emotional and mental needs, and all of the other million details of human experience bubbling on the surface of eternity. Because this part of us sees the big picture, it can seem uncompromising to the rest of our inner self. The best way to train it is to give it something to do, rather than let it take over, which can lead to an efficient yet strangely unfulfilling life. Overcontrol is not the way forward here.

Mullah Nasruddin again decided to change occupations. Instead of breeding donkeys, he decided to raise carrier pigeons. Upon consulting the best minds, he determined that the main difficulty with the whole system of using carrier pigeons was that the bird could easily lose the message wrapped around its leg. Mullah thought long and hard, and then hit upon a brilliant idea. If he could cross a carrier pigeon with a talking parrot, the bird could simply memorize the message at one end and repeat it at the other—no scrap of paper to lose.

Somehow Mullah succeeded. The bird had a wonderful sense of direction and could also talk. Before he put the bird on the market, Mul-

lah decided to do a trial (some medieval beta testing). He taught the bird a message, then gave it to a friend to take to his own village. He told the friend to release the bird in the morning at a particular time. Then he waited. And waited.

Finally, at the end of the day, many hours after the bird should have arrived, it showed up.

"You idiot! What took you so long?" asked Mullah. "You should have been here hours ago!"

"Ah well," replied the bird. "It was such a nice day that I decided to walk!"

Perhaps life is calling you right now to put your outer life in order. Or, an overactive inner critic, who is always attempting to make you more efficient, is plaguing you. In either case, the best approach is love. Allow this self within you to have its say. Is it speaking in your own voice or in that of another—for instance, a parent, relative, or former teacher? If so, send the part of this quality that is not yours back home. What remains can join the circle of your self and help you find proportion in your life.

～ Roots and Branches ～

Traditional translations of this quality include "the just" and "the equitable." The roots of this name point to the distribution and mastery (*DL*) of formed existence (*'A*). On one level, this quality of the heart's surface (which we could call the "mind") realizes that our existence in the flesh is limited, and so it wishes to make the best use of time. `Adl*, like the previous pathway, *Hakam*, is another endowment of our earlier, instinctive human consciousness. The Qur'an uses the word to refer to the fulfillment of the promises of the One with respect to time, proportion, and justice.

Meditation

Center again in the heart. Breathe in with the feeling of the sound *Ya `A* (the *A* is guttural and backward into the throat), and breathe out the sound *DiL* (expanding and opening within). Use this breath to gently remind yourself that all reckoning belongs to the One, who is compassion and mercy. Then look through the heart's eyes at the way you live your life right now. How do you spend your time each day? What is most important now in order to further your purpose in life?

30. Subtle Mystery

اللَّطِيفُ

Al-Latif

When you are guided to this pathway,
take the opportunity to contact the part of your being that reflects,
and can reflect upon, mystery and subtlety.

I N EXPLORING OUR INNER self through the pathways of the heart, we may be tempted to believe that we could one day understand everything. We could explain all miracles if only we could train our senses and feelings to be subtle enough (for instance, by exploring the previous pathways *Hakam* and *`Adl*). This pathway and the next (which are often linked) tell us that whatever sensitivity we may develop through our bodies, nervous systems, and senses, whatever self-control we may master, divine mystery will remain. The following Quranic meditation (Sura 22.63) expresses this:

> *My Beloved, please ask everyone to notice how*
> *the One Being sends rain from the sky*
> *and immediately the fields green.*
> *The One's sight and sense cannot be fathomed,*
> *so subtle, nurturing, mysterious*
> *bringing the seed-self of all beings to fruition.*[17]

Mystery remains an active force in the universe, like a wild card in the game of existence. As the saying goes, this could be good news or bad news, depending upon how your life is going at the moment. All other things being equal, the Sufi usually opts for mystery. As Rumi says:

> *Be empty of what you think you know.*
> *That's why Muhammad said,*
> *"Fools will take up the most of paradise."*

Your clever mind just whips up
a dust storm of pride.
Allow yourself to be fooled and
peace clowns its way into your heart.
If your head would shatter in wonder
at what Reality really is,
reason's tyranny would end and
every hair on your head would
become an oracle.[18]

Perhaps life is calling you right now to contemplate subtlety and mystery and to stand in awe of the One Reality of life. Don't try to explain things, just add wonder and gratitude. When we begin to see with the eyes of *Latif,* everything around us seems to have its own, uniquely beautiful, secret place inside. And Allah protects Allah's secret in us all.

∾ Roots and Branches ∾

Traditional translations of this quality include "subtle" and "gracious." The roots of *Latif* show something that gets our attention (the sound *LA*), within which lies a mystery (*T*) of great charm and beauty (*IF*). The subtle centers of the body—for instance, heart, throat, third eye, crown, solar plexus, sexual center, and root—are called by a related word, *lata'if,* in the Sufi tradition. *Latif* and the next pathway, *Khabir,* growing inner awareness, are often linked in Quranic passages that encourage one to look deeply into the wonders of nature to discover the living presence of the divine.

Meditation

Center again in the heart. Breathe in the sound *LA-* fully and gently, and then breathe out the sound *-Teeef* even more gently, feeling the sound vibrating the subtle centers of the body. Feel the breath massaging the whole nervous system, and allow the subtlest wavelengths of Unity to heal your whole self.

31. The Seed of Potential

Al-Khabir

When you are guided to this pathway,
take the opportunity to rest in the place in your inner being that is
germinating like a seed.

MANY TIMES WE CAN catch glimpses of a new way of being or acting, but we feel a voice inside telling us that we're not ready for it yet. When this voice carries an edge of fear or sounds like someone in our previous life, we'd do best to release it. When it comes clearly and with love, it may be the inner voice of wisdom, to which this pathway directs us.

The previous pathway asked us to embrace mystery and subtlety in our lives. This one directs us further inside to recognize that deep within us lies a seed of potential, waiting for the right time, place, soil, weather, sun, and position to sprout. On another level, *Khabir* is the "still, small voice" of the Holy One heard by Elijah in the cave, as described in the Hebrew Bible. This voice of guidance arrives unexpectedly, or from a seemingly insignificant source. Its message is this: What's of value may take time to grow. Saadi of Shiraz says:

Things that come easily don't last long.
In China it took forty years to make a porcelain bowl,
while a hundred a day pour out of a kiln in Baghdad.
Which is worth more?
A chick fresh out of the egg pecks its own food,
while an infant remains helpless for many years.
The first never raises its gaze from the ground,
while the second can find stars and galaxies inside.

Perhaps now is a seed-time for you, and life is calling you to provide subtle love and attention to this face of Allah in yourself or in another. Don't dig up the seed (as the man in the story related at the end of the Introduction did), just warm it with the radiance of divine compassion, expressing itself through you. When anything comes into awareness, it proceeds from the depths to the surface, from seed to plant. What universe is waiting to be born in your heart?

—ᷜ *Roots and Branches* ᷜ—

Traditional translations of this quality include "the knower" and "the aware." As mentioned, *Khabir* is related by root to *Khafid* (22), honoring the small within us. What felt restricted or contracted (*Kh*) and so diminished and ignored (-*FID*) is now reborn (*B-*) into awareness (-*IR*) and becomes part of the divine plan for your life. In comparison with *Alim* (19), the understanding of names and forms, this type of knowing illuminates a process of growth. When *Khabir* grows into full manifestation, it becomes *Kabir* (37), outward creative power. From this externalized form it can again return to its seed-self, and the cycle of growth repeats.

Meditation

Center again in the heart. Breathe with the sound *Ya KhaBeer* and allow it to sink into your being like rain into dry ground, like the sun warming the earth in the spring. Breathe the initial sound *Kha-* into the heart, and then breathe the sound -*BeeR* outward, feeling the potential for growth. Find the place inside where a new awareness dawns, and what is waiting to be born begins to stir. Nurture that feeling by breathing softly from the heart into the inner self.

32. Dissolving Chains

Al-Halim

When you are guided to this pathway,
take the opportunity to feel the ropes that entangle you stretching until they
dissolve and fall away.

S UDDENLY, WITHOUT WARNING, AN expanded state of awareness can come upon us. Many people have experienced this
when walking in nature, being in love, or playing a sport. If we shrug
off this experience or push it away, we've missed a door into another
world. The classical Sufis called this momentary epiphany by the
name of *hal*. They distinguished these "states of grace" from the
awareness that we gain by effort in everyday life (which they called
maqam). However, the division is not so neat. Something that passes
away may be just as valuable as what remains, if it shows us a new
possibility or unties the knots of the moment. The eleventh-century
Sufi Al-Qushayri compared these states to:

> *First, flashes of lightning*
> *   from an unknown horizon,*
> *then rays of light*
> *   showing the path ahead,*
> *finally, light all around,*
> *   the full brilliance revealed*
> *only to those who*
> *   turn their senses within.*

This pathway reveals a part of our inner being through which the
Holy One dissolves tension and frees us from our conceptions of
the past. This is why Sufis emphasize unlearning. What we need is
not more information, but a deeper knowledge of ourselves. And if

our way of knowing ourselves is faulty, all the teachers and books in the world can't help us. It is like the famous story of the men in the dark:

> *Some men took refuge from a storm in a barn that was pitch-black inside. "There's something in here with us!" exclaimed one. "I can hear it breathing."*
>
> *"You're right. I'm reaching out and feeling a large, rough wall that seems to be moving."*
>
> *"No! From where I am it feels like a snake."*
>
> *"Over here I feel a very large leaf moving up and down."*
>
> *"Over here I feel the trunk of a tree."*
>
> *The men argued for a while longer and then decided to light a torch. When they did, they found that they were all looking at an elephant.*

Perhaps life is calling you right now to relax into the divine hands that can loosen the knots in your muscles, whether emotional, physical, mental, or psychic. These hands can knead forever. All we need to remember is that they are always there, ready and waiting. Or, perhaps you are being called upon to release and forgive another person. In one of his poems, the twentieth-century Sufi Samuel L. Lewis recounts a vision of the heaven of Isaac, over the doorway of which was written, "Abandon tension all ye who enter here." This pathway opens the door to that heaven.

⌒ Roots and Branches ⌒

Traditional translations of this quality include "forbearing" and "clement." As indicated above, this pathway shares its main root with the word *hal,* which can mean an accommodation for something, a tent, or a spiritual state. A spiritual state can hold us and release us; its nature is to come and go. A state that descends upon us in tune with the purpose of our lives can free us from a rigid view of who we think we are. *Halim* is also related to the Arabic word for dreams and visions. The Islamic tradition gives the name *Halim Allah* to the prophet Ismail, the first son of Abraham. In the Qur'an's version of the story, it was Ismail whom God ordered Abraham to sacrifice, and upon hearing this, Ismail remained serene and calm.

Meditation

Center again in the heart. Allow your breath to go wherever you feel any unnecessary tension. Breathe the sound *Ya Ha-LeeM*, and feel it massaging and loosening your being, bringing it back into the right tuning for the moment.

33. *Flexible Strength*

Al-`Azim

When you are guided to this pathway,
take the opportunity to feel a flexible strength that can adapt to any
situation and yet remain rooted in, and moving toward,
the purpose of your life.

ONE OF LIFE'S GREATEST obstacles can be regret. "If only . . ." leads us down a path upon which we become weaker and weaker with every step we take. However, if we listen deeply inside, a part of our being says, "Forget the past. . . . Just keep going!" This pathway provides a reservoir of resolution and flexibility, which allows us to overcome despair at the way things have gone, or are going, in the outer drama of our lives. It offers us the hope that we can redeem any situation by realigning ourselves with the Source of Life. Rumi says:

Never give up hope in the Beloved.
Hope is the trailhead of the path to refuge.
Even if you're not on the path,
at least guard the trailhead.
"I've acted crookedly," you say.
Remember Moses' staff, which,
becoming a snake, ate the wands
of Pharaoh's magicians.
When you find the straight way
it eats up all the crookedness of your past.

Perhaps life is calling you right now to find a place in yourself that reflects this divine audacity and flexible strength in the face of all odds. Or, perhaps you are being asked to notice this quality in others as they express the sacred in their own unique ways. Sometimes the worst of life can bring out the best in us. It's then that we come closer to what is truly divine within.

∽ Roots and Branches ∽

Traditional translations of this quality include "supreme" and "the greatest." *Azim* is indirectly related to *Aziz* (8), which is the One working through the strength of form. As in that word, the beginning sound `AZ* shows breath condensing and focusing itself. The ending *-M* shows that this condensed, energized substance can also be flexible and fluid. It can adapt to any situation, or appear in any person. The same root helps form the Arabic word for *bone*. As this condensed yet flexible strength, *Azim* becomes the definition of what it means to be great. When the Persian dervishes saw this quality in another, they would greet each other with this name, using the Persian pronunciation *ya az'm*.

Meditation

Center again in the heart. Breathe in the sound `A- (with the sound going backward into the body), and breathe out the sound -ZeeM, feeling it spread from the heart to the solar plexus and the third eye (with the heart remaining at the center). Breathe until you feel the sensation balanced in these centers. Can you allow the breath of this quality to bring out the best in all the strengths that you bring to life? Remember in your heart some of the people you know—friends, family, coworkers, teachers. How do they express this flexible strength in the ways they uniquely approach life's challenges?

BATHING IN UNITY

The prophet Muhammad was once on a journey with some companions.
Some of the men stood up and began chanting very loudly "Allaho Akbar!"
("Unity Is Always Greater"). The Prophet told them, "Friends, please go
easy on yourselves, and don't raise your voices. You're not calling to
one who is deaf or absent. The One is here. The Reality to whom you're
praying is closer to you than the neck of your camel."

When we get enthused about something, it's easy to get carried away. We may then find ourselves simply following others, without any real consciousness of what we're doing. The Sufis recognize that ecstasy can transform our ordinary consciousness. They also, however, warn us to keep one eye open on our common sense, and to not follow along simply because it seems the right thing to do. Here's a famous story about this warning, told by Rumi:

Once upon a time, a community of poor dervishes invited Mullah Nasrud-
din to a banquet in his honor. At the time, Mullah was becoming
renowned as some sort of sage, and he turned to his servant and said,
"This is the way a great Sufi should be treated! Pack the donkey and
let's go!"

When he arrived, the dervishes greeted Mullah with all the appropriate
honors: "Ya Az'm! O Great One, Sufi of Sufis! You are most welcome, and
we are not worthy! Please come and rest from your long journey. When
you awaken, all will be prepared."

"See," said Mullah to his servant, "this is how it should be. . . . Remem-
ber! Now, don't bother me until the banquet."

Unknown to Mullah, once he had gone to a tent to rest, the poor
dervishes took his donkey and sold it to buy provisions for the meal and to
hire entertainers. Mullah's servant saw this, but because he had been in-
structed to not bother Mullah, he didn't. Hours later, the dervishes woke

Mullah and said, "O Great One! All is prepared. Please don't trouble your-self about anything, and come and join us." Mullah's servant tried to tell him about the donkey, but Mullah brushed him off. "Not now! Can't you see that this is my night? Everything is ready!"

As great evenings went, it was truly great—all the best food, delica-cies, and music (a good donkey was worth a lot in those days!). Then, without pause, as such gatherings went, the dervishes broke into sacred song and chant. These things went on for hours, or all night.

"Mullah! Mullah!" said his servant.

"Not now—didn't I tell you?" said Mullah.

The chants of the Sufis are often many-layered. One part comes in for a while, then another group joins with another praise or affirmation, then another. Soon everything is going on at once. The conventional wisdom is "just follow along." As the hours passed, Mullah was getting higher and higher. Whether it was the food, the drink, the music, or the chant, he couldn't tell, but he just joined in as best he could. Soon he began to hear a very high musical part coming in over the top of all the chants of "Allah! Allah!" As he could just make out the words, he heard: "The donkey is gone, the donkey is gone, donkey is gone, is gone, the donkey, the donkey, is gone, is gone, donkey gone, donkey, donkey, gone, gone . . ."

"Hmm," thought Mullah to himself. "Must be some local chant I've never heard before." And he joined in. After a while the chant moved on to something else, and finally Mullah just passed out.

The next thing he knew, he felt the sun on his face and heard the birds singing in the trees of the oasis. As he sat up and looked around, he saw that the banquet, tents, and dervishes had vanished. Only his servant was left, who was sitting looking at him.

"Wow! Some evening!" said Mullah. "Fetch the donkey and let's head home."

"But Mullah," said his servant, "They sold your donkey to pay for the banquet. I thought you knew, and that's why you were singing, 'The don-key is gone!'"

On its surface, this story tells us that imitation can be dangerous on the spiritual path. If we look a bit deeper, we can also see that the animal part of our inner self, or *nafs*, represented by the donkey, literally gets carried away when we become addicted to a certain type of ecstasy. This can happen when we have a genuine spiritual experience, an altered state of consciousness, and then find ourselves simply wanting to repeat it again and again. We then need to recover our "donkey" later, by bringing our supposed (yet ungrounded) spirituality into everyday life. This was obviously a problem even in Rumi's time. Yet it's even more of a problem today because Western culture constantly directs us to fulfill our desires *now*, without regard to past or future. No doubt real spiritual experiences do happen in a very present, timeless moment (which the Sufis call a *waqt*). Yet we have to ask ourselves, as the Nasruddin story illustrates: When does the power of *now* become the narcissism of now?

Meditation

Center again in the heart. Breathe in the sound *Al-*, and out the sound *-lah*, with as much ease and release of tension as you can feel in this moment. Find your home in the breath. Is there any part of your life in which you are simply following along and imitating others, while an essential feature of your inner self goes missing? Is there a way in which you can bring your awareness of the sacred in the present moment to bear on your entire life—past, present, and future?

34. The Forgiveness of Light

الغَفُورُ

Al-Ghafur

*When you are guided to this pathway,
take the opportunity to touch the place in you that can deeply understand a
situation, and so release an impression you are holding or heal a wound
you are nursing.*

IN AN EARLIER PATHWAY, *Ghaffar* (14), we saw that sometimes an impression that we want to release needs to be burned away. As we circle around something that has lodged itself in our heart, the heat generated from going deeper and deeper can often heal the wound. In this case, the circling draws us in upon ourselves, as though boiling or cooking us. The present pathway, by contrast, shows us that some impressions yield instead to greater wisdom. In this case, circling around the situation draws us outward to a wider, healing perspective of the situation. The divine Beloved seems to take whatever pain we're holding into another universe, simply causing it to disappear. What remains is a broader, deeper understanding of the situation or person involved.

One day, when the Prophet Muhammad was sitting with his companions, one of them saw him smiling and asked about it. The Prophet responded:

"One day two believers will kneel before Allah, and one will ask for compensation for the wrong that the other has done to him. Allah will then ask the accused to make this compensation, but he will respond,

'O Sustainer, I don't have a single good action left to give him.'

'Then can't he carry some of my burdens?' the accuser will ask."

Muhammad commented, "It will be a truly terrible day in human history when people are not able to carry their own burdens."

"Then Allah will ask the accuser to look into the garden of paradise and describe what he sees.

'I see cities of silver, palaces of gold crowned with pearls. What great prophet will possess these?'

'Only those who can pay the full price,' said the One Being.

'But who, O Sustainer, could possibly do that?'

'You can—by forgiving your brother.'

'O Sustaining One, I do so immediately.'

'Then take your brother's hand and enter paradise together.' "

Muhammad told his companions: "Be astounded by the love of the One. Make peace among yourselves now, or Allah will establish his own peace among you on the day of resurrection."[19]

Perhaps life is calling you right now to open your heart to the miraculous healing power of the One and to a wider, deeper insight into the situation that troubles you. How this forgiveness happens is as mysterious as the passage from one world to the next. At some point, we simply need to let the One Being do the forgiving. A large part of this pathway is "Thy will be done."

⌒ Roots and Branches ⌒

Traditional translations of this quality include "pardoner" and "all-forgiving." The roots of *Ghafur* are similar to the earlier pathway *Ghaffar* (14), burning away tension. The *GhF* shows a constriction of breath, something that we hold rigidly and unconsciously. In this case, the release comes from light (*UR*) rather than from fire and heat (*AR*). Strictly speaking, in Semitic languages, *light* means intelligence, or what is known. *Darkness* simply means what is unknown. Both are part of the One's universe. In this case, as with the pathway *Nur* (93), the light of intelligence, we are not talking about the surface intelligence of the mind, but a deeper knowing that includes heart and mind. By another rendering, the roots of *Ghafur* and *Ghaffar* can also point to a shroud or veil between a person and the ultimate Reality. In this sense, forgiveness can be a protective veil in that it reminds us that we are not always in a state of unity with Unity. We are still on the way.

Meditation

Center again in the heart. Hold your hands cupped together before you, as though offering your heart to Allah to heal. Breathe with the atmosphere of this pathway.

Or, place one hand lightly over your chest, and breathe with the sound *Ya Gha-Foor*. Call a circle of your inner self, and invite the various feelings, sensations, and voices within you to Wisdom's table. Ask who may be holding on to anything that they would like to release. Allow the light of the One Being to descend through you as a blessing of forgiveness.

35. *Gratitude, Giving Back*

الشَّكُورُ

Ash-Shakur

When you are drawn to this pathway,
take the opportunity to feel simple gratitude and follow all the divine light
you have received back to its source.

THE QUR'AN MENTIONS THAT all sacred books of all traditions have their origins in the "Mother of the Book," which resides at the primordial beginning, with Allah. This is not a book with words, but rather the archetype of all the sacred teachings of humanity. In addition, the Qur'an (in verse 42:29) teaches that the Arabic words that manifested to the Prophet Muhammad only reflect the larger "Qur'an of creation," which is the universe that the One Being has created. In this sense, each individual being is really a verse of the "sacred manuscript of nature" (as the twentieth-century Sufi Inayat Khan rendered the idea), which transcends all holy books.

After we release the constriction caused by holding on to perceived offenses against us (*Ghafur,* 34), we are free to see the divine intelligence circulating through all the circumstances of our lives. This is the essence of gratitude. As Shabistari puts it:

In the Secret Rose Garden,
roses bloom that reveal
the mysteries of the human heart.
Lilies sing and the narcissus
sees everything perfectly.
To enter this garden,
see with your heart's eyes and
gaze gently on these blossoms.
All your doubts will fade away.
Don't look for mistakes:
The roses may turn to thorns.

Ingratitude reveals ignorance,
and the friends of truth are truly thankful.

Perhaps life is calling you right now to investigate gratitude: Try to see its signs everywhere. If you find this difficult, begin with the small things closest to you. Even thank before you receive. This pathway is not a matter of business, of give and take. It is the sign of a heart that remembers Unity.

—❧ *Roots and Branches* ❧—

Traditional translations of this quality include "thankful" and "grateful." In Arabic, the word *Shakur* has to do with an attitude of recognition and appreciation, rather than with the specific "facts" of a situation. The latter is expressed by another pathway, *Hamid* (56). The root *SH* indicates a circle opening to include more, like the rays of the sun that, in Jesus' words, shine on the just and the unjust. Follow these rays, not the shadow. The sound *-KUR* takes us from the small, particular, formed gifts of the universe back to the Source of eternal light (related to the old Semitic root *AOR*, for "light" and "intelligence"). This light can transform us: Thankfulness changes things.

Meditation

Center again in the heart. Any doorway into this pathway is a good place to start, but they all start and end in the heart. As you walk down the street, begin to look outside of your own envelope of concerns and to-do lists. Look around for things for which to be thankful, and people who are expressing their own unique melodies and fragrances in life. In this way, gradually enter the "secret rose garden."

During a midday break, imagine your own heart as a garden of beauty and invite in the various voices of the inner self. As each enters, welcome and thank them. Then, with your feeling of your inner community united in the only "I Am," look outward and thank your friends, family, community, and all beings.

36. *Experiencing Life at Its Peak*

العَلِيُّ

Al-`Ali

When you are guided to this pathway,
take the opportunity to feel yourself at the peak of everything, including
letting any thought of your self disappear.

REAL ECSTASY IS ONE of life's rare gifts. Sometimes—especially when we're not expecting or seeking it—one of life's "peak experiences" can transform our whole view of life in a radical way. Rumi talks about one such experience in poetic form:

> *At dawn, the moon appeared*
> > *and swooped down from the sky to look at me.*
> *Like a falcon hunting a meal,*
> > *the moon grabbed me and away we went!*
> *I looked for my self, but my self was gone:*
> > *In the moon, by grace, my body became like soul.*
> *Luminous, I journeyed on as soul,*
> > *until the mystery of Self and self was clear.*
> *Nine shimmering heavens mingled in that moon,*
> > *and the boundaries of my being disappeared in the sea.*

Such an experience challenges us to see and live our lives differently. In most cases, it's best to say nothing about such an experience, even to those closest to us, until we have discovered how to integrate it into our everyday lives. Once words enter the picture, the surface mind is not far behind, and at that point our own (or another's) concepts take us further from the experience itself. Part of our consciousness would like to pull us back to a more cozy and comfortable existence, one that doesn't challenge us so profoundly. The following Sufi story illustrates how this part of our mind can gradually take over an experience, until there's no experience left!

Once upon a time a bedouin was crossing the desert with his camel, and lay down to sleep for the night. The night became very cold, and the bedouin was glad that he had a tent. The camel, however, became cold in the night and woke his master, saying,

"O master, couldn't I just stick my nose inside the tent? I'm so cold!"

"All right," said the bedouin, and turned over again. A short while later, the bedouin woke up, hearing the camel say,

"It's much colder now. Couldn't I just put my whole head inside?"

"All right!"

This went on. Next came the neck. Then, without even asking, the camel moved his whole body inside the tent. At that point the bedouin awoke to find himself lying beside the camel, and the tent nowhere to be seen. It was above him, draped over the camel's hump.

Perhaps you have experienced, or are experiencing, a "peak moment" through the grace of the One. Meet and acknowledge it as part of Allah's universe. Don't worry about its meaning or significance now. Avoid the "trough" experience that frequently follows the peak by seeing it as a reflection of the One in you. It is not "your" experience, only a loan from the One to remind you that there is more work to be done. Or, perhaps life is calling you right now to act in a public, outward role that helps others recognize the sacred nature of the universe. Realize that in this role you are only—no more and no less—the reflection of the ultimate Unity of life.

~ Roots and Branches ~

Traditional translations of this quality include "grand" and "exalted." The sound *'AL* in *Ali* goes backward into the body, not outward, and is similar to the beginning *Al* in *Alim* (19), the understanding of forms. This sound points to the material reflection of the divine being, which moves toward a purpose. The outward projection of this *AL* sound appears in the word *Allah* as the great "Yes" of the universe. Many Sufi circles also share this name in remembrance of the fourth Khalif Ali, the Prophet Muhammad's son-in-law and, according to some traditions, the person who, along with Ali's Fatima, received Muhammad's esoteric transmission.

Meditation

Center again in the heart. The One Being can reflect itself in myriad ways, many more than ninety-nine, or even 99 million. With the feeling of this pathway, call a circle of your inner self. Breathe in the sound *Ya 'A-* (bringing the sound backward into the body), and breathe out the sound *-Lee*, bathing the self in the remembrance of its divine potential.

37. Outward Creative Power

Al-Kabir

When you are guided to this pathway,
take the opportunity to reflect on the power that carved creation out of chaos
and that sustains creativity throughout the universe.

WE ARE OCCASIONALLY REQUIRED BY life to demonstrate our creativity outwardly, or to make a presentation that requires us to be more visible than we normally are. It's sometimes called "making an impact." Some of us are used to this and, in fact, we may tend to do it more than necessary, and not let anyone else get a word in edgewise. Others of us habitually shrink to the periphery when it looks like we may have to put ourselves on the line. We are not so much afraid of failure as we are of success. If we do make an impact, how will we deal with others' views of us? Some will admire us, but others undoubtedly will try to pick us apart. Then life could become one long series of dealing with other people's concepts. Why bother?

The secret offered by this pathway is to remember that each of our smaller acts of creativity connects with a much larger one: the creation of the cosmos. Each of our own actions, no matter how great, is a small part of a much larger picture. The Beloved made a big impact in creating the universe—and as its evolution proceeds, creative acts happen all the time. We simply don't notice them. When we start to notice the interrelationship of things, we also realize that we are not the center of things, we are just part of the process. As Rumi commented to his students, life's appearances sometimes distract us from seeing the creative energy and intention behind them, which are the expression of this pathway:

When a strong wind blows,
it rushes through windows

and lifts carpets or levitates straw.
A pond looks like rippled armor.
Branches, leaves, and trees dance.
All these things look different,
but in root and reality they're one:
the wind.

Listen to this story: A poet once visited the court of a king who ruled in Arab lands yet knew no Arabic or Persian, only Turkish. The poet brought a beautiful eulogy to the king, but it was written, of course, in Arabic. When he recited the poem, however, the king nodded at all the right places; laughed where he was supposed to; looked sad or amazed or contemplative at just the right moments. After the poet left, the king's courtiers were worried. Had the king known Arabic all along? If so, they could be in trouble for all the sarcastic asides they'd spoken to each other over the years in Arabic. They bribed the king's favorite slave to find out.

One day, when the king was in a good mood, his servant asked him straight out—did he know Arabic? If not, how did he know how to respond to the poet?

"Of course I don't know Arabic," said the king. "But I knew what the poet's purpose was. His purpose wasn't the poem, it was to impress, amuse, and entertain me. I understood him, so I didn't need to understand the poem."

Perhaps life is calling you right now to act publicly and creatively in service to the One Being. Or, you may be called to work internally with those parts of your own inner being that are either afraid of showing this power or feel hurt from having become inflated or grandiose in the past. By following the internal energy of creativity back to its source, we have the opportunity to remember our connection to Sacred Unity. When we rest in the source of this power, we can find protection and peace. Nothing can harm us, and nothing can disturb us, including our own concepts.

⌒ *Roots and Branches* ⌒

A traditional translation of this quality is "the most great." Compared to the earlier, similar pathway *Khabir* (31), the "seed" awareness, the roots of *Kabir* (beginning with a different K sound in Arabic) show the more definite, outward manifestation and carving (*K*) of the One's creativity (*AB*), life force (*I*), and radiance (*-R*). Whereas *Khabir* includes the unbroken awareness of the One held within, *Kabir* shows us the concentration of that awareness turned outward in form. In Sufi views of the creation of the universe, first Allah becomes conscious of Allah's Self, and then creates beings to make that process more diverse, definite, and powerful. *Kabir* can mean (and is often translated as) "great," but great not in comparison to anything that is "good" or "better." The One Being expresses through the myriad forms and faces in the universe a greatness that is singular and unique. So Unity itself is the essence of what the Sufi calls good, better, and best. When we focus on the many forms, we enter the related pathway of *Karim* (42). As a spiritual practice, *Kabir* is often done in the form of the phrase *allahu akbar,* which can be translated "Unity is all the power there is." The realization of this leads to the experience that "peace is power," as the twentieth-century Sufi Samuel Lewis translated the phrase.

Meditation

Center again in the heart. With equal attention and breath on both syllables, breathe in the sound *Ka-,* and breathe out the sound *-BeeR,* allowing the feeling to radiate outwardly from the heart. Realize that each breath is part of the divine re-creating the universe. Nothing is outside this power or opposed to it. Breathe the strength of this peace with your whole inner self.

38. Remembrance and Preservation

Al-Hafiz

When you are guided to this pathway,
take the opportunity to sense the part of you that can quietly and
confidently protect the remembrance of Sacred Unity in your inner being.

SOMETIMES PROFESSIONAL ATHLETES TALK about "staying within themselves" when they have competed particularly well. This refers not simply to mental concentration, but to a sense of remaining centered within and not getting pulled off-balance by apparent success or failure from one moment to the next. The next few pathways show various shades of this consciousness, all of which the Sufi sees as qualities of the One Beloved. They also balance the more outer pathways we just passed, *Ali* and *Kabir.*

The first "staying within" focuses on remembrance. What are we about? What is the purpose of what we're doing? It can be very easy to forget when caught up in the excitement of the moment. For instance:

There was once a king who wanted to commemorate the anniversary of his reign with a big public spectacle. So he commissioned a team to build a beautiful and ornate triumphal arch, under which he would ride on the day of celebration. When the time came for the procession, everything was ready. Heralds, footmen, and the king's knights all went under the arch. But when it came to the king himself, he couldn't get through. He was too tall. The celebration had to be canceled.

How could this have happened? The king instituted a public inquiry. The builders blamed the suppliers ("The bricks were too short!"). The suppliers blamed the architect ("We only followed the plans!"). And the architect reminded the king that he had made some last-minute alterations.

The king called on his palace sage, who recommended that the sensible thing was to punish the real culprit, the arch itself. So a scaffold was built to hang the arch. However, it was pointed out that, since the top of the arch had touched the king's head, it was immune from prosecution, so they would have to hang the bottom only. Then they discovered that the rope was too short to do this. The rope maker blamed the carpenters.

"The crowd is getting ugly," said the king. "We need to hang someone, and determine guilt or innocence later." However, in checking the whole crowd, they couldn't find anyone tall enough to fit the scaffold—except the king. So they hanged him.

When the people realized what they'd done, they consulted their book of traditions. There they found that the new king was to be chosen by the next person who walked through the town gates. The next person, as luck would have it, was the town idiot, who always replied to any question with the word melon.

So it was that many years later, a visitor to the kingdom found a melon sitting on the palace throne. "We don't know why its majesty, in its infinite wisdom, prefers to be a melon," said one of the courtiers, "but we presume that when it chooses to be otherwise, it will tell us."

Perhaps life is calling you right now to remember what you're really about. Or, you may be called upon to protect or defend someone else, or to preserve a trust or spiritual transmission. We can place a shield of *Hafiz* before us in order to remind a part of our inner self that divine safety is always present. This pathway asks us to act our part, even if we are not used to it. Allah acts through those who say, like the Hebrew prophets of old, "See, here I am, use me." Sometimes what we are asked to preserve has to be put in storage for a time to come, when it will be able to be used and appreciated fully.

─∽ *Roots and Branches* ∾─

Traditional translations of this quality include "preserver" and "guardian." The word *Hafiz* unites a root that shows a protection, cover, or guarantee (*HF*) with one that tells us this preservation is for the purposes of passing something valuable on to others (*-FIZ*). Like its cousin, *Aziz* (8), the strength of the earth, this protecting, preserving quality is brought fully into action and form. In the Islamic tradition, a person who has memorized the entire Qur'an is called a *Hafiz*. That wonderful act of memory reflects an even greater one: remembering the Unity of Being.

Meditation

Center again in the heart. Call a circle of your inner self and offer a breath of this quality to each sensation, feeling, or voice that arises. Breathe the sound and feel the initial sound *H-* slightly aspirated, and the sound *-FeeZ* (with a long *I*, or *ee* sound) radiating throughout your being, reaching every boundary. Feel a circle of protection acting around and through you. This path of remembrance is particularly useful when you need to consider leakage in your psychic or emotional boundaries.

39. *Embodying a Steady State*

الْمُقِيتُ

Al-Muqit

When you are guided to this pathway,
take the opportunity to feel a very steady yet powerful state of awareness in
your being that maintains and nourishes you and others.

SOME OF US ARE good at beginning things; others are good at ending them. Still others are good at maintaining something in a living "steady state." While our culture has given much of its attention to seducing us with what is "new" (if only in appearance), it often overlooks or devalues the roles of nurturing and maintaining. Nothing lasts forever, but from this it doesn't follow that we need to plan obsolescence into everything we do.

Like the previous pathway of the heart, this one is also about "staying within" while we play the game of life. More may be at stake than we realize. As Rumi says:

Outer form means more than we know,
since it's joined to inner substance.
A seed cannot grow without its kernel,
but it also fails if it doesn't have a husk.
So the body has importance too.
Without it, purpose fails.
Look at reality from Reality's viewpoint.
The body is like Mary.
We all have Jesus within us
waiting to be born, but
until the birth pains come, no Jesus.
If the pain never comes, he just returns
to Source by the secret way he came.

Perhaps you are experiencing a powerful state of being that wants to maintain itself until it becomes your everyday stage of consciousness. Or perhaps you are being called upon to distribute some kind of nourishment or sustenance given to you by someone else, or by your own spirit of guidance. In such situations, *Muqit* helps us to remember that we need not, and must not, overextend ourselves. The power of the One that we carry will radiate its own authority and have its own influence by working through us.

—∾ Roots and Branches ∾—

Traditional translations of this quality include "sustainer" and "maintainer." *Muqit* combines sounds indicating the embodiment (*Mu-*) of manifested power (*QI*), which resists extending or dispersing itself (*T*). By another rendering of the roots, the sound of life (*I*) takes up a home between the root *Q*, which carves space out of the sphere of life, and the root (*T*), which maintains it over a period of time. The root Arabic verb means to nourish or feed. A related pathway is *Muqsit* (86), establishing a new foundation or "bottom line" in life.

Meditation

Center again in the heart. Consider the arenas of your life where you are called upon to nurture and sustain something or someone over a period of time. Feel the breath of this pathway surrounding each person or situation with protection and energy. This support does not want things to stay the same, but for them to grow and continue at their right tempo and timing.

Next, or later, call a circle of your inner selves and see who responds to this pathway and the energy it offers. Feel this nourishment being offered to your whole inner family, so that they can all continue to grow toward the fulfillment of their purposes in life.

40. Feeling Divinity in the Details

Al-Hasib

When you are guided to this pathway,
take the opportunity to find "Allah in the details"
of the living process of your life.

SOMETIMES WE ARE CALLED upon to be aware of many distinctions in life, like keeping track of different relationships or the details of a particular project that is in development. We do this all the time with many simple occupations, like driving a car, which actually calls for many coordinated skills and awarenesses simultaneously. Or, in some occupations, like playing a musical instrument, a beginner must keep many different details of new behavior simultaneously in his or her consciousness until they become "second nature."

Keeping in tune with this pathway can save us a lot of time and trouble when we find life's details distracting and misleading. Without accessing this intuitive practicality, our surface minds can run rampant with all sorts of imagined consequences, which may have no basis in reality. The following story of Mullah Nasruddin shows how combining logic with detailed observation doesn't necessarily equal truth:

One night Mullah Nasruddin ran into the street yelling, "I'm being robbed! I'm being robbed!"

His neighbors came out of their houses and asked him, "Where's the robber?"

"In my house," the man replied.

"Did you see him?" they asked.

"No."

"Was anything missing?"

"No."

"Then how do you know a robber is there?"

"I was told that robbers work in absolute silence in the middle of the night. So when I woke up in the middle of the night and didn't hear anything, I knew that a robber must be there!"

Perhaps life is asking you right now to find a face of Unity in each individual, seemingly insignificant aspect of something, while still keeping track of the overall process. Sometimes we can reach an agreement with our inner self, or some part of it, to help in this accounting work. This is a use of the deep mind that helps unclutter the surface.

⌁ Roots and Branches ⌁

Traditional translations of this quality include "reckoner" and "accountant." The roots of *Hasib* show a silent or secret action happening inside (*HS*), which produces gradual creative growth (*IB*). *Hasib* can be another way to enter the flowing space of "staying within." This pathway is also related to *Muhsi* (57), which focuses more on content than on the process aspect, as with *Hasib*. Like the previous two pathways, *Hafiz* (38) and *Muqit* (39), this one provides access to the particular energy of the Holy One that is neither power nor beauty, neither starting nor finishing, rather maintaining things in a very living, steady state.

Meditation

Center again in the heart. Breathe the sound of *Hasib* while walking in rhythm, always centered in the heart. Feel the sound leading you and sense the walking itself as innumerable small motions coordinated by one intelligence, the reflection of the One.

41. *Pooling Strength*

الجَليلُ

Al-Jalil

When you are guided to this pathway,
take the opportunity to affirm the deep ocean of resources in you that builds
up internal power.

AS WE COME TO the edge of this neighborhood of pathways leading to "staying within," we find one that deals with pooling strength until it is the right time to act. Like building up a reservoir of water in times of rain to prepare for seasons of drought, this pathway shows us another way to work inwardly while showing very little outwardly. Sometimes this just means saying "no" to the part of us that always likes to have things to do and thoughts to think. In the following story, Mullah Nasruddin represents the part of our mind that resists staying inside and not expressing itself outwardly:

> *Mullah Nasruddin was always getting in trouble with his wife. He often brought friends home for dinner without telling her beforehand. By the Middle Eastern custom of hospitality, she felt bound to feed them. But if she didn't know they were coming, she usually didn't have enough food in the house, and that was a big problem. "That's it, husband!" she said one day. "No more." So Mullah promised to tell her before bringing friends home.*
>
> *However, the next night he forgot again, until he was just about to go through the door of his house, his friends in tow. "Oops! Please wait here," he told them as he entered.*
>
> *His wife, hearing the footsteps, was ready. "No, husband! I told you! Either send them away or I'm leaving you."*
>
> *"But I can't send them away," replied Mullah. "I'll lose face, and that would be terrible for both of us!"*

"All right," said his wife. "You go upstairs and hide. I'll tell them you had to go out on a family emergency and that dinner is off for tonight."

Mullah went upstairs and hid under the bed. He could hear through the open window his wife making apologies, but his friends weren't easily put off.

"O gracious lady, you say he's gone out, but we didn't see him leave. How could he have left except passing by us?"

Mullah's wife was temporarily stumped and an awkward silence ensued. As Mullah listened, the silence became longer and longer. Finally, he couldn't take it any longer and yelled out the window, "Tell them I went out the back door!"

On the surface level, this story is not about refusing hospitality, which would be unthinkable in the Middle East. Instead, it's about the overexpressive part of our being that resists the energy of *Jalil*, pooling up power (or "food") so that when we do express it, it really makes a difference.

Perhaps life is calling you to rebuild your inner resources or to unclutter your life. Or, perhaps you find yourself in a situation where nothing can be done outwardly, but you can still develop inner qualities such as certainty, confidence, strength, or devotion. This pathway teaches you to allow these qualities to build within, like a wave swelling into fullness.

⌒ *Roots and Branches* ⌒

Traditional translations of this quality include "glorious" and "sublime." The roots of *Jalil* show the divine manifested power welling up and beginning to spread (*JaL*), then piling up, internalizing, and doubling back on itself (*IL*). This is like the deep ocean, far from shore. When this power comes out, it is expressed as *Jalal* (85). Here this power is sublimated in the original sense of the word *sublime*. It need not act outwardly because it radiates without speaking or acting. In contrast to *Kabir* (37), outward creative power in action, *Jalil* expresses the contents of a reservoir of power in repose. *Azim* (33), flexible strength, expresses a power that can act either outwardly or inwardly, as the needs of the moment dictate.

Meditation

Center again in the heart. Call a circle of your inner self and invite all the feelings, sensations and voices within you to Wisdom's table. Breathe in the sound *Ya Ja-*, and breathe out the sound *-LeeL*. Invite whoever shows up to allow themselves to feel a wave of divine resources slowly building within. You can be borne upward by this ocean, without having to do anything but surrender.

42. *Abundant Expression*

Al-Karim

*When you are guided to this pathway,
take the opportunity to feel yourself as part of Allah's continual, creative
expression, which carves out new realities each instant through an
abundance of forms.*

W E LIVE IN A culture in which personal wealth confers great sta-
tus, and one of the most popular themes in self-development
tells us that we all need to develop a greater inner sense of abundance. The Sufis have traditionally regarded wealth with suspicion,
not because there is anything intrinsically wrong with it but because
the self can easily get lost in the personal power and freedom that
wealth seems to purchase. For this reason, many Sufis have followed
the principle of giving away whatever they don't need. Imam Ali, the
Prophet Muhammad's son-in-law, gives a succinct reason for this:

> *O child of Adam! Whatever you have collected more than you actually
> need, you are not going to use, so you will end up only acting as its
> trustee for another person.*
>
> *If you want to pray to the Sustainer for a better way of making a
> living, first give something in charity.*

Rumi regards personal wealth as a test from the Beloved, but one
that a person can, with difficulty, pass:

> *God afflicts many with the trial of wealth and power,
> but their souls run away from it.
> A dervish once saw a prince riding on a horse,
> his face illuminated like a prophet or a saint.
> "Praise to the One," he said, "who can
> test his servants even using affluence!"*

Perhaps you are experiencing the feeling that there is not enough, or precisely the opposite: It's all too much. There may be an aspect of your inner self that feels something is lacking or that can't hold the abundance you have already received. This pathway opens a door for the soul to remember that Allah's creative sound constantly reverberates throughout the cosmos, forming new universes as we breathe each breath. As reflections of Reality here, we already have this quality within us; we don't need to import this abundance from some other realm.

❧ Roots and Branches ❧

Traditional translations of this quality include "bountiful" and "generous." The root *KR* shows the way in which old Semitic language cultures imagined the Holy One continually speaking and engraving the universe into existence (like the Old Hebrew word *ikera* in Genesis 1, usually translated as "said"). This creation is not a "once and for all" occurrence; rather, it happens constantly. The divine mind expresses itself each moment in the countless forms that we see manifested, symbolized by the ending *-IM*. Every living being participates in this divine creation of abundance. It should be noted that *Karim* is not particularly abundant wealth, honor, or any of the things to which the grasping mind may be attracted in its search for a magic mantra. *Karim* is simply abundant expression of forms. When we focus on the activity of outward creation itself, we enter the pathway of *Kabir* (37). We find another, more intensified form of the previous two pathways in a later one, *Dhul Jalal Wal Ikram* (85). We are encouraged to feel the pathways in this neighborhood as part of Allah expressing itself through us. In the later pathway, we are encouraged to remain in awe in the midst of a living, sacred universe, through which one Reality constantly expresses power and abundance.

Meditation

Center again in the heart. At first breathe out the sound KAR-, and feel it clearing space within. Then breathe in the sound -eeM, and feel the divine life force reverberating within through all the inner pulsations of the body. As a rhythm establishes itself, feel the outward carving of reality on KAR-, and the inward renewal from the divine spring of life on -eeM. As you breathe in the heart, feel that giving away actually means filling up.

43. *Watching with Presence*

Ar-Raqib

When you are guided to this pathway,
take the opportunity to view some person or relationship in your life with
the clear, compassionate gaze of Unity.

*I*T CAN BE DIFFICULT to watch a process in which we are deeply interested with a dispassionate gaze, even when we know that this might be the wisest course of action. The secret of this pathway is identifying our view with something greater, as grandiose as this might sound. Just as the pathway of *Basir* (27) led us to the doorway of seeing with the eyes of the Beloved, so this one takes us further, from seeing to watching.

On the Sufi path, the student proceeds step by step: first discovering the relationship between seeing and feeling, head and heart, so to speak; then learning to see from the point of view of the guide by looking through the eyes of his or her heart. Then one can extend this view to all other beings, as the twentieth-century Sufi Inayat Khan commented:

> *The Sufi's tendency is to look at everything from two points of view:*
> *from his own and that of another.*[20]

However, none of this can be done without love and surrender. Paradoxically, we must build an ideal of the divine for ourselves, one that we use as a means to experience something much greater than ourselves and which transcends the ideal itself. Developing a type of fierce devotion goes against the "everything and everyone is equal" point of view on which our consumer society is based. Yet if we look deeply, we can see that all beings show their own unique potential and evolution, and that nothing is really equal. Would it be possible for us to allow ourselves to be "seen by God" and pray in the intense, heartfelt way that the eighth-century Sufi Rabia Al-Adawiyya did?

Eyes heavy with sleep, unaware, forgetful.
Still Rabia remains in your presence,
hoping that you will look on her
with a gaze that keeps her awake to your service.
By your power, Beloved, keep me
serving you day and night until
I meet you face to face.

Such devotion may seem outmoded or, at worst, dualistic. A mystic like Rabia already knows that "Allah" is the only Reality that exists, so why express herself in this way? Because it allows her to include the part of her being that is still growing, still "watching," still outside the circle of unity. So even the parts of our being that are "dualistic" can serve the expression of our life's purpose.

Perhaps life is offering you the opportunity to see from the point of view of another in your outer or inner community. This pathway allows us to watch anything upon which our gaze falls with compassion and presence because we're seeing the world from a wider perspective. The word *watchful* in English sometimes conjures an image of a parent watching so that a child doesn't do something wrong. The sense of *Raqib,* however, is that of watching attentively, not so that something doesn't happen, but so that natural growth—in tune with our own or another's purpose in life—does.

❧ *Roots and Branches* ❧

Traditional translations of this quality include "watchful" and "observer." The roots of *Raqib* show rays of light (*Ra*) illuminating something focused and growing within a certain sphere (*QIB*). Using a musical metaphor, this would be like "keeping to the keynote" of a piece of music, or staying in pitch. In *Raqib,* we also find part of the root for the word *qibla,* the direction in which Islamic prayer is offered, facing the Kaaba in Mecca. We also find a link to the Hebrew word *qabbala,* which means "what is revealed" and refers to one type of Jewish mysticism. This pathway—a compassionate, focused view in which we see everything as within the heart of One Being—can lead us to a deeper revelation of the whole universe as a living symbol.

Meditation

Center again in the heart. With eyes open, breathe in and out the sound *Ya Ra-Qeeb* and feel a connection between your eyes and heart. Feel the heart as a mirror, able to reflect whatever it focuses on. Imagine very strong boundaries, and a very clear surface. Practice wiping the surface clear with the feeling of a compassionate breath. Try turning the mirror outside, toward a situation or person that has you puzzled. What do you see?

44. Reflective Listening

لُمُجِيب

Al-Mujib

*When you are guided to this pathway,
take the opportunity to practice listening with presence. Feel as though you
are a full moon reflecting the light of the sun.*

MANY COURSES TODAY TEACH "good listening skills." The relentless draw of Western culture toward outer life and individual goals forces us to admit that we have forgotten how to really take in the concerns of another person. Perhaps this lack has, in part, driven the rise of Western psychotherapy in the last hundred years. Because we can no longer really listen to each other, we train professionals to do it for us. Some research has concluded that whether psychotherapy works for a person depends mainly on whether there is a good relationship between therapist and client. Trust, a feeling of give and take, and focus all seem essential.

The Sufis would call this the pathway of *Mujib,* sacred listening. This quality can develop from strengthening the heart and making it a conscious container for what enters it. The training of the heart also allows one to empty the container, so to speak, so that it can receive more and not hold on to what has been received. This takes one into what the twentieth-century Sufi Inayat Khan called the "silent life," which is nothing other than the original creative silence that began the universe. Touching this type of silence can give one hope, because in touching the mystery of original creation, all things are possible. Inayat Khan comments on how few people actually understand this language of silence:

People often ask me questions that I cannot very well answer in words, and it makes me sad to think they are unable to hear the voice of my silence.[21]

Perhaps life is calling you to be more flexible or reflective in your outer life, or with a part of your inner being. As with the previous pathway, *Raqib* (being present, witnessing), reflective listening can have strong effects and requires concentration. This is not passivity, which, on spiritual and psychic levels, takes energy for itself instead of reflecting it or passing it along. In this pathway, the responder clarifies, enlarges, and serves the source of what it hears. Ultimately one experiences the source as another part of oneself.

～ *Roots and Branches* ～

Traditional translations of this quality include "hearer of prayer" and "responsive." The roots of *Mujib* show the embodiment (*Mu-*) of something convex, which reflects a source that seems to be other than itself (*-JIB*). The Arabic word *jaba* means to bore a hole in something. So to really hear and reflect others, we need to carve out space for them in our inner being. The Qur'an uses this quality of the One to indicate that Allah is always ready to respond to whoever calls, at any time.

Meditation

Center again in the heart. Breathe the sound of *Ya Mu-Jeeb* in and out. Call a circle of your inner self and listen reflectively, with heart, to each voice within you.

Or hold in your heart a situation in your outer life and practice listening to the different points of view that surround you. Can you find space for each within you? Can you hear the meeting place of wisdom behind them all?

BATHING IN UNITY

*H*ere's another story told by Rumi that invites us to bathe in the ocean of Unity, without the need to compare ourselves to anyone.

Once upon a time, a sultan set up a competition with a very rich prize for the most accomplished visual artistry. He invited teams from around the world. Both China and Greece sent delegations of artists. Each side could order whatever materials it wanted, and the wall of a room was provided for each to do its work. A curtain separated the two rooms.

The Chinese team asked for a plethora of paints made from many different plants and minerals, which provided an unimaginable array of colors. The Greek team asked only for materials for sanding and polishing.

When the two teams were finally ready, the Chinese unveiled their wall first. They had used every color of the rainbow, in a most harmonious design. The sultan was dazzled. Then the Greeks unveiled their work, throwing back the curtain between the two rooms. They had used no paint, but had polished their wall to such a degree that it reflected the work on the Chinese side. Through the play of light and air, the Chinese design seemed to move, and was even more fantastic and beautiful.

Comments Rumi:

Be like the Greeks, O Sufis,
without pedagogy, books, or erudition,
sand away greed and hatred from your hearts,
so that they can reflect all the
million signs and colors of the One.

Meditation

Breathe with a peaceful feeling and allow the mirror of the heart to clear. We don't need to paint our hearts with qualities and names, only burnish them to reveal what is already there.

45. *The Heart Has No Limits*

الوَاسِعُ

Al-Wasi

When you are guided to this pathway,
take the opportunity to touch the part of your deepest being that has a
limitless capacity to hold and embrace whatever comes into its orbit.

THE LAST TWO PATHWAYS, seeing and hearing with presence, lead us deeper to a path behind them—increasing the capacity of the heart. This may be the hardest for most of us to understand. We know how to accomplish things. When we consider the idea of simply *being*, we may have the impression that this means being passive. We don't know how to do without doing, or how to speak without speaking. Much of the Sufi path aims to expand our "heart-sense," a capacity that we often use without thinking about it. How, for instance, do we know whether a person is telling the truth? (And why do children and animals seem to have a better sense of this than do adults?)

The key to beginning this pathway may simply be need. If life calls us to a greater capacity to feel deeply, we have two choices: stretch or break. The training of the heart in Sufism begins from this interplay of need and capacity. The student brings the need, the guide brings the capacity. On another level, it is as Rumi once said:

> *Bring to God even your dry, hypocritical, agnostic prayer, since the One Being in its infinite compassion accepts bad currency as well as good. Increase your need so that Allah can give you more.*

In this sense, even if we bring doubt to the spiritual path, we are bringing something. The Beloved can hold it. The twentieth-century British Sufi Irina Tweedie described how doubt helped her own process of awakening:

The value of the doubt is: who or what is doubting? It is always the ego. The little self is a covering on your higher self. The grace of the teacher will activate those doubts in you in order that you should see the light. How does it activate? How can you see the light better through doubts? Doubts are obstacles. To overcome the obstacles you make an effort and you will progress. Sufis say the devil is very useful to you if you overcome him, but woe to you if you don't. So doubts are extremely helpful. Doubt is power. It is energy you have to overcome. It's like a frontier, like an obstacle. You have to jump over it. That's why [my teacher] said you have to write down all the doubts—it will help people.[22]

Perhaps life is asking you to stretch to include aspects of your inner being that you have not encountered previously—even your own doubts—or to simply hold another being in the light of the One. We do not need to do anything for them, but rather need to be there as a presence, reminding them of the divine embrace. Holding with the capacity of *Wasi* does not mean carrying someone: This is being, not doing.

❧ Roots and Branches ❧

Traditional translations of this quality include "all-comprehending" and "all-embracing." The roots of *Wasi*, the letters *WAS*, show a stream flowing without effort, embracing everything within it, or a container of limitless capacity that can hold all without being full. The secret of this ability lies in the One Being's emptiness, which complements its fullness in you. The root *WA-* can mean "and," indicating mystically a state that is "between," that transforms a being, for instance, from existence to nonexistence. With this name, you have the opportunity to cultivate the sort of spacious capacity that can hold all because it knows that ultimately it holds nothing.

Meditation

Center in the heart and breathe, feeling the heart as a container, bounded by the sensation of your heartbeat and the rhythm of your breath. Begin to breathe out the sound *Ya Waa-*, and breathe in the sound *-See* (with the *ee* sound going backward into the body). Feel the various sounds resonate and melt any inner restriction. Then allow your being to open and receive its natural capacity from the Source. This breath of the heart is already part of your divine nature.

46. *Discriminating Wisdom*

Al-Hakim

When you are guided to this pathway,
take the opportunity to connect with the part of your being that expresses
the One's discriminating wisdom.

ONCE WE LEARN TO hold something clearly in the heart (as the previous pathway teaches), we can practice sacred discrimination. This is yet another aspect of the inner capacity that we began to develop with *Raqib* (43), watching with presence. We could call all these abilities—seeing, listening, and holding someone with heart—the tools of Holy Wisdom. As noted in the Introduction ("Calling a Circle of Your Inner Self"), the biblical book of Proverbs tells us that Holy Wisdom gathers all of our inner voices around a table to eat and drink together. From this gathering a new sense of "self" arises, a new version of our "I am." Ultimately, of course, our own "I am" is only virtual—it is part of the Divine Beloved.

This pathway directs us to our innate capacity to judge what is important in our lives at this moment and exclude all superfluous details. Sometimes this means including some of our less-integrated inner voices indirectly, by allowing their usual distraction to become part of the work. Because it's actually impossible to describe something that one has not experienced, the Sufis tell stories about how our different tendencies of mind operate:

Once Mullah Nasruddin was on his roof, fixing some loose tiles. A friend of his happened by and called to him, "Mullah! Could you please come down here for just a moment?" Mullah groaned because he didn't want to be interrupted. It took a while to get down and up again.

"Yes?" he said to his friend when he had reached the ground.

"Mullah," he whispered in his ear, "could you loan me ten dinars until tomorrow?"

"My friend, why did I have come down here? Couldn't you have yelled up to me?"

"Well, I didn't want the neighbors to hear me asking."

"Okay, well . . . can you give me a minute, helping me up on the roof?"

Mullah and his friend climbed up to the roof, and Mullah gave him a hammer and set him to work fixing tiles. When they finished, Mullah said, "My friend, I'm sorry, but I'm flat broke. I don't even have five dinars for you."

"But couldn't you have told me earlier?"

"No, my friend, I didn't want to turn you away immediately because then people would know that I have no money."

One way to look at this story is to think of "money" as life energy. In this (but not all) stories, Mullah might be the action of our "higher" guidance, engaged in an occupation that it feels is the most important in this moment. One of our "lower" inner voices tries to distract him, to obtain some energy. The charade about not wanting others to hear shows how the higher self can use the excuses of the *nafs* to include the lower self in the integrated work of the self.

Perhaps life is calling you right now to look carefully at a situation where the context—setting, timing, and presence—plays an important part. The primary question raised is "What is really important *now*?" Often we don't need to choose between what is "good" and "bad," but between two "goods" that seem to conflict with one another. In these cases, we need all the wisdom this pathway of our heart can provide. Or, in working with your inner community of feelings, thoughts, and voices, your higher guidance may need to work through this quality of discriminating wisdom in teaching the aspects of your lower self, which are still growing toward maturity in the One.

～ *Roots and Branches* ～

Traditional translations of this quality include "wise" and "judge of judges." Like the earlier pathway *Hakam* (28), this one is another face of the Arabic form of the older sacred phrase that probably originated in the Hebrew *Hochmah* or the Egyptian *Hek-Mat*, that is, Holy Wisdom or Sacred Sense. In specific, this pathway shows that the Sense behind all senses works not only subconsciously (*Hakam*) to make sense of the diverse impressions that come to us but also actively (*Hakim*) as an aspect of our conscious mind. *Hakim* is the spoken word that finds common ground and unites opposites. It is the part of our being that is able to live with the paradoxes of being alive. The Qur'an often pairs this word with either *Aziz* (8), embodied strength, or *Alim* (19), understanding differences in names and forms.

Meditation

Center again in the heart. Feel a breath beginning in the heart, then radiating out to include both the center of your forehead and your solar plexus. Then feel all these centers united within the heart of the divine Beloved. Using the sound of the word to center you, begin with a gentle spoken sound, *ya HaaK-eeM*. As with *Hakam*, the initial *h* sound is aspirated. After a rhythm establishes itself, the sound practice can develop in a more inner or outer way, depending upon how you are guided.

47. Love Is a Give and Take

لَوَدُودُ

Al-Wadud

When you are guided to this pathway,
take the opportunity to call to the part of yourself that reflects the constant
exchange between lover and beloved in every particle of the universe.

WE KNOW THAT LOVE brings heat, as the eighth-century Iraqi Sufi Ruqayya expressed in her poetry:

I love my Sustainer with a fierce love.
Should he order me to the fire
I would feel none of its heat
for the heat of this love.

But does this heat, as many Sufis have pointed out, bring blinding smoke with it? This pathway of the heart asks us to notice how the universe turns with the constant give and take of love. Seeing life in this way, Hakim Sanai speaks here to the Beloved behind all relationships:

How can I be a friend to anyone but you?
All the rest of them are dead.
All friendship grows in your garden.
Does duality make any sense—
this illusion that you are you and I am I?
Why all this smoke from your fire?
Since you exist, why not let
everything else return to nonbeing?
Everything breathes the breath of your loving,
your being loved, your pleasure.

I prefer even the pain of your love
to all the wealth of this world.

While some have accused the Sufis of taking divine love too far, into divine masochism, Sufis themselves see things differently. The only way to understand love is to love. The only way to experience friendship is to be a friend. If this creates pain, that's better than allowing the heart to shrink. Even the discrimination of the last pathway, *Hakim*, which we could compare to the cutting power of a diamond, can't touch this love. As Abil Khayr says:

Love is not something one can talk about,
this gem no diamond can cut.
All we say and do are naught but speculations.
Love comes undetected and leaves undefined.[23]

Perhaps life is calling you right now to take a chance on loving another or becoming a friend. Or, you may already find yourself in a love relationship, where the going has become hard and going deeper seems a better alternative than bailing out. This pathway shows that the essence of deep relationship lies in the gradually kindled fire of friendship rather than in the more surface and immediate blaze of attraction. In all of these circumstances, *Wadud* can help clarify and refine the love that keeps on loving.

My love belongs to those who love each other in Me, who experience intimacy in Me, who shower each other with goodness for My Sake, and who visit each other joyfully for My Sake.[24]

—Sacred Hadith, words of Allah spoken
through Prophet Muhammad

⌐ Roots and Branches ⌐

A traditional translation of this quality is "the loving." The roots of *Wadud* show an unlimited supply of love (*WA-*) in the heart of the Only Being, which reveals itself as a mutual affinity between all individual containers for the divine life (*DD*). Another form of this root appears in the the Sufi expressions *mahbud Allah* and *mahbud lil-lah,* in which the give and take between lover and beloved, as well as love itself, are identified as the Only Being expressing itself. Love changes the fabric of reality. The Qur'an often uses this word in conjunction with *Ghafur* (34), illuminating forgiveness.

Meditation

Center again in the heart. Breathe with the sound of *Ya Wa-DooD*, with hands clasped over your own heart. Then bring your hands to the belly, and later to your forehead. Feel the One Being's love for every particle of your being. Extend this breath so that your heart is now part of the heart of the Holy One, loving all beings.

Call an inner circle of your self and allow the various voices within you to be showered with the unconditional love of Allah through the channel of your highest guidance. Let the One be the ideal therapist for you, with an unlimited capacity for rapport with even the most challenging place within you.

48. *Dazzling Energy*

المَجِيدُ

Al-Ma'jid

When you are guided to this pathway,
take the opportunity to celebrate the life energy that acts visibly, in a
memorable and stunning way, through you and all beings.

SOMETIMES LIFE'S ENERGY, WHETHER in nature or in another person, stops us in our tracks. The Sufis would say *"alhamdulillah"*—"everything praiseworthy returns to the One!" Or, they might say *"ya Ma'jid"*—"yet another magnificent face of divine life energy!"

Many Sufi poets rhapsodize on this theme, and one might wonder how they get themselves into such a state. After all of the pathways about presence, watching, listening, and staying within that we just passed, doesn't this unbridled wonder seem a bit over the top? It does indeed, and it is to accommodate these large emotional paradoxes within one heart that the Sufi follows the path of love. For the heart to become flexible and wide, it must become strong. Holding on to the highs or lows of existence just becomes another habit pattern or generates another dogma.

This pathway challenges us to enjoy a stunning moment while it lasts, and to receive the life force behind it, but not hold on to it. If we are the one in whom someone else sees this dazzling energy, the challenge is a bit more complicated. We can certainly receive the impression, but then what do we do with it? Does it support the growth of our inner self, and if so, when does support turn into a seduction that causes us to forget the real source of energy or beauty? We could end up believing that we are the source and therefore can act as we choose, without considering the feelings of others—a very modern dilemma, and a very difficult dance. The challenges of glamour and charisma center another of the sayings of Allah through a "sacred tradition" of Muhammad,

My mysterious robes are Transcendence and Magnificence. Whoever contends with me for one of these will encounter the fire.[25]

Sometimes we simply have to go through the fire of forgetting. When we learn the lesson the hard way, we can then return to a view of our small selves connected one-to-One.

Perhaps you are in a situation in which you have been struck by the divine energy and glory in someone else, or in all living beings. Or, perhaps you find yourself the subject of this kind of adulation. As with the previous pathway, *Wadud* (47), this pathway can also help your inner selves grow into a more mature and complete relationship with Sacred Unity. *Ma`jid* helps us trace the divine life force in action to its source. And in the form we find it as *Ma`jid*, the distance to trace is not very far.

～ Roots and Branches ～

A traditional translation of this quality is "the glorious." The roots of *Ma`jid* show a very subtle notion of the way manifestation may occur, according to old Semitic cosmology: *MA-* indicates the potential substance of anything before it takes individual form; this is its "plastic" nature—it can take any shape. With the ending sound *-ID*, we have the divine life and power in manifestation—not potential but actively moving and shaping. In the middle stands J, which in this position provides the organic shape or cover for this power. *Ma`jid* is related to its twin *Ma'jid* (65), with the emphasis on the first syllable. This quality has the same roots, but focuses on the instrument of divine life force, rather than its action. It is also related to *Wajid* (64), which emphasizes the ability to actively sense and find the divine life energy manifested in a particular form, whenever needed, like a dowser finding water.

Meditation

Center again in the heart. Breathe with the sound *Ya Ma-Jeed*. Feel the heart as a mirror and breathe for a few moments, allowing the mirror to clear. Then turn the mirror downward and inward to view with compassion the various aspects of your inner self, gathered at Wisdom's table. Breathe with life energy with each aspect of your being, and see each as a unique face of the divine life given you to work with in this lifetime.

49. The Return of What Passes Away

البَاعِثُ

Al-Ba`ith

When you are guided to this pathway,
take the opportunity to celebrate the divine quality that recycles everything
that, within and around you, fades away and has only limited life span.

ACCORDING TO THE SUFIS, one part of our being, the soul (or *ruh*), travels further after physical death; other parts get left behind. But even the aspects that get left behind persist in a certain way. Our physical flesh, for instance, returns to the earth and feeds those who come after us. Various thoughts and feelings that we leave behind might also yield energy for others. Many Sufis believe that a saint also leaves behind a "subtle flesh," which provides blessing and guidance for those who remember the way that she or he moved, walked, or breathed. This subtle flesh then provides a doorway into another realm for those who come after. It's a recycled form of our physical life.

While it might not be pleasant to contemplate our own recycling, the Sufis have done so for centuries by widening the vision of the heart. Rumi comments:

Bees bring wax and honey together,
then fly away to another,
farther corner of the garden.
Our parents are like the bees—
seeker unites with sought,
lover with beloved—
then they leave us.
Wax, honey, and garden remain.
Our body is like a beehive made of
the wax and honey of the love of God.
The Beloved gives bees other forms

when they no longer need the old ones.
The same with our souls.
If you sit in a grave with a corpse,
even for a moment,
you might feel you're going mad.
Why, then, would you remain
in the corpse once you're freed?
The fear of death is just a subtle reminder,
like the way people pile up stones
where a caravan has been ambushed:
"Warning! Danger here!"

Perhaps life is calling you right now to view a situation in its larger context. Something may be passing away or wearing out. How might it be recycled? When we are confronted with a world full of impermanence, this pathway prompts our conscious mind to reflect more deeply upon the purpose of our lives. It can help the voices of our inner self remember that selfhood continually changes and leads to a more expanded life.

⌁ *Roots and Branches* ⌁

Traditional translations of this quality include "raiser from death" and "awakener." The final root (*'ITH*) points to something that has only a limited lifetime, a relative existence. This aspect of our being returns in another form, or recycles itself (*BA*). It goes its own way when the eternal part of our being continues its journey. The remembrance of *Ba`ith* also prepares for two later pathways of the heart: *Mu`id* (59), restoring that which still contains life, and *Mumit* (61), changing state completely—that is, what we normally call "dying."

Meditation

Center again in the heart. Breathe out with the sound *Baa-* radiating from the self to all parts of your being. Breathe in the sound `*eeTH* (not a normal *ee* sound, but more guttural, backward into the depths of the body. Keeping a bit of the *a* sound with the *ee* will help). Consider the various projects and relationships in your life through the eyes of this quality. Each has a limited life span, and each, as it passes away, is recycled into the heart of Allah.

50. Experiencing a Universe of Unity

Ash-Shahid

When you are guided to this pathway,
take the opportunity to speak and act from your experience of
the Reality shared by all beings.

THE SUFIS SPEAK OF lover and beloved, seeker and sought, human and divine. Yet we can experience a moment when all the "ands" fall away. In these moments, we cannot speak about "we," "I," or "you." Everything is united. In small ways, many of us may have experienced this. Attar tells this story of the famous lovers Leyla and Majnun:

> Majnun knocked on Leyla's door.
> "Who's there?"
> "It is I."
> "Go away. There is no room here for you and I."
> Majnun retreated to the forest, meditated for a long time, and then returned.
> "Who is it?"
> "It is you."
> The door opened.

Other pathways tell us that life's diversity, the "you" and "I," also serves a purpose, yet the present one offers us the deeper view, the wider picture. A moment of such direct experience of unity alerts us to settle for nothing less. The twentieth-century Sufi Samuel Lewis writes:

> *It is not necessarily reading and studying, or even devotion and practice, that lead one to the desired goal. Every word of every prayer may be taken seriously, used as subject matter in both meditation and con-*

centration and allowed to come to fulfillment through realization. As Al-Ghazali has said: "Sufism is based upon experience and not premises." Many ancient Sufi writers stressed the lifting of veils. As veils are lifted, a whole new universe seems to come to consciousness. It has always been there; each new vista only makes one better aware of what has always been there.

Perhaps life is calling you to experience life at the center of a dynamic, interconnected, changing cosmos, or to publicly share an experience of this unity with others. As with the previous pathway *Raqib* (43), this pathway can also help in training your inner self, especially when you feel upset or confused. Allow *Shahid* to help your highest inner guidance (the *ruh,* in Sufi terms) clarify and reestablish its firmest connection with the One Being, and then to share this experience with the rest of the inner community of your lower selves, the *nafs.*

~ Roots and Branches ~

A traditional translation of this quality is "the witness." The roots of *Shahid* shows a being that is calm and empty, within a whirlpool of sensations and impressions (*SHa*). This being sees and experiences the divine life in action (*HID*). We find such a state at the center of a hurricane or tornado. These roots also serve as the basis for the word *shahada,* which most often refers to testifying to the Unity of God and Muhammad's prophethood in the Islamic tradition. As a number of mystics have pointed out, this testifying is not merely verbal; it is, or can be, an actual experience. The One Life displayed itself gloriously in *Ma'jid* (48). Here we empty ourselves to allow the One to give us this direct experience through all of life's experiences, whether they are outwardly glorious or not.

Meditation

Center again in the heart. With eyes open, breathe through the heart and feel that you are seeing through its "eyes." Make a space for the possibility of seeing, feeling, and experiencing One Life behind all of the various forms. Like all the pathways, this experience cannot be forced or commanded, and yet we can practice and prepare ourselves for its unveiling through us at the right moment.

51. The Truth in Each Moment

Al-Haqq

When you are drawn to this pathway,
take the opportunity to make space for the amount of divine life energy
you are able to embody at this moment, and experience this as
your "truth" in this moment.

*E*ARLIER, THE PATHWAY OF *Halim* (32) showed us the value of temporary, altered states of consciousness. Here we focus on the extent of the divine qualities that we are able to fully embody at this moment, in a consistent way of living our everyday life. This extent depends upon the flexibility of the *nafs,* our inner community of voices, and its ability to reflect and express our sacred purpose in life right now.

The Sufis also use this attribute of the One Being to point to its "real Reality"; that is, the reality beyond words and concepts. As Rumi told his students:

That Reality, as Reality itself, has no opposite. It only has an opposite when viewed through form, like Iblis compared with Adam, Moses compared with Pharaoh, and Abraham compared with Nimrod. The "opposite" of the saints also served their purpose. Through their opposition, the saints prospered and became known:

The moon shines in the darkness,
bringing joy to all.
A dog howls in response,
according to its nature.
We can't blame the moon
just because the dog disturbs us.

Perhaps you have had a peak or trough experience—a high or a low. Where did this leave you? The Sufis would call this your *maqam*, or stage of spiritual development for the moment. Perhaps you are facing choices in your life. If so, consolidate and solidify all the possibilities and intangibles. What part of your realization can you bring into action *now*?

∼ Roots and Branches ∼

Traditional translations of this quality include "the truth" and "the only reality." The roots of *Haqq*, the letters *HQ*, show a definite impression being made, like a character pressed into clay. This writing *into* your being is your character. This quality is also indirectly related to the pathways *Hakam* (28) and *Hakim* (46). The gathering of sense and discrimination that these two pathways offer fully manifests itself here as the "truth" of one's being in the present moment. The Qur'an often uses this name for the One Being to remind its listeners that the "Allah" it is speaking about is not another theological thought-form or ideal, but the basis of reality itself, no matter what it is named.

Meditation

Center again in the heart. Breathe the sound *Ya* into the heart, and breathe out the sound *Haqq* from the heart, downward, all the way to your feet. Allow a door to be open to the inner self. Then release any tension you feel. Relax and allow the full embodiment of the One's truth for this moment to be absorbed into you like rain into the fertile soil. Breathe rhythmically in and out. As you feel more force in the sound, keep releasing more. Let go. It is Allah's force, not your thought of yourself, that does the work.

52. *Meeting Challenges*

الوَكِيلُ

Al-Wakil

When you are drawn to this pathway,
take the opportunity to affirm the sacred power within you to meet
challenges and obstacles, and to bring all circles full.

THIS PATHWAY TAKES US down the "problem-solving" lane of existence. It reveals that there is a particular faculty of our heart-mind that can meet our life's challenges in the right way at the right time, and that helps us untie the knots these challenges present. Many of us experience this aspect of our being when, after contemplating a problem for a while and then giving up, we receive the answer in an instant.

When this happens, it mirrors the progress of our spiritual path. We begin by using our minds to wrestle with life, then we give up (a stage the Sufis call *tawbah*). After we give up, the solution reveals itself in the form of spiritual guidance, from our own higher self or through another person. For this reason, the Sufi does not withdraw from ordinary society, except for periods of spiritual retreat. Life itself provides the substance to make spiritual practice a reality.

The classical Sufis prized the sense of confidence and trust (called *tawwakul*, based on the name of this pathway) that allowed them to believe that whatever life could throw at them, divine guidance would provide a response. Sometimes the message is that we need to allow the situation to really reveal itself to us, rather than focus on external details. Once again, Mullah Nasruddin teaches us the lesson by showing us the opposite, the habit of mind in which we become so engrossed in the details, or in ourselves, that we fail to understand what's really going on:

One night Mullah Nasruddin awoke to hear a thief entering his house. Mullah went downstairs and began to help the thief load possessions into a bag.

"What are you doing?" asked the thief.

"It looks like I'm moving, so I'm helping you!" said Mullah.

Another time Mullah woke up to hear the thief breaking in again. This time Mullah hid in the closet and listened to the thief banging around, trying to find something to steal. Finally the thief came to the closet and opened it to find Mullah there.

"What? Have you been there all along?" said the thief, afraid that Mullah would call the police.

"Yes," said Mullah. "I was so embarrassed that I had nothing to steal that I thought I should hide."

Perhaps life is calling you to solve a puzzle in the best way possible. You need the practical hand of the Only Being in your life, working through your own hands. Don't presume to know the solution; ask the One to reveal it. As you work with your inner self, this pathway can remind the many voices in you that, while each has its own purposes and needs, all find their needs best fulfilled within an integrated "I am"—that is, ultimately in the only "I Am."

∾ Roots and Branches ∾

Traditional translations of this quality include "trustee," "guardian," and "disposer of affairs." The roots of *Wakil* show the whole circle of being, nurtured and tended by Allah. The divine life compresses itself into form (*WaK-*), then spreads toward its own purpose in individual life and returns to the One (*IL*). This process goes on continually. Like other names beginning with *WA*, such as *Wahhab* (16) and *Warith* (97), *Wakil* reminds us that there is always more of this divine quality; it never runs out. The heart of the Holy One holds within itself all circles of being, the completion of every destiny, the solution to all seeming obstacles. The Sufis also use this name in its Persian form, *Vakil*, which may derive from that of an ancient, pre-Islamic angel of protection.

Meditation

Center again in the heart. Breathe *Ya Wa-Keel* with the inner self, and allow your highest guidance to offer a feeling of nurturance to the various voices gathered around Wisdom's table. Rest in a feeling of confidence that the One Being will provide you with the intuitive responses to meet the inner and outer challenges that you face in life.

53. Winds of Change

القَوِيُّ

Al-Qawi

When you are guided to this pathway,
take the opportunity to feel the winds of change blowing the superficiality of
your life away.

"*I* GOT CARRIED AWAY!" Virtually everyone has had this experience, and anyone who has not has missed part of life. Events overtake us, and life becomes a blur of confusion. We feel that we have been dropped into the middle of a desert wilderness with none of our usual bearings to guide us. Most of us experience this energy in our dream lives, where we are carried from one bewildering event to the next. Even Rumi had dreams like this, one of which he shared with his students:

> *I saw someone like a wild fox, sitting on small balcony, looking down the stairs. I tried to grab him, but he leaped away. Then I saw Jelal [a former student] with him in the form of a stoat. He tried to escape, and then to bite me, but I was able to grab him. I put my foot on his head and pressed down hard until the contents of his brains ran out. Then I looked at the empty skin and said, "This deserves to be filled with gold and precious stones. I have what I want, so go ahead and leap off now, wherever you want to go!" He jumped around, because he didn't want to be mastered, but undoubtedly this was where he found his true happiness. He was formed of meteor fragments. The divine drenched his heart, and he wanted to experience everything, but he had set out on a road that he couldn't follow to the end.*

> *Nets cannot capture the one who knows. She is completely free to determine who shall capture her, and no one does so without her free will. You sit behind your cover watching for prey, but the prey sees you, your cover, and the cunning behind it all. He doesn't even pass by your cover. He only travels by the paths he has created.*

As Rumi comments, spiritual guidance often arrives in forms that we can't fathom. We think we have life figured out, and then something happens that squeezes the brains from our heads. Sometimes we think we are the hunter but find that we are the prey, and that the Beloved is hunting us rather than we it.

Perhaps you are experiencing a storm in your inner or outer life. Does the awareness of the unlimited expression of the One Being's power of change change your perspective (or that of your inner selves)? The conscious mind, the limited ego, cannot talk to this power, or else it will be shattered; it would be like trying to hitch a ride on a hurricane. Or, perhaps the hurricane has already blown through your life. If so, you can use the opportunity to pick up only what you need, and leave the rest behind. As the twentieth-century American mystic Ruth St. Denis once wrote, "I stand willingly in the way of storms, that all my dead leaves may swirl away and be lost."

∽ Roots and Branches ∾

Traditional translations of this quality include "full of strength" and "powerful." The roots of *Qawi* show the natural power of the One expressing universal change (W) and continued life (I). Like *Qahhar* (15), which expresses power in potential and in fire, *Qawi* expresses the same force rolling over and through any obstacle like a powerful desert wind that drives us into the wilderness. *Qawi* is also linked as a name of the One's "natural" power to *Qadir* (69), the force acting through individual forms, and to *Qayyum* (63), expressing the power that rises again after subsiding (the alternating movement and rest of cosmic creation). It is also related to *Muqaddim* (71), natural force expressing itself at the beginning of time.

Meditation

Center in the heart: Breathe in the sound QA-, feeling it fall backward into the body, and then breath out the sound -Wee, feeling it sweep through your whole self. Feel the divine wind moving through your life, rolling over obstacles, blowing away any dead leaves.

54. Step-by-Step Persistence

المَتِينُ

Al-Matin

When you are guided to this pathway,
take the opportunity to connect with the sacred qualities of practicality and
deliberation, of small steps taken over a long period of time.

WE ALL KNOW CERTAIN situations call for taking things "one step at a time." But sometimes it is difficult to have the patience to do so. With all the Sufi's emphasis on love, surprise, and grace, you may wonder what role persistence pays. This pathway keeps us going even when we don't receive positive feedback from our surroundings, yet our heart of hearts tells us that we're on the right path. You could say that nothing really worthwhile has ever been accomplished on earth without this pathway. In the following story, Mullah Nasruddin demonstrates that this sort of persistence can seem crazy, but often accomplishes what's needed:

At one time in his life, Mullah Nasruddin was "riding the circuit" as an independent qadi, *or arbiter of local, personal disputes. It was a way for a wise (or in Mullah's case, only semi-wise) man to make a living. One day, Mullah Nasruddin ran into one of the villages on his route yelling, "Where's my donkey's saddlebag? I've lost my saddlebag! Unless someone finds it immediately, I'll do to you what I did to the village I just visited!"*

After a long search, someone did find Mullah's saddlebag.

"What would you have done if we hadn't found it?" someone asked.

"I would have left here and gone to the next village," said Mullah.

Love also demands this type of persistence, especially when the relationship has begun to mature beyond attraction, into something deeper. As the fourteenth-century Sufi Hafiz puts it:

If you wait until the end of time,
you will never smell love's perfume
until you kneel at the doorstep
of your heart's tavern and sweep it,
night after night, with your forehead.

Likewise, if you want to taste
the pure wine in this
jewel-encrusted cup of love,
you may have to bump
your head on its rim
countless times
before you get a sip.

Perhaps you are facing a long, uphill journey, or a project of many years, in which there may be many distractions. Take this pathway to heart and look at the unfolding of the universe and the evolution of life on earth as examples of the amazing feats that can result from perseverance.

⌒ Roots and Branches ⌒

Traditional translations of this quality include "steadfast power" and "firm." The roots of *Matin* show a basket perfectly woven to form a whole (*MT*), which can resist disintegration for a long time (*N*). When this quality of active persistence awakens within you, you do not become tired of taking things one step—or even one part of a step—at a time. *Matin* conforms to whatever circumstances it meets and keeps going until the task is finished. In this sense, it is similar to *Sabur* (99), but the latter expresses itself through light or intelligence, while *Matin* expresses itself through form.

Meditation

Center again in the heart. Try breathing and walking with the name in a rhythm of four: *ya-Ma-Teen* (the last syllable held for two counts). Or, while sitting, allow the sound to find a regular rhythm and tempo that harmonize with your breathing rhythm and heartbeat. Keep the breath strong and stay with this feeling as you look ahead at the day before you to see what is important right now.

Call a circle of your inner selves to Widsom's table. Allow all the feelings, sensations, and voices within you to participate in breathing *Matin*, which can remind them that the long journey of evolution begins with individual steps.

55. Friendship

الوَلِيُّ

Al-Wa`li

When you are guided to this pathway,
take the opportunity to reflect on friendship in your life, or to befriend a
voice of your self's inner community.

THE SENSE OF FRIENDSHIP and companionship that we seek outside must first be found inside. This has become a truism in popular culture, but how do we actually accomplish it in practice?

This pathway attempts to teach us real friendship, which is something beyond acquaintance or codependence. Inayat Khan once commented that learning how to be a friend is really the essence of the Sufi path:

> There are many things in the life of a Sufi, but the greatest is to have a tendency to friendship; this is expressed in the form of tolerance and forgiveness, in the form of service and trust. In whatever form he may express it this is the central theme: the constant desire to prove one's love for humanity, to be the friend of all.[26]

It's true that friends can often let you down, and so some people find they can establish an easier relationship with beings that aren't physically present. Samuel Lewis warns about the dangers of this attitude:

> One sees so many faults in humanity. But those who affirm love for God, or friendship with angels, are often deluded. The scriptures posit love for humankind and this is one of the bases of Sufism. Metaphysical knowledge without such an expanded heart is useless, has always been declared useless by the wise and yet been sought by the unwise in all times.[27]

Perhaps life is calling you right now to first befriend yourself, and then to dare to be a friend to someone else. Begin with the feelings of tolerance and respect for yourself. Then apply these to your outer relationships and allow them to develop your interest in others. As life draws you out of yourself more and more, your heart begins to naturally reach out to others. Before you know it, you've forgotten yourself in friendship.

◦— *Roots and Branches* ◦—

Traditional translations of this quality include "protecting friend" and "the one who is near." The roots of *Wali* emphasize the second root and syllable (*-LI*), which shows the divine Unity inclining, leaning, or moving toward individual life, and doing so continually (*W*). The One Being extends itself toward all beings under all circumstances, every moment embracing us as the closest friends. To paraphrase the saying of Allah through one of the sacred traditions of Muhammad: "As you move one step toward the One, the One moves ten steps toward you." The "twin name" *Wa'li* (77) emphasizes the first syllable and root and adds the letter *alef* (*A*) to it, which shows the power of Unity to direct or command life as it manifests. The Sufis also use the term *wali* to indicate a saint or "friend of God"—one who has drawn close to divine Unity.

Meditation

Center again in the heart. Breathe the sound *ya Wa-Lee* (with accent on the second syllable) and allow it to radiate out and down into the belly. Try crossing your arms over your heart (right over left), with your hands touching your shoulders. Feel your own arms as the arms of the divine, embracing you in friendship.

BATHING IN UNITY

Sometimes it helps us to clarify things if we notice when we're doing something that doesn't match what we say (or think to ourselves) we're doing. For instance, we may be spending more energy enduring a work situation than actually accomplishing anything. Or, we may find that we have created a whole story about how we're living our lives that doesn't actually match what's really going on. In the following story, Mullah Nasruddin reveals such a situation by taking it to an extreme:

> Mullah Nasrudin was back in the business of selling donkeys. This time, he really seemed to have cracked the formula for success. Each week he brought a very well-bred, well-fed, high-class donkey to the market and sold it for a price much lower than any other donkey dealer could.
>
> Week after week this went on, and the other donkey sellers began to grumble among themselves.
>
> Finally, one of them pulled Mullah aside.
>
> "Mullah, I appreciate good business as much as the next person, but you're putting me out of business. I'm very rich, and I've already tried low-balling the competition, selling below cost to drive them away. I own a lot of land and rent it back to peasant farmers. They pay me in grain, so I get the donkeys' food free. I also have servants who groom and care for them, clean out their stables, the whole works. I pay the servants virtually nothing. But I still can't sell my donkeys as low as you're selling them. Please tell me your secret, and I'll make it worth your while."
>
> "My friend, I see your problem immediately," said Mullah. "You're only stealing the land, the grain, and the labor. I'm stealing the donkeys."

Meditation

Breathing with the sound or feeling of Allah in the heart, ask yourself what message this moment offers. No matter what your mind
says, what does your heart tell you is really important in your life
right now? How could you spend more time with this heart-work
each day?

56. The Gift of Purpose

الحَمِيدُ

Al-Hamid

When you are guided to this pathway,
take the opportunity to affirm the place in your being that expresses your
unique purpose in life, that quality or gift that only you can offer.

I ONCE HAD THE privilege of studying with a "hidden saint," a Pakistani bookseller by the name of Shemseddin Ahmed, who had a deep knowledge of the Qur'an. He taught classical Arabic to a young Sufi student by going through the Qur'an virtually word for word. Surprisingly, he started beginners on the most advanced practice: using the roots of the Arabic text to see into the "Mother of the Book," Allah's creation itself. Whenever he would come to a form of the root *hamd* in the text, from which this pathway derives, he would say, "Don't think of this as something only high. Allah has created each being with such a *hamd,* an essence that it wants to bring out. Milk has a *hamd,* water has a *hamd,* and you have a *hamd.* That *hamd* is your gift that you bring out for God. That's why we say *alhamdulillah*—all *hamd* is praising God."

Like a number of other mystics, including Walt Whitman and William Blake, Shabistari also had a vision of the richness that resides within each being:

Dive deeply into a drop of water, and
a hundred oceans will flood you.
Look into a mote of dust, and
a million nameless beings will jump out.
A hundred harvests rest in a germ of barley seed, and
in the right light, an insect's wing reflects the sea.
Why be surprised?
Deep in the pupil of my eye lie cosmic rays,

and the center of my heart
beats with the pulse of the cosmos.

Perhaps life is calling you now to find the essence of your own purpose in life, or to see and acknowledge that divine purpose in another. Sometimes simply seeing it is enough: Recognition can shine through the eyes and illuminate your whole self. In working with the inner self, this pathway can help affirm the purpose of each individual voice, which ultimately returns to unity with Unity, losing its small "I" in the greater "I Am."

๑~ Roots and Branches ๑~

Traditional translations of this quality include "worthy of praise" and "owner of praise." The roots of *Hamid* show something warm and enveloped, like a seed before it sprouts (*HaM-*), getting ready to unfold itself to fulfill the full extent of its capabilities (*-ID*). The One has given each being, each element, each particle of the universe a unique essence, or *hamd,* with which to express itself and give back, enriching the whole. Whereas *Khabir* is the form of this seed-gift as light or intelligence (the "wave" form, so to speak), *Hamid* expresses its "particle" form.

Meditation

Center in the heart. Intone *Ya Haa-meed,* feeling the sound uniting the heart and belly on *Ham-*, with the first *h* slightly aspirated, and then on *-eed* rising to include the upper body, and showering over you. Then breathe the sound with the same feeling.

Or, using the word *al-ham-du-lillah,* place your fingertips on your heart and allow them to rise upward (on the sound *hamd*). Praise the One in all the growing seeds in which it expresses itself in your life right now.

57. *Assessing What Is*

المُحْصِي

Al-Muhsi

When you are drawn to this pathway,
take the opportunity to stop and look through the eyes of divine clarity
at your life as it is right now.

*I*N SOME INSTANCES, WE may need to view a process unfolding over time. In others, we may be called upon to "take a snapshot" of this moment, to look clearly at a situation as it is right now—not as it would be, could be, or might be. Fittingly, one traditional definition of a Sufi is "a child of the instant."

In search of this moment of clarity, Sufis try to cut through irrelevant discussions of ritual or metaphysics. For instance, Ruqayya of Mosul, who was skilled in *fiqh,* the legal jurisprudence of the Quran, once told her listeners:

> *Why not study* fiqh *in the university of your heart's sincerity, rather than argue about the ritually proper way to mount a female camel?*

As we saw in the previous pathway *Hasib* (40), sometimes we need to view the details of a process over time. This pathway, however, tells us the best thing we can do right now is to not be distracted by details that don't mean anything for the moment. Another Mullah Nasruddin story illustrates this:

> *Some religious scholars were having a field day discussing the question of which side one should stand on when carrying a coffin. Some said right, others said left. Finally they went to Mullah Nasruddin to settle the matter.*
>
> *"What does it matter," said Mullah, "as long as you're not in the coffin."*

Perhaps life is calling you to clearly assess the way things are right now. This pathway recommends that you use the eyes of the heart to allow Allah to see through you to help achieve your purpose in life. This pathway can clarify outer relationships as well as states of the inner self. Bringing this level of clarity to either promotes further change and growth.

—❧ Roots and Branches ❧—

Traditional translations of this quality include "counter" and "reckoner of value." *Muhsi* comes from the same roots as the earlier pathway *Hasib* (40), but adds the prefix *Mu-*, indicating a more thoroughly manifested or embodied form of the quality. It deletes the *-B* of *Hasib*, which as an ending would symbolize a process extending over time. Looked at this way, *Hasib* has more to do with feeling accurately the unfolding growth of a process. *Muhsi*, on the other hand, focuses on a situation in its particular form, exactly as it is at the present moment. As we have done previously, one could articulate the difference as that between content (*Muhsi*) and process (*Hasib*).

Meditation

Center again in the heart. Breathe through the heart as if seeing through a clear lens. Then look at the various situations of your outer life, or in your community of inner self, just as they are at this moment, without expectation or judgment. What does this snapshot tell you about fulfilling your heart's purpose as you continue on the path?

58. *Individuated Creation*

الْمُبْدِئُ

Al-Mubdi

When you are guided to this pathway,
take the opportunity to find the place in you that is helping you grow more
and more into yourself—a unique, fully human, being.

THE CREATION STORY IN the Hebrew Bible account of Genesis 1 relates that the One "divided" light from dark. This "dividing" (the Hebrew *yabdel,* from the same root as the present pathway) was not simply separating two things that were already themselves. Rather, it points to a process of two beings individuating from one shared existence. To "divide" them means to draw out the unique potential of each by using sound and "calling" their names.

Similarly, the Qur'an contains an account of Allah calling all our human names when we were still a potential within the womb of the first human being. We were asked, individually and collectively, "Am I not your sustainer, and the sustainer of all beings? Am I not reflected in your heart and the heart of all beings?" According to the Qur'an, we answer, "Why not? We agree to experience this, live it, and pass it on to others."

By undertaking the "divine experiment" to reflect the moving, growing, evolving, creative nature of Reality, we discover our full humanity. Life becomes not an instant replay of someone else's movements, but a caravan of discovery and adventure, in which we follow a long train of ancestors, including all the beings who preceded us on this planet.

Sufis also talk about a saint who functions as an *Abdal,* also from the same root as *Mubdi.* This person serves, often secretly, as the touchstone or philosopher's stone to change one thing into another. Under the guidance of the One, the *abdal* may him- or herself change forms or roles to suit the needs of the moment.

Perhaps life is calling you right now to the real alchemy of the heart, in which Allah takes your inner community of voices, needs and wants, and changes them into something more uniquely themselves. We may find that what we thought was a liability becomes a gift. For instance, shyness might transmute itself into subtlety, or an overactive temper might become creative fire. In this way, *Mubdi* can operate dynamically on a practical level.

⌒ Roots and Branches ⌒

Traditional translations of this quality include "originator" and "creator." The roots of *Mubdi* show the embodiment (*Mu-*) of something that individuates (*BD*) and so expresses life energy (*I*). *Mubdi* is related to another pathway, *Badi* (95), which could be translated "creative surprise" or "unexpected wonder." *Badi* is the quality that begins the process of creation in the heart of the One in pre-eternity. *Mubdi* shows that this quality and activity is fully embodied in every particle of the cosmos, which continues to grow and evolve creatively. The Quranic accounts of creation make clear (as do the Genesis ones, when read in Hebrew) that creation is an ongoing, evolutionary process. It is not over and done with, nor a "historical fact" that occurred in seven twenty-four-hour days. We are each being called upon every moment to manifest the spark of creativity that the One embedded in our hearts at the beginning.

Meditation

Center again in the heart. Breathe *Ya MuB-Dee* with a deep, refined breath, and feel the various roots resonating. Call a circle of your inner self. Breathing into the inner community of voices, invite them to come together at Wisdom's table. Who resonates with the transformative power of *Mubdi*? Who is ready to change to suit the creative needs of the moment?

59. Reviving What Is Worn Down
المُعِيدُ
Al-Mu'id

When you are guided to this pathway,
take the opportunity to breathe new energy into something in your life
that seems tired or worn down.

IN THE HEBREW BIBLE, the prophet Ezekiel has a vision in which he is taken to a valley full of dry bones. The voice of the Holy One asks him: "Can these bones live?" Then he is commanded to prophesy to the bones and to the breath so that they can reform to make living bodies. To "prophesy" in the old Hebrew sense did not mean to predict the future; it meant to activate the living, sacred essence within oneself or someone else, so that this life energy could create something in the world. A prophet (*nabiya*) activated or stirred a community in this way.

Living as we do, in what has been called a "throwaway society," some of us have become increasingly aware of our inability to make things last, be they consumer goods or relationships. It takes discrimination to discover how to reuse or recycle something that seems worn out, rather than to simply replace it. This pathway asks us to cultivate this ability to revive and enliven others, a situation in our lives, or a part of ourselves. This pathway does not ask us, however, to simply hold on to old forms without breathing life into them. This can create disastrous consequences, as the following story illustrates:

> There was once a forest of trees, which lived a magnificent and beautiful life. Due to the natural development of their surroundings, the trees "climaxed," and then gradually died, giving way to smaller species that lived below them. Various groups of bees made their nests in the hollow trunks of the trees and became very happy making honey. Gradually, the trees, one by one, began to decay and fall.

The various groups of bees debated amongst themselves why this should be and concluded that it must have something to do with the various merits of their hives. Some felt that when a tree fell, the bees in it were being punished for improper belief. Others felt more charitable and wanted to bring the homeless bees to their hive, saying "It could have been us, after all." Still others felt that the hives of the homeless bees must have been flawed in some way from the beginning and so were predestined to fail.

The trees gradually continued to fall, one by one, and each time one did the bees in those trees still standing developed more speculations. Finally, all the bees were homeless and had to move on. Each group had been caught by surprise, believing their hive to be the true one destined to survive and bring in a new age. Each had failed to recognize that all trees fall eventually, and so it should finish its work and find another forest before it lost its tree. Each had failed to look further than its own hive and consider the effects of the tree, the soil and the rest of their ecology on its own survival.[28]

On one level this story provides a Sufi commentary on what we commonly call "religion" or "tradition." By mistaking the form of their trees for their real function, the various groups of bees are caught by surprise when their trees finally fall. They deny the need to change by making up all sorts of ideas about why their own trees are better than others. This has always been the Sufi critique of religious or cultural institutions: These institutions are human creations, intended to serve human development and happiness. The real religion behind all religions, according to the Qur'an, is that there is only one Reality, and all people and all cultures share it, no matter which sacred names they use or stories they tell.

Perhaps you are facing a situation in which the form of a project, organization, relationship, or community needs to change. What may be revived will not necessarily take the same form, but will be connected to the past with the same life energy. Perhaps part of your inner self needs some renewal. One voice or capability within you (for instance, the inner friend or lover) may be growing and changing, and this may require rearranging the relationships you find when you call a circle at Wisdom's table. Or, one part of your being may feel that it is dying and being revived in a new form that fits your purpose in life better right now.

~ Roots and Branches ~

Traditional translations of this quality include "restorer" and "the one who brings forth things anew." This is practical embodiment (*Mu-*) that affects what is worn down (`) by infusing new life (*I*), which results in a new expression (*D*). Along with *Mu`id,* the next four pathways all focus on the ways in which the divine life energy comes into form, infuses it, becomes part of it, leaves it, and continues on.

Meditation

Center in the heart and belly. Breathe out, feeling the sound *Ya Mu-* going out from the heart, and then relax and breathe in the sound -`*eeD*, feeling it go backward into the body. Feel the final *-D* sound at the end, touching your bones and the densest parts of your being, reviving all of them. Look into the mirror of your heart and view the relationships and projects in your life. Which need restoration? Into which can you bring new life—and how?

60. Personal Life Energy

المُحْيِ

Al-Muhyi

*When you are guided to this pathway,
take the opportunity to focus on the ways in which life energy already
embodies itself in your life.*

WE OFTEN TALK ABOUT someone's "personal energy," or magnetism, and how it affects his or her surroundings. This vibrancy comes from within and reveals itself no matter what the circumstances. When someone can direct this type of personal magnetism, we often call the combination of ego and energy *charisma*. In addition, many alternative and complementary therapies make use of the "energy," "prana," or "chi" that various traditional medicines of the world believed could be directed for healing.

In the pathways of the heart, we find several ways of looking at the phenomenon of life energy. This pathway tells us that every particle of the universe already contains a kind of life energy, and so ultimately nothing needs to be received or given. When the Sufi penetrates the depths of life, she finds what she was looking for already there. From such an experience, the twentieth-century Sufi Shah Maghsoud speaks of the divine Beloved in this way:

*The sun's radiance in her face is in
the heart of every particle,
and I am like a wave
glimpsing into every cell.
Through her parting elixir of alchemy
my face becomes golden,
and so I could plunge the heart
of the universe into red fire.*[29]

Deep love, which often comes along with pain, draws out a life energy inside of us. It's not imported from elsewhere; it's already there. We feel our own heart as part of the heart of the universe, and both are tempered by love's fire. In a small way, this happens whenever we find that we suddenly have more energy simply because something in which we're interested is happening or being talked about. For this reason, the Sufis try to encourage their students to develop their interests, so that they can consciously discover the relationship between love and life energy for themselves. When the student does this, she or he discovers that everything we need—love, energy, healing—is right here and now, and no one can take it away from us. This gives one the strength and freedom expressed by Rabia in the following prayer:

Allah, you know the secret of all things—
help all my enemies succeed in this world,
and help my friends succeed in the next.
As for me, I am free of both.
Even if I gained this world and the next,
it would not be worth trading for your presence.
Desire for anything but you
makes me a heretic.

Perhaps life is calling you to look within yourself for the energy that you have been trying to find outside. What would help you awaken it? This is not the superficial energy raised by passive entertainment; it is more like the energy that comes after playing a musical instrument, telling a story, hiking, or making love.

❧ Roots and Branches ❧

Traditional translations of this quality include "giver of life" and "quickener." Compared to its parent *Hayy* (62), universal life energy, *Muhyi* indicates the life energy that suffuses every particle of the universe (*Mu*) in its own unique way. This is not life energy held like water in a sponge. The sponge, so to speak, is already an expression of divine energy, and could not exist without it. This recognition can, like the previous pathway, *Mu'id*, help us to distinguish what is already life-filled in our lives. The Qur'an typically uses this word in connection with the next, *Mumit,* to indicate that the same Being shuttles us back and forth between life embodied and life disembodied.

Meditation

Center again in the heart. Call a circle of your inner self, and breathe *Ya Moo-hee* as an affirmation of the way each part of you embodies the divine life energy at this moment in your life. What would allow your inner self to express more life energy and grow stronger in the fulfillment of its purpose in life? Ask for the help of your highest guidance and allow a solution to appear.

61. *Transition*

المُمِيتُ

Al-Mumit

When you are guided to this pathway,
take the opportunity to remember that all formed, embodied existence—
thoughts, feelings, identities, and bodies—comes to an end, and opens a
door to another world.

L IKE THE OLD HEBREW word usually translated "death" (*mawet*), the Arabic *maut* (from which this pathway comes) shows not an end, but a transition from one state to another, one that returns a being to the Universal Self. We may experience such transitions in small ways many times throughout our lives, but we often fail to go through them consciously. They can happen at a time of crisis for us: the death of a loved one, the breakup of a relationship, or the loss of work.

In Sufi terms, the experiences we have of dying within everyday life are called *fana*, passing away from one image, concept, or configuration of our self to another. When we go through these transitions consciously, the self that resurrects itself reflects more of the whole, more of its purpose in life, and more of the Beloved than the one that passed away. Hence the Sufi adage, often attributed to Imam Ali, "Die before you die."

The Sufis tell many stories about this experience, but none more famous or poignant than the following, as retold by Attar:

Once a group of moths fell in love with a flame. They consulted together and decided to send someone to investigate their beloved more closely because from their vantage they could see only a blinding light. One moth went out and returned, then gave a fuller description: three parts to the flame—the dark underneath, the light in the middle, and an aura around it. The wise moth that chaired the meeting decided this wasn't good enough, so another volunteered to go. This one singed its wings on the flame and returned, describing the burning sensation, the pain, and the heat. This report was still deemed unsatisfying to the rest. Finally, a third moth flew right into the flame, embraced and made love to it. Flame and moth were one. "This one knows and understands," said the wise moth, "but it can't say anything."

Perhaps life is presenting you with a situation where something must die in order for something else to live. Or, perhaps you face a change in your situation, which feels like death to your self, or to part of it. Sometimes, in the work with one's inner self, one part of the self passes away to make room for another. This can happen in various ways, but the essential dynamic is that the vehicle of "self" that was serving your soul's development is no longer necessary or helpful. This pathway will not cause this process to happen, but it will support such a process that is already underway.

~ Roots and Branches ~

Traditional translations of this quality include "slayer" and "giver of death." The roots of *Mumit* show: M—formed, fluid existence; U—Allah's power of transition, to bring something into or out of manifestation; M—more form; I—divine life energy; T—the goal, opening into something else. Following on from the previous names—*Mu'id* and *Muhyi*—and followed next by *Hayy* and *Qayyum*, this sequence of pathways shows various interplays between divine life energy and embodied forms: revival, full embodiment, death, liberation, and resurrection.

Meditation

Center again in the heart. Call a circle of your inner self of feelings, thoughts, and voices. Breathe with the feeling of this name and re-mind all the voices gathered around Holy Wisdom's table that forms have a limited life span in Allah's universe. What aspects of your inner or outer lives are ripe for death and rebirth? What masks of your self can you dispense with?

62. Universal Life Energy

الحَيُّ

Al-Hayy

When you are guided to this pathway,
take the opportunity to drink in the universal life energy of the One,
wherever you find it around you.

TWO PATHWAYS AGO, WE saw that according to the Sufis, we live and have our being in an ocean of divine life energy—if we only knew it. As the Indian Sufi Kabir described the situation, "The fish in the sea is not thirsty." Everything we need can be found within us, when we feel our personal "I am" connected to the universal "I Am."

Despite this, part of our being is still growing and developing. It often feels itself separate from the widest community of life, and so we also fail to find the energy hidden deeply within us, in the "wilder" territories of our inner life. At these times, we experience a personal lack of energy and begin to look for it around us. There is nothing wrong with this; asking for help can reconnect us to our relationships with others.

This pathway, *Hayy*, introduces us to the source of the personal energy we find embodied within us (*Muhyi*). According to the Sufis, this subtle life force infuses the air we breathe and invigorates our food. How much energy we receive from our food is determined both by how much it contains and by our ability to absorb it, which in turn derives from the quality of our breathing. The twentieth-century Sufi Samuel Lewis commented:

> *Life-force enters with the breath and leaves with the breath. This life-force is stored in the body. It is not the result of caloric intake through food. A stout person may obtain many calories from food without being able to utilize this in action. If the caloric theory alone were true, the stout would always be superior to the thin. The energy in an electric*

battery is derived from the chemicals introduced, and not from the material of the battery. In a similar way, the life-force vitalizes the body, and the body utilizes the life-force. Therefore, the body is an accommodation and not a person.[30]

To the Sufi, our preoccupations with our own concerns, hopes, and fears blind us to the life energy moving around and through us. We believe that we live practical lives, but ignore the exchange of energy going on beneath the surface. Or, when we do look outside for the "energy" or "healing" that will rescue us, we constantly affirm the extraordinary abilities and energy of others, but deny our own. When we wake up, we may find ourselves only playing at being alive. In the following story, Mullah Nasruddin exaggerates this natural tendency for us to want to find someone who will tell us what to do:

One day a neighbor found Mullah Nasruddin sitting in a tree in his garden, in the process of sawing off the limb on which he was sitting.

"Mullah, you'd better stop, otherwise you'll fall down," said the neighbor, then went back inside his house. Sure enough, Mullah kept sawing, the limb broke, and he fell. Mullah ran next door and pounded on his neighbor's door.

"O, great one, please forgive me," said Mullah, "I didn't know I had a psychic for a neighbor! Could you please predict what will happen to me tomorrow?"

The neighbor tried to deny that he could predict the future, saying that what he had told Mullah was just common sense. But Mullah wouldn't listen and kept after him. Finally, the neighbor became exasperated and said, "Mullah, for heaven's sake, for all I care you can drop dead tomorrow!"

The next morning, Mullah woke and said to his wife, "Our neighbor is a psychic and he told me that I would drop dead today, so I have to prepare." He took his donkey along for company and went to the graveyard, then dug a grave for himself and lay down in it. As the day ended, he was still lying there and thought, "I must be dead now. This isn't really so bad!"

Then a pack of dogs came by and started harassing his donkey. The donkey began to bray and make a racket. Finally, Mullah yelled from the grave, "You dogs—get out of here! If I weren't dead I'd get out of my grave and give you a thrashing!"

By giving all our power away, in the end we completely cut ourselves off from the energy within us and so become like the living dead.

Perhaps you feel in need of more life energy. Imagine yourself as a sponge, absorbing the divine life that surrounds you every moment. Perhaps life is asking you to find this energy through establishing more rhythm in your spiritual, mental, emotional, or physical life. Or, you may be asked to share the life energy of the One Being with others in some directed way, as in one of the healing professions. This pathway is not a magic potion. At some point, the sponge gets full, and you must discover the ways in which you hold and contain energy in your deepest self, as we saw in the previous pathway *Muhyi* (60). The present pathway will, however, open the surface of your being, which may have forgotten that the divine life energy suffuses the universe.

⌒ Roots and Branches ⌒

Traditional translations of this quality include "alive" and "everliving." Like *Muhyi* (60), the roots of *Hayy* come from ancient names of the divine used by many Semitic peoples, which center on the sound of the breath expressed by the letter *H*. In Hebrew, one of these sacred names was YHWH, the Ever-Living Life that was, is, and will be. Semitic languages developed variations of this *H* sound to express the action of the breath when free (breathed *H*), coming into flesh (lightly aspirated, *cH*), fully enfleshed (a hard, breathed *kH*), and ready to leave an enfleshed form (no equivalent in European languages; `*uH*). The Qur'an often uses *Hayy* in connection with the next pathway, *Qayyum*, which together can be expressed as "the Life that keeps living, coming to standing again and again in all beings."

Meditation

Center again in the heart. Call a circle of your inner self and breathe the sound *ya Hayy* with the inner voices that gather at Wisdom's table. Who needs more energy? Allow this sacred energy to flood your being through your higher guidance. Absorb what you need at this moment. There is always enough. Or perhaps one part of you has plenty of energy but doesn't know what to do with it. Ask for direction from the Source in using this energy to further your creative purpose in life.

63. Rebounding

القَيُّومُ

Al-Qayyum

When you are guided to this pathway,
feel the "rebound" of Reality that allows you to pick yourself up
and come to standing again.

SOMETIMES WE GET KNOCKED down by something that happens, for instance, the breakup of a relationship, and then feel an inner rebound, a "second wind" that keeps us going. Jesus, at the end of his Beatitudes (or "blessed are . . .") sayings, as viewed from the Aramaic language, recommends that his students consciously use the path of rebound. He tells them that when others direct insults or defamation toward them, they should use the energy behind it to propel them further on their path. He recommends, "Go further, do everything extreme, including letting your ego disappear. Your greater universe of life opens around you from the blows on your heart."[31]

The life of the nature around us abounds in growth and decay, waxing and waning, flow and ebb. We can remember this when we experience a setback in life, and use it as a theme for meditation. It will allow us to come back more consciously. For instance, Moineddin Chishti offered the following saying as a meditation to his students:

Listen to the voice from the incoming waves; it is loud.
But when the tide goes out, the voice becomes silent.

If we experience our voice becoming silent, it will come back again.

Perhaps life is calling you to take the path of rebound. Feel the circumstances that have brought you low, let go of all the details and use the energy that remains to bring you back up. When a spring is pressed downward, it gathers even greater force. When life has brought you low, feel yourself gathering even more strength for when your season comes around again. As *Mumit* (61) showed us, all forms do pass away, but the energy within them resurrects itself in another way, and as Einstein discovered, matter becomes energy when it is accelerated to the speed of light squared. This pathway helps us to discover and experience the inner equivalent of this transformation.

∾ *Roots and Branches* ∾

Traditional translations of this quality include "eternal" and "self-sustaining." The roots of *Qayyum* show a process of coming again to standing (*Qa*), which involves a luminous body (*YM*) rising after being seated. The second root of the word is related to the old Hebrew word for "day," *yom*, meaning embodied light or intelligence. Early Syriac Christian monks used a spiritual practice in which they imagined they were Jesus rising from the dead. The practice, called *qayima* in Syriac, is also related to the word for this pathway. We find the same Arabic root in the word *maqam*, mentioned earlier as the station or "standing" of consciousness from which we live our lives. Another branch from *Qayyum* connects to the QA- family of qualities of divine power, like *Qahhar* (15), primordial fire, and *Qadir* (69), particle power.

Meditation

Center again in the heart. Breathe the name *QaY-Yoom* in rhythm, feeling the final *m* sound resonating in the heart and belly. This name can also be practiced in combination with *Hayy* in the form *Ya Hayyo Ya Qayyum*, which affirms the ever-living Life along with, so to speak, the "eternal Matter" that resurrects itself. This practice is helpful during transitions in life, for purifying dwelling places, or upon the passing of a relative or friend.

∾   ∾

64. *Extraordinary Sensing*

الوَاجِدُ

Al-Wajid

When you are guided to this pathway,
take the opportunity to contact the place in you where the One Being opens
your inner senses to the subtle activities of the divine life around you.

To THE SUFI, WHAT we call extrasensory perception and similar unusual abilities are not miraculous. They are simply part of the many qualities that Allah wished to express by creating humanity. This pathway emphasizes a particular kind of sensing, like the capabilities that a dowser uses when looking for water under the earth.

While the Sufi sees these abilities as completely natural, she also realizes that they can be a hindrance on the path. The opinions of others, as well as the image of oneself as "psychic" or special in some way, can create a great deal of inertia as we continue to change and evolve. To avoid this problem, Sufis sometimes use their powers only secretly.

Irina Tweedie described how her own awakening to divine sensing occurred with her teacher:

> If I see a rose for the first time, not knowing what it is, something can happen in that moment of suspension between naming the rose and knowing that it is the rose. If a long enough interval passes in between, something can happen. The intuitional quality will rise through. That's what [my teacher] did to me. The secret is, and the miracle is, that there is no dilemma.[32]

Even developing such abilities does not guarantee that one has the common sense to use them correctly, as Rumi describes in the following story, which he told to his students:

Once a king had a very ignorant son. So he called all the wisest teachers in the kingdom and instructed them to teach his son astrology, geomancy, divining, dowsing, and every other occult science. Over a period of time, the son became a complete master of these arts. One day the king decided to test him.

"I'm holding something in my fist. Can you tell me what it is?"

The prince reached out with his psychic abilities and said, "What you're holding is round, yellow, and hollow."

"That's right!" said his father. "So can you tell me what it is?"

"It must be a golden sieve," said the prince.

The king threw up his hands. "No, it's a ring! You intuited all the signs. How could you not realize that a sieve wouldn't fit in my hand?"

Just like this, scholars split hairs on everything—what is permitted, what is not permitted. They know everything outside them, but they don't know themselves. Being yellow, hollow, and round is only accidental. Cast the object into the fire and none of these remains. It returns to its essential self, just like us, in the heat of divine Unity.

Perhaps you have experienced such capacities and are wondering how to integrate them into your life. Or, maybe you have not been aware that such psychic abilities are also part of the universe of Unity. Rather than focus on their effects, or on yourself as someone special, why not see the ability as another pathway of the heart, reminding you of your connection to the divine Beloved?

⌒ Roots and Branches ⌒

Traditional translations of this quality include "all-perceiving" and "all-perfect." The roots of *Wajid* show the divine awareness (*WA-*) focusing on the life energy within every particular manifestation of it (*-JiD*). With the emphasis placed on the first syllable, this name focuses on the ability to see, sense, and find things. The next pathway, *Majid,* emphasizes the ability to publicly work with and alter things using a similar extraordinary ability.

Meditation

Center again in the heart. Focus on the heart as an empty mirror and breathe the sound of *Waa-JiD* into it. Is there a situation in your outer life that calls for this quality of inner sensing?

Call a circle of your inner self and allow your highest guidance to use this capability to sense into each sensation, feeling, or voice that arises, feeling its ultimate purpose in life.

65. Channeling Extraordinary Power

المَاجِدُ

Al-Ma'jid

When you are guided to this pathway,
take the opportunity to affirm the magic of life. Remember that anything
you do displays the power and life energy of the One.

IN THE HASIDIC CULTURE of nineteenth-century Europe, the Hebrew term *maggid* meant an itinerant preacher, as well as one who channeled the divine power through a particular angel or other divine spirit. It's probably the source of the Persian word *magus*, which is the origin of our word *magician*. The name of this pathway comes from the same roots and opens a door to our ability to channel and embody sacred power in a public way. These days, this happens most often in the realms of healing and teaching. If we look at people who have acted in this capacity throughout history, they have often found the role to be both a blessing and a curse. Those who channel the divine life in a particular area and are able to do things that seem miraculous often have difficulty distinguishing for themselves and others that the power comes not from their own person but from the Holy One itself. People may become dependent upon them, or they may become deluded into thinking that they are the source of the power they exhibit. Today we live in a culture looking for the next thing to get excited about, the newest celebrity healer, channel, or psychic.

For this reason, as noted in the previous pathway, *Wajid*, the Sufis have often hidden any miraculous abilities from public view. This pathway also speaks to situations in which we are asked to act the part of "superstar" in someone else's drama. The early twentieth-century Sufi Inayat Khan found himself in such a situation when a particular esoteric society wanted to declare him the "world avatar" they had been awaiting. He refused. Later the same group realized that they must have been mistaken because Inayat Khan was not a vegetarian, which was one of their pre-conditions for sainthood.

Working with the pathway of *Majid* means understanding and working internally with our reactions to being a "success" or a "failure." Inayat Khan commented on his experience of these in this way:

What the world calls success is, to me, like a doll's wedding.
Failure in life does not matter; the greatest misfortune is standing
still.[33]

About the latter saying, his student Samuel Lewis commented:

For life is action, action in any direction. Vibrations are like waves that rise and fall. The wave travels in a definite direction as towards a goal and yet in its movement rises and falls to crest and trough. So people rise and fall, have apparent successes and failures, but all the time may be moving towards their true destination without even knowing it. It is only the one who does not move who does not arrive.[34]

Perhaps life has called you to act in a public, noticeable way, manifesting divine energy on life's stage. This may be in a sacred or a secular context. Use this pathway to help you remember that all life energy, and the means to work with it, come from the Beloved. Likewise, in working with the inner self, *Majid* (like *Wajid*) can help your highest guidance effect change in your inner self.

⌒ Roots and Branches ⌒

Traditional translations of this quality include "all-excellent" and "almightiness." *Ma'jid*, with emphasis on the first syllable, *MA*, shows us a vehicle with the ability to direct divine life energy. Its companion name *Ma'jid* (48; accent on the second syllable) reminds us that the same, dazzling power already exists in all beings. The Qur'an uses this word in connection with the expression *al-arsh al-majid* to indicate the "throne" from which the One's creation constantly arises each moment. Early Jewish and Jewish-Christian "throne" (or *merkabah*) mysticism reflected the same idea. Both encouraged devotees to experience the "place," or *makom*, of living creation within their own beings.

Meditation

Center again in the heart. Breathe with the feeling of the sound *Ya Maa-Jid* (accent on the first syllable) and find a rhythm that includes the rhythm of your heartbeat. Call a circle of your inner self and remind all the voices within you that their ability to act publicly as vehicles of the One's life energy depends upon receptivity. Allow this breath of remembrance to resonate through your whole inner community with love and respect.

66. *Counting to One*

الْوَاحِدُ

Al-Wahid

When you are guided to this pathway,
take the opportunity to breathe and "count to one" with each breath. In
whatever situation you are facing, no matter how it appears, feel the divine
heart within your own heart.

LIKE THE PREVIOUS INTERLUDES that invited us to "bathe in Unity," this pathway and the next two ask us to consider more deeply the nature of our own individuality in relation to the only "I Am," Sacred Unity.

The idealization of the divine mystery as "One," or "Unity," which seems native to the ancient Semitic peoples, has—as do all idealizations—its advantages and disadvantages. On one hand, it avoids the problem of imagining the divine as only "good" (which probably forms the original derivation of the word *God* from the Germanic languages). Imagining the divine as only good creates the need to explain "evil" as something "anti-God." At that point, we've created the idea of a dualistic universe, where some people or beings are separate from the divine realm. Many of these ideas come into Christianity from Greek philosophy, which, after Plato, imagined the divine world as separate from the human. As we have noted, all the various Semitic names for God—*Elohim, Alaha, Allah*—can be translated as "One" or "Unity." Strictly speaking, we should understand them as saying "Everything's included in God." And yet the notion of the divine as "one" has led some people in the Middle Eastern traditions to believe that "my One is the only (or real) One."

The Sufis, looking deeply into the Qur'an and its mystical use of various names, attempt to avoid this problem by distinguishing two different types of divine Oneness. The thirteenth-century Andalusian Sufi Ibn Arabi delved very deeply into this mystery. In a vision he says he received from the Prophet Muhammad, he saw that the

One Being used the ninety-nine pathways or sacred qualities, as well as an unlimited number of others, to shape creation. As we saw under the pathway *Bari* (12), creation happened because the Divine Unknowableness needed a home for these qualities in manifestation ("I was a hidden treasure," in the words of the sacred tradition). In particular, Allah designed the human being to be the complete reflection of all these qualities; that is, the divine consciousness of the universe as a whole.

Ibn Arabi compares the pathway *Wahid* to the number one (as understood like the Roman numeral I), which forever appears in all successive numbers, which are only "one" multiplied. For instance, I-I is what we call "two," and I-I-I is what we call "three." So just as this "one" is within all numbers, so the same divine One is within all "numbers" of existence; that is, within all processes, beings, forms, and substances. This is how we can say that the divine heart is within our heart. According to Ibn Arabi, it was the confusing of *Wahid* with the next pathway, *Ahad* (divine uniqueness), that led certain mystics to, in an ecstatic state of consciousness, proclaim that they were the Unique One (*Ahad*); that is, "God" itself. In reality, said Ibn Arabi, they were experiencing the One that reappears in everything (*Wahid*); that is, the consciousness of Unity acting through them. An example of this seeming confusion appears in the case of the tenth-century Sufi Mansur al-Hallaj, who was martyred by Islamic authorities for seeming to claim that he was Allah when he used such expressions as "I am the Truth" (*ana 'l haqq*). In other sayings, however, Hallaj seems to distinguish, albeit ambiguously, between the "Ones":

> *I am the One whom I love*
> *and the One whom I love is I—*
> *two breaths and spirits inhabiting one body.*
> *When you see me, you see the One*
> *and when you see the One you see us both.*

Perhaps life is calling you right now to notice that whatever situation, person, being, or process you're facing, no matter how unpleasant it may be, contains teaching, healing, or energy meant for you. This can be tough medicine. Breathe and relax into Unity. Can you include this, too, as a small part of expanding your conscious-

ness to include all the beings, thoughts, and sensations created before you?

∽ Roots and Branches ∽

The traditional translation of this quality is "the one." The roots of
Wahid show constant (*WA*) guidance toward the source of life
(*-HiD*), a guidance that constantly changes faces but remains the
same behind various masks. Linked with the latter root is the pathway *Shahid* (50). The difference here is that *Wahid*, through the root
WA (also meaning "and") asks us to affirm that Sacred Unity includes "and even this" or "this, too." Both this word and the next,
Ahad, stem from the same ancient Semitic root, which we can see reflected in, for instance, the Hebrew *echad* and the Aramaic *yihidaya*.
The Qur'an uses both forms of the root (*Wahid* three times, *Ahad*
only once) to impress upon its listeners that there is only one source
of divine guidance, and only one reality worthy of honor.

Meditation

Center again in the heart. Breathe the quality *Ya Waa-Hid* rhythmically, with your eyes open. With one hand lightly on your chest, remain centered in the heart. Acknowledge every situation and
appearance before you as another face of the One. Call a circle of
your inner self and invite again every feeling, thought, and sensation
to the table of Wisdom. Can you include ". . . and this, too?"

BATHING IN UNITY

$\mathcal{T}$he Sufis tell various versions of the story in which Rumi meets the dervish Shams-i-Tabriz, who was to set his heart ablaze and turn him from a very competent religious philosopher and teacher into a Sufi master whose mystical love poetry is still able to move people eight hundred years later. The version this writer heard goes like this:

> Shams had come to Konya under the cover of being a merchant, even though he owned nothing. One day, he waited in the lane where Rumi usually went riding with his students. As Rumi's donkey passed, Shams jumped out, grabbed the bridle, and asked, "Look—they say you know the hidden secrets of all the beautiful names. Tell me this: Who was greater, the Prophet Muhammad or Abu Yazid Bistami?"
>
> "Clearly Prophet Muhammad," said Rumi. "How can you even compare him to Abu Yazid?"
>
> "Because," replied Shams, "Muhammad said, 'O Allah, we have not known you as you really are!' And Abu Yazid said, in a state of unity with Allah, 'Glory be to me!'"
>
> Rumi was startled, and by some accounts passed out. But then he regained consciousness and said, "That's because Abu Yazid's cup was filled by a single drop, while the cup of Muhammad was as vast as the ocean."
>
> After that Rumi and Shams became inseparable.

Meditation

Center again in the heart. Breathe a full, refined breath and feel your heart as a cup that can hold more and more of the divine qualities that you find within you. Ask that it be malleable enough to keep expanding and contracting to accommodate every realization that life brings you.

67. *Uniquely One*

الأَحَدُ

Al-Ahad

When you are guided to this pathway,
take the opportunity to touch the place in your heart that feels uniquely you.
Then feel your own heart as part of the heart of Sacred Unity.

A S MENTIONED IN THE previous pathway, the difference between the Sufi notions of "single" (*Wahid*) and "unique" (*Ahad*) are not easy to grasp. Experientially, we could state the difference like this: When I feel that the divine heart is within my heart, this is the experience of *Wahid*. When I feel that my heart is within the heart of the divine, this is the experience of *Ahad*. If one tries to make logical or metaphysical sense of it, the mind boggles. Fortunately, the spiritual path has little to do with logic or metaphysics.

Here's how the ninth-century Sufi Abu Yazid Bistami wrestled with it:

In the beginning I made four mistakes. I tried to remember, know, love, and seek Allah. When I came to the end of this, I realized that Allah had remembered me even before I remembered Allah. And it was the same with knowing, loving, and seeking. Allah knew, loved, and sought me first.

By that time I thought that I had reached the "throne of glory." I said, "O throne, they say that Allah rests on you." The throne replied, "We were told that Allah rests in a humble heart."

For thirty years, Allah served as my mirror, but now it seems I am my own mirror. "I" and "Allah" denies Unity. Since "I" am no more, Allah is Allah's own mirror, or perhaps Allah is the mirror of myself, for I have passed away.

Meditating upon the same theme, Inayat Khan phrased the combination of these two pathways beautifully when he called God "the Only Being."

Perhaps life is calling you right now to rediscover the part of your being that feels unique and will always remain mysterious and unknowable. It cannot be expressed in words and does not express itself outwardly to others. It is not growing toward anything (like *Khabir,* 31), nor is it the divine gift we give to the Universe (*Hamid,* 56). Remaining at the core of your being, it is, in a paradoxical way, your own personal doorway to the uniqueness of Sacred Unity.

～ Roots and Branches ～

A traditional translation of this quality is "the one and only." The roots of *Ahad* show the absolute extent of Being (*A-*) expressing itself through the point, summit, or drop of existence (*HD*). Some Islamic commentators have called this the intrinsically unknowable aspect of the divine (like the *Ein Sof* of Jewish mysticism), which cannot be applied to or known by human beings. According to Ibn Arabi, if *Wahid* is like the number one (*1*) that reappears in all beings, *Ahad* (like the name *Allah* itself) can be compared to the number zero (0), which is the absence of number. In this sense, he compares it to the divine essence (*Dhat*), which encloses and includes all being without being enclosed by or included in anything else.

Meditation

Center again in the heart. Breathe with the sound *Ya Aa-Had* (with the *h* slightly aspirated). Take this feeling inside and let it lead you to the secret place in your heart, the place that the Sufi poet Kabir advises us to "wrap up carefully" because it includes stars and planets, as well as the unknowable mystery that preceded the cosmos. Continue to breathe and feel your own "I am," finding its resting place within the heart of the only "I Am."

68. Refuge for Every Need

الصَّمَدُ

As-Samad

When you are guided to this pathway,
take the opportunity to remember that the One Being is a refuge for all
circumstances in life. It has no boundary that limits the sphere of life into
which it can bring comfort.

THE QUR'AN USES THE word for this pathway and the previous one (*Ahad*) only once, in a mystical passage (Sura 112) that attempts to explain that the "Allah" speaking through it is not another idea, myth, or cult; it is the inexpressible source of a shared reality that ultimately has no fixed name or form. In poetic form, the expression *Allahu Samad* from this passage could be translated as follows:

> *Ultimate Unity throughout the cosmos*
> *envelops and surrounds all dimensions,*
>   *measurements, laws, and tendencies.*
> *It fulfills and completes all potentials that*
> *unfold in joy throughout the Universe.*

Two ideas combine here. One asks us to imagine a refuge, uniquely suited to us, from whatever trouble we're facing in life. The other depicts a source of whatever remedy we need for what ails us, or of whatever we need to complete any lack we feel within. Ultimately, the last three pathways ask us to live as though there is ultimately a wordless Reality behind all our projections and ideals of the sacred. Even if we were to realize within us all of these pathways, as well as all the other names of the sacred from all traditions throughout history, there would still be more to this Reality.

This represents a leap of faith for many of us who style ourselves "postmodern" and affirm that there is nothing beyond various "points of view" and cultural constructions of reality. The Sufi believes that the Source of Love has a reality as sure as the reality of the air we breathe. This pathway warns us to not trap the Real within our own conceptions, no matter how broad or universal we think they may be. Again, in an absurd way, Mullah Nasruddin shows us how easy it is to do this:

> *Once Mullah Nasruddin's favorite clock stopped working, so he took it for repair. When the repairperson took the back off the clock and turned it over, a dead fly fell out.*
> *"So that's the problem," said Nasruddin. "The little mechanic who operated it has died!"*

Today, the "little mechanic" might be represented by genetics or some "theory of everything" that leads us to the false conclusion that we have everything figured out. This is the antithesis of touching the place in us that can reflect and participate in the sacred source of remedy.

Perhaps life is challenging you in a particular avenue of your life, one in which you feel no one and nothing can help. This pathway serves as a reminder that the possibilities of the Holy One are limitless, its remedies endless. There is no one else to turn to, since the Beloved's universe has no edge. In working with the inner self, this pathway can also help your highest guidance remind each inner voice of the divine sound and wave that bring relief from the pain we sometimes feel in the struggle of life.

~ Roots and Branches ~

Traditional translations of this quality include "eternal" and "uncaused cause of all being." The roots of *Samad* show a wave of sound (SM), repairing, saving and meeting all needs, plugging all gaps in existence (-AD). To say that the One is "eternal" could lead us to believe that the One's existence is limited to our own sense of time. Allah includes all senses of time, including Western linear time, Middle Eastern pulse time, Eastern reincarnational spiral time, circle time, no-time, and every other possibility. Within all this spacious possibility, the One provides saving grace for every need. For this reason, Ibn Arabi called this quality the "universal support and refuge."

Meditation

Center again in the heart. Place one hand over your heart and feel the pulse there in rhythm with your breath. Feel this pulse resonating through your bloodstream to include your whole body as it brings new life to every part of you. Now feel your own heart within the heart of the divine, and sense the way in which the divine heart can pulse each moment, bringing comfort and healing that can recreate the universe in each instant.

69. *Holding the Center*

القَادِرُ

Al-Qadir

When you are guided to this pathway,
take the opportunity to contact the part of you that can hold the center point
while everything else swirls around you.

THIS PATHWAY TAKES US into another neighborhood of qualities, which invite us to become more familiar with the ways that divine power works through us. This "power" differs from "life energy" in that it actively changes manifested reality. In comparison with *Qahhar* (15), which figuratively works through fire, and *Qawi* (53), which works through wind, *Qadir* works through earth, in and on the particles of formed existence. Why all the different "power" names that we have seen so far? Because it is easy for a part of the inner self (*nafs*) to assume ownership of what does not belong to it, and to forget that every "self"—every center of existence—already contains the divine power. Power is intoxicating. By becoming familiar with all the different ways that "doing something" can feel within us, we can connect these more easily with the action of the divine Beloved.

The relative merits of different kinds of power form the theme of a sacred tradition through Muhammad, expressing the voice of Allah:

> *When the earth was first created, it began to wobble, and so Allah created the mountains to stabilize it. Amazed by this power, the angels asked, "O Sustainer, is there anything in creation more powerful than these primeval mountains?"*

> *"Iron is more powerful."*
> *"Is there anything more powerful than iron?"*
> *"Fire is more powerful."*

"Is there anything more powerful than fire?"

"Water is more powerful."

"Is there anything more powerful than water?"

"Wind is more powerful."

"Is there anything more powerful than wind?"

"Yes. The children of Adam who give with their whole hearts but without the left hand knowing what the right is doing."[35]

The Sufis have sometimes speculated that if God is all there is, why do we need to do anything? "God will provide." This pathway tells us that we need to center ourselves in life and grasp life's challenges. Saadi tells the following story about this:

Once a dervish wandering through a forest happened upon a fox that had lost its legs. "How does the poor thing manage to survive?" the dervish asked himself. Just then a tiger happened along, carrying its prey. The tiger ate what it wanted and left the rest for the fox. The next day the dervish came back, and the same thing happened.

"So that's how it's done," thought the dervish. "I'll try the same." So he went home, sat in a corner, and waited for the universe to provide for him. He waited for days, and nothing came. Finally, becoming famished, he heard a voice: "You're following the wrong example. You have legs. Be like the tiger, not the fox."

Perhaps you are being called upon right now to hold a strong center in your life. The situation into which you are stepping, or feel that you have been thrust, may seem too much for you. You may know what you are able to do, or you may not. Perhaps you are being called upon to awaken in yourself some practical ability, to direct the divine power you have felt in a focused, embodied way. In all cases, this pathway helps us to remember that it is really the One Being working through us that accomplishes what needs to be done.

⁀ *Roots and Branches* ⁀

Traditional translations of this quality include "the able" and "providence." The roots of *Qadir* show the unlimited divine power (*QA*) applying itself to individual forms by centering on a point (*D*) and radiating this power outward (*R*). Other meanings of the Arabic word include to arrange, dispose, devise, or assign. These all point to the development of a type of mastery through the manipulation of the "stuff" of life. The Qur'an frequently uses this word in connection with the One Being's ability to bring what seems to be dead back to life.

Meditation

Center again in the heart. Breathe with the feeling of this pathway, and place the sound *Ya Qaa-Dir* on your breath in a rhythm of four beats in and four out (the last beat being a rest). Feel the sound anchoring you in the heart and linking heart and solar plexus in a very centered, grounded way. Try this practice as a walking meditation. It is especially good when walking over uneven ground, during which you may experience the sensation of a "larger heart" stabilizing you.

70. *Embodying Power in Action*

المُقْتَدِرُ

Al-Muqtadir

When you are guided to this pathway,
take the opportunity to feel the actual process of expressing divine power
while you are acting and to see everything around you expressing this same
power to do and arrange things.

SOMETIMES LIFE CALLS US to act forcefully with compassion, knowing that the effort may not be understood. The work of the spiritual guide is often compared to that of the horseman in the following story:

> *Once, a man woke after camping out for the night. He felt terrible and began to cough and shake violently. A horseman rode by and immediately understood the problem. He jumped down and started pounding the man on the back and squeezing his stomach forcefully from behind. He kept doing this for some minutes, while the man, gasping, tried to tell him to stop. All of a sudden the man threw up a scorpion, and before he could thank the horseman, the horseman jumped on his horse and rode away.*

I once met and was able to work with a Sufi who was one of the most unassuming yet powerful people I have ever met. He was very mild-mannered and peaceful, but had tremendous energy. I met him while he was in his eighties, working as an engineer in a research project at a local university that was investigating a new way to harness the solar energy collected by the ocean. In his past, he had fought with the Norwegian resistance during World War II. He had worked as an economist on an alternative system of large-scale bartering, which was used to rebuild Norway after the war. He had traveled the world, and he had been both penniless and wealthy. I never saw him wear a robe, or even let on to most people that he was a Sufi, yet he had a vast knowledge of Sufi practice and had the initiation of a senior teacher, or *murshid*. He felt that people were too easily attracted by charisma and costumes, and that these were side trips on the spiritual path. I remember him telling me that whenever he received a letter attacking him or the projects on which he was working, he tried never to write a letter in anger but to always find the place where he and his perceived opponent agreed. For me, twenty years after his passing, he still expresses an example of divine power in action, without spotlight or publicity.

Perhaps life is calling you to remember that, in the middle of acting (which is often the most intoxicating moment), the energy of your action is Allah expressing the One Self through you. As we saw in the pathway of *Ma'jid* (65), when we find ourselves in situations involving healing or another outward, obvious use of power, others can project the archetype of hero or heroine onto us. If we accept this, it is a big step toward forgetfulness. In this sense, *Muqtadir* reminds us that Allah is the only hero or heroine. It also reminds us that all beings already embody sacred power—nothing needs to be added from the "outside."

❧ Roots and Branches ❧

Traditional translations of this quality include "powerful," "omnipotent," and "determining all things." *Muqtadir* bears the same relationship to *Qadir*, the previous pathway, as *Muhyi* (60) does to *Hayy* (62). The divine power not only operates through particular centers, but also already exists in every particle of existence, which already *is* (that is, it does not simply contain) divine power.

Meditation

Center again in the heart. Breathe with the feeling of the name *Ya MooQ-Ta-Deer* and allow every particle of your being—every thought, emotion, sensation, and voice that arises—to be included in it. Continue to breathe with this feeling for a while. Then, while in action, breathe with the name or its feeling. See all of creation suffused with the divine power, and see yourself as just another particle of it.

71. Preparing the Way

المُقَدِّمُ

Al-Muqaddim

*When you are guided to this pathway,
take the opportunity to acknowledge the part of your being that feels
"oldest," and prepare the way for power to flow through your life.*

IN THE GOSPELS, JESUS reportedly says that "the first shall be last and the last shall be first" (Matt. 19:30). In the Aramaic version of this saying, the first (*qadim*) are the older parts of our psyche, which prepare the way for the younger, more facile parts, such as our "modern" logical intelligence. In our inner circle of self, this pathway leads us to the voice that embodies practicality and initiates things.

In a larger sense, this pathway connects us to the souls who are traveling ahead of us on the caravan of creation. The sense of time in old Semitic languages places the moving past ahead of us, with the "front of the caravan" moving with the beginning of creation, when everything remained as potential within the heart of the Only Being. The future generations come along behind us. In this sense, the journey of which the Sufis speak is a journey back to our original image in the heart of Allah, before we were called into existence, along with all the other "beautiful names" of the One. Ibn Arabi comments on this:

> *The universe is composed of gatherings of signs. Every being is a sign or symbol that points to the divine reality upon which it is based, and which forms its foundation in the primordial beginning. It is to this beginning that each returns when it leaves this existence.*

Likewise, Abil Khayr related this larger cosmic movement of souls to the affinity felt by those who travel together in this lifetime.

Allah created souls thousands of years before their bodies. The One kept them near and nourished them with divine light. Those who live in this world in friendship and agreement must have known each other in the heart of God. Here they live in agreement and love each other. They find comfort in each other's company, even if they are separated by distance or by time.

The Qur'an says that there was also a "primordial religion," upon which all subsequent religions were based. Not the cultural form of Islam, Christianity, Judaism, or any religion that today has a name, but the essence of simple surrender to the one Reality behind creation:

So turn your face and purpose towards the primordial religion of the upright, the hanif—*the nature innately formed by the One Reality in which the One created humanity. Let there be no change in this work created by One. This religion is self-subsisting, the standard, always resurrecting itself* (qayyim). *But most among humanity do not understand. Turn to and remain conscious only of the One, remaining constant in prayer. Don't deify anything else in your life, not concepts or beliefs. Don't divide yourselves into sects that congratulate themselves on their own ideas.*

—Sura 30, 30–32[36]

Perhaps life is calling you to prepare the way for the future, to scout ahead, or to remember and connect with those who have done so—the ancestors. Sometimes what we set in motion does not bear fruit during our lifetime, but leaves a legacy for those who come after us.

❧ Roots and Branches ❧

Traditional translations of this quality include "advancer" and "forewarner." The roots of *Muqaddim* are related to the other names of power beginning with *Qa-*: Qahhar (15), Qawi (53), Qayyum (63), Qadir (69), and *Muqtadir* (70). In this case, the ending -*M* indicates that the divine power expresses itself in different ways that have led to a diversity of beings. The *MU-* prefix shows that remembrance of the ancient is already deeply embedded in every being. It is the natural religion of humanity.

Meditation

Center again in the heart. Breathe with the feeling of the sound *Ya Mu-Qaa-dim*. Feel the past ahead of you, with your caravan of ancestors before you. Gently sway forward and back, breathing out as you lean forward, in as you lean back, and feel the ever-moving caravan of life. After some moments, gradually come back into stillness, and feel the movement continue in the sensation of your heartbeat and breathing. Everything continues to move and change in the divine Heart.

72. Doubling Back on the Path

المُؤَخِّرُ

Al-Mu'akhkhir

When you are guided to this pathway,
take the opportunity to see the divine in situations in which you have to
repeat yourself or double back on your path.

YOU MAY BE SURPRISED to learn that the pathways of the heart include having to repeat yourself. Yet how often do we find that repetition helps us learn something we didn't really understand the first time around or notice an essential detail that we missed?

As we explored in the previous pathway, *Muqaddim*, we are always in one sense repeating the journey to the One and, as we do so, completing our humanity by widening our hearts to include more and more of the unknown potential within us. While we travel, we enrich ourselves and existence through the love we are able to express. This is why the Sufis talk about the path of the mystic being "to the One, with the One, and in the One."

Sometimes we find ourselves repeating an emotional or mental habit that we thought we had released. Another gift of this pathway is the opportunity to observe that one part of our being only pretended to let go. It was all a bit of a show on our inner stage, like the charade that Mullah Nasruddin acts out in the following story:

One day, Mullah Nasruddin told his wife that he was going to take his favorite donkey to market to sell.

"But husband," said his wife. "That's the donkey you use every day. How will you ever get along without it?"

"Don't worry," said Mullah. "I'm going to price it so high that no one will buy it."

Sometimes we price our "hang-ups" so high that even when we claim to be letting go of them, we're holding on to them more tightly. This pathway presents us with a mirror in which we can clearly see this tendency. This can happen, for instance, in group therapy, where one person competes with another for the honor of who has the worst story. Mullah acts this one out for us as well:

One day Mullah Nasruddin brought a donkey to market that was very ill-tempered. It kicked everyone who looked at it and brayed constantly.

"Mullah, how do you expect to sell a donkey like that?" someone asked him.

"I don't want to sell it," said Mullah. "I just want everyone to realize what I have to put up with all the time!"

Perhaps life is calling you right now to repeat a step, or to re-feel something you thought you had finished. The first sura of the Qur'an, *Fateha,* says, "Show us the most direct way," but sometimes the One Being's "direct way" is really crooked, roundabout, or spiral. We may not know the reason for this repeated step immediately, and perhaps we will never know it. Yet we can still celebrate that even something that can cause us aggravation finds a home in the heart of the One. It can also relieve our compulsion to fix everything or to get it right the first time.

❦ *Roots and Branches* ❦

Traditional translations of this quality include "deferrer" and "fulfiller." The primary root, *KHR,* shows something turning back on itself, an action that serves to engrave or preserve something in memory. What we thought was the end doubles back on itself, like the doubled *Kh* sound in the word itself. *Mu'akhkhir* is also related to *Akhir* (74), which indicates real completion or the end result of some process.

Meditation

Center again in the heart. Breathe with the sound *Ya Moo-aKh-KheeR.* Feel the dense *Kh* sounds of this word creating the feeling of delay or doubling back. Find a way to integrate this with your breath.

With eyes either open or closed, feel all of nature involved in a process that repeats itself, with small changes producing great consequences over a long period of time. Why not use this opportunity to notice any small changes in your own path or being?

73. *Sacred Surprise*

الأَوَّلُ

Al-Awwal

When you are guided to this pathway,
take the opportunity to open yourself to the unexpected,
the face of Allah as Sacred Surprise.

THE BELOVED SOMETIMES CONSCIOUSLY breaks into our lives with something completely different and unexpected. Whether we can benefit from it has much to do with our willingness to be or look foolish. Rumi has this to say about how surprising events can bring wisdom:

> *The Prophet said, "Fools will occupy most of paradise."*
> *Your cleverness is what creates dust storms of pride.*
> *Be willing to be fooled and you'll find real peace.*
> *If bewilderment can drive reason's babble from your head,*
> *then every hair has a chance to become wise.*

Similar to the previous pathway *Muqaddim* (71), *Awwal* also directs our attention ahead of us, but this time to the very front of our moving caravan of ancestors. What did, for instance, the very first moment of human consciousness feel like? What was there before the big bang? These kinds of questions lead us to dive deeply into ourselves to experience, for instance, the moment that each breath, feeling, or sensation arises in us. Balancing the feeling of *Mu'akhkhir* (72) that we just passed, perhaps nothing is ever really repeated.

Perhaps life is calling you to notice that surprise has entered your life. You thought you were going in one direction and toward a specific goal, but a mysterious doorway has appeared that seems to lead in a new direction. Suddenly, like Alice in Wonderland, you are in an entirely different universe. Or, perhaps through a sudden inspiration you feel called upon to initiate some process or to start a project totally unlike anything you have done before.

Roots and Branches

A traditional translation of this quality is "the first." The roots of *Awwal* show a direction of movement, symbolically from *A* toward *L*, beginning to end. Appearing in the middle of the word is *W*, which symbolizes the portal between being and nothingness, and which can be heard as a *U* sound (*oo*). In all the ancient Semitic languages this sound indicates the mysterious power of the divine to convey us from one realm or world to another, or from one type of life to another. Related to this word is the Arabic *ta'wil*, which means to interpret a sacred text mystically by conveying a meaning from its inner intention that can apply to a situation right now. The Qur'an uses this quality in connection with the next pathway, *Akhir*, to indicate that Sacred Unity includes both the beginning and end of all imaginable processes.

Meditation

Center again in the heart. Call a circle of your inner self and allow the sound *Ya AW-Wal* to bring spaciousness and possibility to any situation that seems to be at a dead end, or where you feel painted into a corner by circumstances. Leave space for surprise.

At the time of the new moon, breathe the sound in your heart and consider any project or relationship that you are about to begin. The unexpected can bring freedom.

74. Completion

Al-Akhir

When you are guided to this pathway,
take the opportunity to feel complete for now
with a state or stage of your life.

THE SUFIS SOMETIMES COMPARE life to singing a musical note. Both the beginning and the end are very important. An audience can feel the intention and emotion we have at the instant we begin to sing. Likewise, the way we release each note can either set if off clearly or slur one note into the next. Depending upon the acoustics of the room and how long the note is held, each sound eventually returns to the silence from which it began. One of the lessons of life, according to the Sufis, is how to consciously pursue something from its beginning, through its middle, and to its end.

For most of our life's projects and accomplishments, completion means letting go, which can be the hardest part of the process. How do we know when it's time to let go, when something is really complete? By way of a story, Shabistari tells us that we can rediscover our own sense of right timing by connecting the feeling of our breathing with nature around us, and ultimately with the sacred breath:

In a particular sea, I have heard,
pearl shells rise from the depths in April,
opening their mouths to the sky.
Mist also rises, then falls as rain.
A few drops fall into each open mouth.
The shells close and fall again,
their hearts full with a pearl-to-be.
Much later, the diver descends
and brings up a gem of great price.

Eons ago, the divine breath dived into us,
and now it dives again and again,
a thousand pearls wrapped in its blanket.

The completion of each stage of the pearl's development was necessary at a particular time to prepare the way for something else. As Shabistari says, a thousand potential pearls lie wrapped within us. To grasp another, we may need to let go of the one already in our hand.

The Sufis also use the word *akhir* to indicate the "end of time," when everything returns to the heart of the One. Dhu'l Nun recounts a story in which he meets a woman mystic walking on a beach, very possibly Fatima of Nishapur, who was one of his spiritual guides:

"What is the end of love?" I asked her.
"Don't be simple," she replied, "Love has no end."
"Why not?" I asked.
"Because there is never an end to the Beloved."

Perhaps you are completing a project, relationship, or phase of your life. You may be willing or unwilling to let go. It may be that what you think is perfectionism is really an unwillingness to complete and release something. Breathe with the feeling of this pathway to illuminate the situation, as well as your next steps, with the light of the One.

～ Roots and Branches ～

A traditional translation of this quality is "the last." The roots of *Akhir* show the most compact form (*AKH-*) giving way—almost leaping—(*-IR*) to a new expression of the divine life, radiating outward. Unlike its sister pathway *Mu'akhkhir* (72), this one shows us that it really is time to let go. The One Being is there at the moment of ripeness, when the fruit is eaten. Imagine the whole universe as fruit. When it is eaten, Allah is still there, so you can't lose by letting go.

Meditation

Center again in the heart. This is a good meditation for the time of the full moon. Breathing with the feeling of the word, bring each of the various areas of your life into the heart and allow the sound *AaKh-eeR* to illuminate them. Feel the compactness of the sound, the way it requires more breath to allow you to release the life in it from being trapped in form. Which projects, relationships, or patterns in your life feel complete for now?

75. *The Star*

الظَّاهِرُ

Az-Zahir

When you are guided to this pathway,
take the opportunity to focus on the face of the One Being in you that is
conspicuous, clear, and radiating.

AFTER A STAR REACHES its full brilliance, it gradually collapses backward into itself, becoming an ultradense black hole. This pathway introduces us to the full radiance of the star. Sometimes we need to do something very clearly and conspicuously in our lives, so that it makes an impression on others. Jesus told his disciples that sometimes they needed to teach obviously and openly, like a dove that flies straight toward its goal. Other times, they needed to teach in a hidden and roundabout way, like a snake that slithers this way and that until it gets to where it's going.

This pathway tells us that working outwardly in life can be just as important as doing inner work. To the theologians of his time who felt that living in the world was not sacred, Ibn Arabi said:

> There is no existence but the one existence. The Prophet Muhammad pointed to this when he said, "Don't abuse the world, for Allah is the world." By this he meant that this world's existence is due solely to Allah, as when the Prophet reported that God said to Moses, "I was sick and you didn't visit me. I asked for help and you didn't give it to me." The beggar's existence, the sick person's existence—both are the existence of the One. When the secret of one atom is clear, the secret of all becomes clear. This is what the Qur'an means when it says, "Everything is passing away except for Allah's face," and "Wherever you turn there is the face of the One."

Similarly, a sacred tradition through Muhammad has the One Being say:

I will appear to my servants at the End of Time in the way in which each expects me to appear. Yet I am with my servants invisibly, even now, whenever they call on me.[37]

Perhaps life is calling you right now to take the role of the star—to be clear, radiating, and out-front. Remember that clear, positive action can cause others to become attached to you personally as the "doer." Use this pathway to meet and purify this starstruck energy with the greater manifested light and life of the One.

⟶ Roots and Branches ⟶

Traditional translations of this quality include "the manifest" and "the evident." From its roots, *Zahir* shows the radiant life of the One (*-HiR*) manifesting in a form that communicates clearly, in a very apparent way (*ZA*). *Zahir* is also related to the previous name, *Akhir*, which shows a movement in the opposite direction. As in breathing, when we fully exhale, expressing ourselves, the divine balance draws us back inside, toward the essence.

Meditation

Center again in the heart. Consider any areas of your life in which you are called to act publicly in service to your purpose in life. Breathe with the feeling of this pathway and feel the breath softening any rigid areas of your body. Flexibility allows for the greatest radiance. Remember that you don't have to do it all. When *Zahir* enters your path, just show up with what you have already cultivated and, like the old Hebrew prophets, tell the One Being, "Here I am!" Then let the divine radiance shine through you.

76. The Hidden Traveler

Al-Batin

When you are guided to this pathway,
take the opportunity to focus on the face of the sacred in you that is hidden
from others, the One who "travels without feet."

IN THE TAROT, THE high priestess archetype can express the aspect of the self that is veiled and acts as "the keeper of the mysteries." This pathway guides us into this hidden realm at the sacred heart of our being. On a practical level, Imam Ali expressed the wisdom of keeping silent when one wishes to accomplish something:

> *Success is the result of foresight and resolution, foresight depends upon*
> *deep thinking and planning, and the most important factor of planning*
> *is keeping your secrets to yourself.*

Just as the previous pathway, *Zahir*, expressed the clear, apparent face of the divine in our lives, this one points us in the other direction, toward what remains hidden yet is very active. Rumi says:

> *O Hidden One, you fill East to West,*
> *behind both moon's reflection and sun's radiance.*
> *You are the water and we are the mill stone.*
> *You are the wind and we are the dust.*
> *You are the spring and we are the garden.*
> *You are the breath, we are the hands and feet.*
> *You are the joy and we are the laughter.*

Perhaps life is calling you right now to withdraw from outer action on a project or relationship and to work behind the scenes. Steps taken in the inner world can have large effects. Or, perhaps you are being called upon to preserve some living wisdom or transmission until the time is ripe for it to be given openly again. Bide your time and reset it to the time of the One Being.

～ Roots and Branches ～

Traditional translations of this quality include "the hidden" and "the immanent." The roots of *Batin* show a movement, coming and going (*BA-*) that is protected as if by a woven screen or basket (*-TiN*). *Batin* is related to *Ba'ith* (49), which shows this movement returning after it appeared to be gone. *Batin* is also related through its ending to *Matin* (54), which shows the screen or resistance persisting over a period of time, conveying the image of firmness. All of the last four pathways appear in one verse of the Qur'an (57:3): "Allah is the first and last, the evident and the hidden, and Allah understands and embraces all the things of manifested existence." These qualities are sometimes called the "mothers of the names" to show their role in the creation of all the others. Sometimes *Batin* is also paired with *Zahir,* the previous pathway, thereby providing a balance between hidden movement and manifested light.

Meditation

Center again in the heart. Begin by breathing the sound *Ya Baa-TiN* inside, feeling the darkness inside the body gradually becoming illuminated. Or, place your hands lightly over your eyes as you breathe the sound, bringing the call deeper and deeper. Allow the sound to call to the inner self, to whichever part represents the most hidden or veiled voice in you.

77. Mastering Life

الوَالِي

Al-Wa'li

*When you are guided to this pathway,
take the opportunity to feel the part of you that can bring harmony and a
sense of accomplishment to your life through loving self-discipline and a
sense of inner mastery.*

THE EXERCISE OF ANY kind of "mastery" has largely fallen out of favor in Western society, except in the areas of professional sports and some types of musical performance. For all the rest, we like to think that one person is pretty much the same as another, even if this is not true. This is the misdirected application of a good principle, democracy, which was intended to maintain that people are equal with regard to their right to govern themselves. It did not originally carry the idea that everyone's abilities are the same, since in most cases they obviously are not.

Jesus tells the story in the Gospels of the servants who are each given a "talent" by their master before he goes away. Two of them develop their talents, and one buries it in the earth for safekeeping. The two who develop their talents are praised, while the one who hordes it is cursed. Likewise, the Sufi makes efforts in the path of attainment, realizing that the inner qualities of self-discipline and mastery that she develops in the process, which can be of service to the Beloved, are greater than any outer product. The twentieth-century Sufi Samuel Lewis described the path like this:

Those who have not gone on the path of attainment cannot surrender to God, for what will they surrender? They cannot surrender that which does not belong to them. So they should try to own something, whether it be things or faculties or powers or anything that can have a name or form, and then bring these in loving self-sacrifice before God, and then not stop but go on and on, always active, whether inwardly or outwardly. By this they show their love for God, a love which means nothing if it be but a word, a love which means everything if it is a way of life in this world or in the world to come.[38]

Of course the attractions of acquisition can always seduce us. Yet the pathway of *Wa'li* can also call us back to harmony when the voice of the ego starts to drown out the voice of guidance. This call to self-awareness and self-discipline can sometimes be blunt, or downright rude, as in the story Attar tells about a Sufi teacher:

Sheikh Abu Bakr was out for a day trip with his disciples. He was riding on a donkey, and they were walking. All of a sudden, the donkey came out with a massive fart. Abu Bakr broke down crying.

"O Master," said one of his disciples. "What's the trouble? Can we help?"

"I was just riding along," said Abu Bakr, "thinking about how good life is. I have my own group of disciples, my own center and community. I was thinking that I must be getting equal to the great Sufis, like Abu Yazid Bistami. It was at that moment, when I was in my glory, that the donkey responded with the noise you heard, as if to say, 'Here's what I think of that!' At that point, my fantasies burned to ashes and I felt sorry for my moment of egotism."

Perhaps life is calling you to bring your life back into a new order that more fully expresses your true being. In work with the inner self, this pathway can help provide a loving form of self-discipline. Perhaps you know that you are living a lie, but one voice within you holds on fearfully to old, self-defeating patterns of behavior. Use *Wa'li* to help this voice realize that there is a strong, disciplined way to bring the whole being back into harmony. This is another way to befriend yourself.

⟶ *Roots and Branches* ⟵

Traditional translations of this quality include "governor" and "guardian." The roots of *Wa'li* show the continually renewing and transforming action of the One, spreading and extending itself (*WAL-*), directing the creation of more life energy (*I*). By emphasizing the first syllable and root, this *Wa'li* distinguishes itself from its sister name *Wa`li* (55), whose action shows a continual movement of friendship rather than of command or mastery.

Meditation

Center again in the heart. Breathe out the sound WAL, and breathe in the sound -I (a short i). Feel the unlimited ability of the One through your highest guidance to regulate and coordinate your life under all circumstances. Spread your hands and arms outward from the heart as you breathe out, feeling your breath directing your life's activities. As you inhale, bring your hands back to your heart and touch the place of love that motivates both self-discipline and mastery in you.

BATHING IN UNITY

Among their many delights, the Mullah Nasruddin stories serve to demonstrate to us that life will not yield its secrets to logical reasoning and understanding. In fact, following logic as a principle can lead to crazy consequences:

> Once upon a time, Mullah was living in a town in which dishonesty and trickery were rife. Everyone was swindling or hustling everyone else. The king decided to put an end to it and declared that anyone entering the city and telling a lie would be promptly hanged.
>
> Mullah was one of the king's counselors and advised against the law, arguing that one could not turn a principle into a law so easily. It would be better to hire more judges to settle disputes between people. The king was not convinced.
>
> "I'll prove it," said Mullah. "Tomorrow morning, I'll enter the city gates. Meet me there and have your guard ask me where I'm going." The king agreed.
>
> The next morning, a guard stopped Mullah at the city gates.
>
> "Halt! Where are you going?"
>
> "I'm going to be hanged," replied Mullah.
>
> "That's a lie," said the guard, "which is against the law."
>
> "Which means you'll have to hang me," said Mullah, "and so it's the truth!"
>
> The king agreed to rescind the law and hire more judges.

Meditation

Center again in the heart. Breathe the sound *Al-lah* in and out, feeling the pores of your skin open to the atmosphere around you. Then notice the sensations of your body inside: breathing, heartbeat, and pulsation. Feel your whole self as a knowing being, not limited to your thoughts or emotional feelings.

78. *Inhabiting an Expanded Consciousness*

Al-Muta`ali

When you are guided to this pathway,
take the opportunity to embody an expanded state of consciousness in order
to serve others. This part of your being is learning by the grace of the One
how to, in a small way, bring heaven to earth.

ALTHOUGH BY DEFINITION THE classical Sufis understood an expanded state of consciousness, or *hal,* to be something that passed away, they also felt that travelers on the path could master a particular *hal* and easily access it. Some people can experience this on an extended retreat, or by repeatedly guiding others into a particular meditative state. Under such circumstances, the One Being teaches us how to expand our awareness and be of service whenever the need arises.

This pathway not only benefits one's own spiritual life; it can also provide a hidden blessing to others. According to Samuel Lewis, the whole purpose of the spiritual path is to enable a person to generate a kind of magnetic heart-blessing (called *baraka* in Sufi terms) wherever they go:

> *The great work of the initiates henceforth will be to spread* baraka. *By so doing they will purify the general atmosphere, and by that the Message of God which belongs to the sphere itself will gradually touch the hearts and minds of all who pass through it, who breathe the air or go to the places where the seeds of* baraka *have been sown. Thus is the selfless propagation of the Message.*[39]

Behind most of the religious rituals of humanity we find the original impulse to bring more blessing and compassion into everyday life, even where the purpose has been lost or misplaced due to a later emphasis on religious dogma. The twentieth-century Sufi Bawa Muhaiyaddeen expressed one experience of inhabiting an expanded state of Unity in this way:

> *My brothers and sisters, if you can know your own life and understand it, you will find the ocean of divine knowledge within you. You will find the Qur'an in you. You are the Qur'an; you are your own book. If you can study that book and reach the state of fully ripened knowledge, then you will be able to speak of its sweetness and know peace and comfort in your life. To establish and understand this state is* Iman-Islam, *the state of the spotlessly pure heart which contains Allah's Holy Qur'an, divine guidance, divine wisdom, truth, prophets, angels and laws.*[40]

Perhaps life is calling you to master a particular expanded state of consciousness, or offering you a glimpse of how it could be helpful to others right now. The best attitude with which to practice this pathway is through celebration and complete relaxation and surrender in the One.

∾ Roots and Branches ∾

Traditional translations of this quality include "the exalted" and "the one far above anything that is or could ever be." The roots of *Muta`ali* are related to those of `Ali (36) and indicate the embodiment of "peak experiencing." If `Ali indicates an expanded state of awareness, which the Sufis call a *hal*, *Muta`ali* represents what they have called the "perfection" of a particular state. This is not *maqam*, the station of living everyday life, but rather the ability to go into and out of a particular expanded state when necessary. From another point of view, this name shows that, like the relationship between *Hayy* (62) and *Muhyi* (60), the activity of the divine peak experience is already in every particle of existence, and nothing could exist without it. The Qur'an uses the word only once (*Sura* 13:9), to indicate once again that the One Being is not limited by any list of attributes or by any concepts of them.

Meditation

Center again in the heart. Breathe with the feeling of this pathway, *Ya Mu-Ta-Aal-ee*, and allow it to take you inside, reconnecting you to the source of all expanded states, the divine Beloved. If one or more of your inner selves have become frightened by or are reacting against an expanded state you have experienced, this name can also help to reassure them. Can you reach an agreement that it's part of your purpose in life to visit this state frequently, in order to provide a blessing to others?

79. *Burnishing*

Al-Barr

When you are guided to this pathway,
take the opportunity to feel the blessing of the One that burnishes and
purifies your heart, which allows you to sort the real from the unreal.

THE NEXT FIVE PATHWAYS introduce us to various ways to purify and heal the heart. This one presents the image of burnishing the heart with breath in order to separate what we need from what we can release. The Sufis often speak of the heart as a mirror. We polish the mirror (or it is polished, through us, by the Beloved) in order to see our real face, the face of eternity. This also makes the heart able to accept and embrace the many paradoxes, misunderstandings, and hardships of life, as well as to enjoy more fully its beautiful variety. As the late-twentieth-century Sufi Moineddin Jablonski said:

Wholeness in variety is Heart; wholeness in unity is Soul.[41]

Through the many pathways of the heart, we gradually discover nooks and crannies of our self that we didn't know existed. At times, the heart needs to release what it holds, even (or especially) what we think we know of ourselves. Rumi tells the following story about this sorting process:

An old man came into a goldsmith's shop and said, "I have some gold here that I'd like to weigh; could I borrow your scales?"
"Sorry," replied the goldsmith, "but I don't have a broom."
"It is your scales I want, not a broom," said the old man.
"I don't have a sieve, either," replied the goldsmith.
"Are you deaf? It's the scales I need."

"No, I'm not deaf, and I have eyes. And I see that your hands are shaking and that your gold is in the form of very fine dust. When you end up dropping it, you'll need to sweep it up. And once you've swept it, you'll need a sieve to separate the gold from the dust of the floor. And I don't have a broom or a sieve."

Often we need to release the impressions we are holding of others, or that we think they are holding of us. When we begin to react to the projections others hold of us, and those we hold of others, and the projections of the projections, we enter what Inayat Khan called "the palace of mirrors." His student Samuel Lewis noted that we cannot entirely escape this effect, but we can learn how to work with it:

> *It is true that a person's mind was meant to be a palace of mirrors, and also it is not necessary to build up ego thoughts. There is a right attitude of response. First one should feel to whom and what to respond. This requires intuition. The intuitive faculty is built up by slow, gentle, rhythmical breathing. There is no insight when the breath operates rapidly, except, perhaps, some instinctive movement. For no one can entirely destroy his instincts, without suffering terribly, mentally and physically.* [42]

Perhaps life is challenging you to breathe more slowly, and to direct your breath to your heart. Is something telling you that you need to sort through the experiences you are undergoing and weigh them in your heart? Or, perhaps now is the time to finally release some impressions you are holding from the past. Use your breath like very fine sandpaper, or like a polishing cloth, in order to allow your heart to reflect more clearly what is really happening right now.

❧ Roots and Branches ☙

Traditional translations of this quality include "benign" and "beneficent." The roots of *Barr* are similar to those of *Bari* (12), the radiation of creativity, and show the active power of the One Being radiating waves of power and heat. With its emphasis on the double *R* sound, *Barr* carries a purifying, burning quality that prepares one to express the divine blessing. The Qur'an uses this word in combination with *Rahim* (2), the moon of love, in songs attributed to the souls in heaven, who recognize the mercy and burnishing blessing that their lives have been (*Sura* 52:28).

Meditation

Center again in the heart. Breathe or whisper the sound *Ya Barr* into the heart. Emphasize internally the final R sound (almost like a rolled Scottish r). Gradually increase the tempo as you feel the sound anneal and burnish your heart. At the end, simply breathe and feel your heart as a purified mirror. Receive from the Source and reflect to your inner self whatever strength, inspiration, or wisdom you need for this moment.

80. *Returning to Rhythm*

التَّوَّابُ

At-Tawwab

When you are guided to this pathway,
take the opportunity to stop what you are doing, soften within,
and allow your heart to return to the right rhythm in time with
the heart of the Beloved.

SOMETIMES THE BEST THING we can do is stop and let go. When we do this our breath naturally returns to a more normal rhythm, and we can clearly assess the situation in front of us. When life pierces our heart, sometimes we need to let the holes remain rather than fill them immediately, as Moineddin Jablonski says in this poem to the Beloved:

> *Note by clay note*
> *pipe me down.*
> *Play the holes in my heart*
> *that swallow love*
> *and slowly heal.*[43]

The realization of the twelfth-century Persian Sufi Abu Hamid Al-Ghazali also helps put things in perspective:

> *A person who owns some snow wouldn't*
> *hesitate to trade it for jewels and pearls.*
> *So life's circumstances are like snow.*
> *When the sun comes out, it all melts,*
> *while the next world, the world of your heart,*
> *is like a precious stone that remains.*

Perhaps life is telling you that it's the right time to stop and turn in another direction, back to the path that takes you to the Beloved.

Or, perhaps you find yourself up against a habit of mind, one of the voices of your inner self that feels like a hard edge in your psyche. This pathway brings softening and letting go. It already resides within you, as a reflection of divine Unity. The One Being waits with open arms like the father of the prodigal son in the story Jesus tells in the Gospels. Open your own arms, and feel the Beloved welcoming you back to your Self.

⁓ *Roots and Branches* ⁓

Traditional translations of this quality include "acceptor of repentance" and "oft-returning." The roots of *Tawwab* show a protected cover (*T*) over something turning within, ripening, and transforming itself (*WB*). This name is related to the Hebrew and Aramaic words usually translated as "repentance" (*tauba, t'yabuta*), as well as to the words for ripeness and blessing (*tob, tub*). In all of these, "goodness" is defined as returning to the right rhythm, timing, and attunement with the Holy One.

Meditation

Center again in the heart. Breathe rhythmically with the sound *Ya Ta-WaaB* in the heart. At the end of each inhalation and exhalation, feel the *B* sound as a release and letting-go into Unity. Then, through the lens of your heart, view the outer situations in your life. Is there a way in which you can bring yourself back into rhythm within and find your way back to what brings you joy and freedom?

81. *Sweeping Out*

الْمُنْتَقِمُ

Al-Muntaqim

When you are guided to this pathway,
take the opportunity to consciously sweep from your heart anything
that feels superficial or affected, anything you have taken on in
order to please others.

SOMETIMES BURNISHING AND FINDING your way back to your own rhythm may not be enough to purify and heal the heart. The two previous pathways lead to this one, a purification envisioned as a forceful sweeping and cleansing action. Shabistari describes the process in this way:

> *The travelers on the path to God know*
> *where they've come from, where they're going, and*
> *they just go—purified from self like flame from smoke.*
> *Why don't you sweep out the rooms of your heart,*
> *and prepare them to be the home of the Beloved?*
> *When you leave, the One can enter.*
> *Freed from self, the Beloved reveals its beauty.*
> *Purified from all impressions,*
> *your real Self outgrows differences—*
> *knower and known become one.*

It's always easier to clean someone else's room—or tell them how to clean it—than to deal with our own. Jesus talks about taking the log out of our own eye before we try to remove the splinter from someone else's. Likewise, this pathway does not give us license to impose on someone else our ideas about what "purity" is. As Bawa Muhaiyaddeen says:

*[I]n every way, we have to look at our own faults and understand the faults of others. Then we must correct our faults and give peace to the others. If we are true believers (*mumim*), we will not see any differences between others and ourselves. We will see only One. We will see Allah, one human race, and one justice for all. That justice and truth is the strength of Islam. That compassion and peace is the strength of Islam . . . It is the completeness and resplendence that gives peace to all lives. It is love, grace, unity and compassion. It is to live as one race and one family. That is Islam.*[44]

Perhaps life is telling us we need to clean house in our hearts. By covering our real natures with affectation or superficial concerns, we may have lost sight of the reflection and image of the divine in us. If this strikes a chord with you, look outwardly—at the situations, conditions, and relationships in your life. Also look inwardly, where some voices of your inner circle may have allowed the impressions of others, which are not yours to deal with, to breach the psychic doorways and take root inside.

➴ Roots and Branches ➴

Traditional translations of this quality include "taker of retribution" and "avenger." The roots of *Muntaqim* derive from NA- (newness, in the sense of what is superficial) and QM (making something clean, sweeping away what has been added that is not natural or related to one's purpose in life). Like other names that use the QA- root (here as part of QM), including *Qahhar* (15) and *Qadir* (69), this name shows that the force needed to do the sweeping and cleaning is strong and irresistible. The equivalent Hebrew word *naqam,* used in Deuteronomy 32 (usually translated *"vengeance* is mine says the Lord . . ."), also comes from the same roots. In both Hebrew and Arabic, all the principal verbs mean "to clean or purify." I have not found an etymological source that can justify the translation of "vengeance" based on anything other than ancient cultural conventions that included blood vengeance—which we can now, in the One's mercy, release.

Meditation

Center again in the heart. Breathe with compassion into your inner being, and look through the eyes of the heart at the situations of your life. What can be straightened, swept, or cleansed? What inner furniture is out of place when you consider the purpose of your life? Take up this pathway with love and respect for all parts of your soul. How can you prepare the chamber of the heart for the divine Beloved?

82. Blowing Away the Ashes

العَفُوُّ

Al-'Afuw

When you are guided to this pathway,
take the opportunity to blow away anything you don't need that is sitting
on the surface of your heart, like blowing away the ashes left after a fire.

ANY IMPRESSION WE RECEIVE from another person or from another part of ourselves, whether positive or negative, can prove a hindrance to fulfilling our purpose in life. When someone blames us, it can set us back by diminshing our courage or causing us to waste time justifying ourselves. Praise can also divert us by causing us to think more about ourselves than is appropriate at the moment. This does not mean we need to guard against every impression; then we might begin to close our hearts toward others, a greater mistake than occasionally opening our hearts too far. Sometimes, however, we need to burn and forcefully blow away an impression, because it has taken deep root and needs strong medicine.

Strong medicine can create a strong reaction. Rumi tells his students a story about a man who came to Muhammad, complaining about the results of the spiritual path:

A man came to Muhammad and said: "Please take back this religion. I haven't had a single day's peace since I began to surrender to Allah. Wealth, wife, children, respect, strength, lust—everything's vanished!"

The Prophet replied, "Wherever our religion goes, it does not return without pulling up people by their roots and sweeping clean their houses. You don't have peace because sorrow is helping you clean what's superficial from your system."

Be patient.
Grieve if you have to
because grieving cleans you out

like a good fast.
After the cleansing, joy returns,
a joy without sorrow,
a rose without thorns.

Attar tells the story of the phoenix, which, after having lived a full life, prepares its own funeral pyre and then rises from the ashes as a new, young bird. We can likewise envision the process this path describes.

Perhaps life is calling you right now to burn and blow away any impressions lodged in your heart that prevent you from seeing your way clearly. Remember that everything is part of Allah's universe. You can't pollute the One's air by burning away a false impression because every impression may have its place in Unity. But this particular impression's time of residence with you is over.

—◦ *Roots and Branches* ◦—

Traditional translations of this quality include "forgiver" and "pardoner." The primary root of `Afuw, `AF (with the guttural *a* sound intoned backward into the body) shows something that has passed through the fire. What remains whole becomes purified and annealed. What has been burned off blows away on the wind. If the previous name, *Muntaqim,* was "taking out the trash," `Afuw is burning it. In this case, we allow ourselves to stand in the fire and let the heat of the One burn away anything that is not of our true nature.

Meditation

Center again in the heart. Inhale the compact sound of `A- into the belly, and then, as you exhale, breathe the sound -*foo* into the furnace of the heart, and breathe away the "ashes." The name can be directed toward a situation in need of releasing or forgiveness, or toward and with a part of the inner self.

83. *Healing Wings*

الرَّءُوفُ

Ar-Ra'uf

When you are guided to this pathway,
take the opportunity to experience and express the compassionate,
regenerative power of the One reconnecting your heart to Unity.

THE GOSPELS RELATE THAT after Jesus was tempted in the wilderness, angels came to heal and minister to him. Many stories of angels fill both the Bible and the Qu'ran. They relate ancient Semitic ideas of healing, which deal with bringing us back into balance with ourselves, with the rest of the cosmos, and with the divine.

When we breathe as if we were the only being in the universe, we can feel cut off from the Sacred Breath (sometimes called the Holy Spirit). When we feel that our breathing is connected with those around us and with nature, when we realize that we all breathe the same air, we're reminded that we do not simply exist for ourselves, nor do we have to do everything ourselves. Often, illness or a traumatic event can throw our breathing and heart out of rhythm, and can remind us that we need help. Healing this separation is expressed by the Semitic root *Rph,* from which derive the angelic names *Raphael* and *Se-raph-im*. Being willing to receive this healing takes some courage and abandon, as Shabistari says:

> *If you want to be free of self,*
> *haunt the tavern of love.*
> *In this sanctuary, egotism is heresy.*
> *Only lovers who have no fear can enter.*
> *Only here the bird of your breath can*
> *nest and rest in the*
> *palm of the Beloved's hand.*

Perhaps life is calling you to receive deeply this quality of healing, or to express it for another. If we feel that Allah does the healing through us, Allah is also the healed. This pathway allows us to feel the wings of healing that can take us back to the source of compassion and consolation.

～ *Roots and Branches* ～

Traditional translations of this quality include "compassionate" and "full of kindness." The principal roots of *Ra'uf* show a radiation (*R*) of recovery, regeneration, redemption, medicine, and health (*UPH*). The Qur'an uses the word frequently, often in combination with *Rahim* (2), the action of receiving deep compassion.

Meditation

Center again in the heart. Breathe the name *Ya Ra'-ooF* with and in the heart, with a definite, strong rhythm. Feel your whole inner self being sheltered by the wings of healing, and being carried back to the heart of the Beloved.

Then, or later, call a circle of your inner self. With your highest guidance directing the process, allow each of your inner selves to bathe in this quality. Then invite them all to join in as the inner sound regenerates each cell of the physical body, as well as the whole emotional body. As the psalmist says, "Let every voice that has breath praise the One."

84. *Passionate Vision*

مَالِكُ الْمُلْكِ

Malik-ul-Mulk

When you are guided to this pathway,
take the opportunity to open your heart to a passionate vision that would
compel you to live your life in service to Unity.

*F*OLLOWING THE FIVE PATHWAYS that led us through various purifications of the heart, the next two offer us a glimpse of the incredible passion, vision, power, and beauty that can fill our lives. In this one, vision and guidance arrive with such force that they grab us and won't let go. Rumi talks about this in the following story:

> *There once was a dervish who was so poor that in the middle of winter he wore only a thin cotton robe. As he was passing by a mountain river that was still in full flow, he saw a bundle of fur being carried downstream. Some nearby children called to him, "Look, man, there's a fur coat for you. You're cold—go for it!"*
>
> *The dervish was very cold, so he jumped in to try to catch the fur coat. Unknown to him, the coat was really a bear whose head was hidden beneath the water. When the dervish grabbed the bear, it grabbed the dervish.*
>
> *Seeing this, the children called out: "Hey, it must be cold in there! Either get the coat or let it go and come on out!"*
>
> *"I am letting go," said the dervish, "but the coat isn't letting go of me. Now what?"*
>
> *So why should the One's passion let you go?*
> *Give thanks that you're not in your own hands!*
> *An infant doesn't know anything but milk and mum,*
> *but God doesn't leave us like that.*

On we go to bread, play, logic, and finally
another world, another breast. As the Prophet said,
"It's incredible that Allah has to drag some of us
to heaven in chains," where, my friends,
we roast in union,
roast in beauty,
and roast in perfection.

Expressing a similar urgency and inner prompting, Rabia said:

O Sustainer,
if fear of hell prompts my devotion, let hell burn me.
If hope of paradise moves it, let heaven spurn me.
But if I worship you only to feel your nearness,
don't hide your beauty from me.

Perhaps life is calling you to reach deeply inside and gather all the power and vision you have received in your life in order to go forward. Or, perhaps it is asking you to open your heart, to live with much greater passion in order to be of service to others. Whether in affirming this quality as part of our inner reality or in facing a particular outward situation, we do not really choose this pathway; it chooses us. To breathe and feel its force with a full heart affirms that all our work, loving, and knowing are really just this pathway expressing itself through us. To actually experience it, at any level of the self, is grace.

~ Roots and Branches ~

Traditional translations of this quality include "possessor of sovereignty" and "lord of power and rule." Derived from the earlier pathway *Malik* (3), this pathway shows us not only the ruling vision and empowerment behind the cosmos, but also the next "power" of it, the "I Can" squared, so to speak. We could call this literally the visioning within all visions, the essence of passion within all passion. This name also reminds us that Reality is not a definition, it is what is doing the defining. It is the *maliki yaumiddin,* mentioned in *Sura Fateha:* the voice that continually affirms creation and power.

Meditation

Center again in the heart. While the tendency is to breathe "strong" (or *jelal*) names strongly, and gentle (*jamal*) names gently, this tendency can hook us into our concepts as well. If we wish any spiritual practice to have an effect in our being, we must dive into it with as full a heart as we can muster in the moment, however much or little this may be. Breathing or saying a sacred phrase is not performing for our parents or teachers, it is speaking to our lover. Breathe the words *Malik-ul-Mulk* and allow this pathway to lead you to the right way to begin, whether strong or gentle, slow or fast. Don't presume to know, simply ask to be led.

85. *Overwhelming Power and Beauty*

ذُوا الْجَلَالِ وَ الإكْرَام

Dhul-Jalal-wal-Ikram

When you are guided to this pathway,
take the opportunity to feel humbled by a wave of divine power
and abundance flowing over and through you.

T HE PREVIOUS PATHWAY INVITED us to new passion in our lives. This one opens the doorway to such an abundance of power and beauty that we can only be humbled to recognize that they are already ours. The eleventh-century Afghani Sufi Al-Hujwiri comments:

> *When the One manifests itself to its servants, it sometimes shows its power, and sometimes its beauty. The power fills us with awe, the beauty with feelings of intimacy. The awe disturbs us, the beauty brings joy. Power burns, beauty illuminates. Touched by the power, our inner self, the* nafs, *remembers its mortality. Touched by the beauty, our heart remembers its communion. Through the vision of divine power, the small self passes away. Through the revelation of divine beauty, our hearts are resurrected.*

Opening the doorway to this path invites us to make a greater commitment to live our lives in service to the Source of Love, in all of its various disguises. Rumi tells the following story of a servant, who was a Muslim, and his master, who was not, living in the time of Muhammad:

> *One day the master said to the servant, "I'd like to go to the baths. Fetch some bowls for washing, and let's go." On the way, they passed the mosque where Muhammad and his companions were praying, and the servant said, "Master, would you please allow me to make a few pros-trations? If you'd just hold these bowls. I won't be a moment."*

The master did so, a bit grudgingly, but he wasn't really a bad sort. After prayers were over, Muhammad left with his companions, and so did everyone else, except the servant. Being a patient person, the master waited until midday, and then called, "Let's go, servant—come out!"

The servant called back, "There's too much work. They won't let me go!"

Looking inside the mosque, the master saw only the shoes of the servant, and shadows. "Who's keeping you? I don't see anyone!"

"The same One who is keeping you out," said the servant. "The One you don't see."

So we are always in love with what
we don't see or hear or understand.
Night after night, day after day,
we search for it.
I'm tired of what I see and hear and understand,
I am the servant of the One whom I don't see.
If the One would reveal itself a million times
it still wouldn't be the same.
You, too, can see God this moment,
always multicolored, changing every instant.

Perhaps life is calling you to notice a great wave of power and beauty washing through or over your life right now. You can begin to release the limiting thoughts of yourself and others, and allow Allah to work through you. If you are called upon to bring this pathway into your inner or outer life, there is nothing to do but let go. Sometimes we need this pathway just to get the attention of our *nafs*. The voices saying "me!" can often become so loud that they can cause us to forget that there is something greater, the only "I Am."

⌒ Roots and Branches ⌒

Traditional translations of this quality include "possessor of majesty and benevolence" and "lord of majesty, bounty, and honor." The root of the first part of this name (*DL*) shows something that humbles and brings us to our knees. This is the extent of the manifest power of the One Being (*AL*) heaping itself up in nature and the cosmos (in the root *JAL*), plus the abundance of diversity of forms and life (*KRAM,* a different form of *Karim,* 42). The Qur'an uses this phrase in one of its best-known passages: "Everything in the universe passes away, but what remains is the face of the Sustainer, full of power and beautiful abundance"(55:26–27).

Meditation

Center again in the heart, and breathe the phrase *Dhul-Jalal-Wal-Ikram.* Look to the ocean, a thunderstorm, or the mountains, as our ancestors did, in order remind yourself of this quality. Or, gaze at one of the photographs from deep space of the stars and galaxies being formed. First gaze with eyes open for a minute, as though breathing in and seeing through the heart. Then close your eyes and hold the feeling that remains in the heart. Can you feel the power and abundance behind the creation that is going on in each instant?

86. New Roots, New Foundation

المُقْسِطُ

Al-Muqsit

When you are guided to this pathway,
take the opportunity to feel your feet, find your roots, and establish
a foundation that cannot be shaken.

AFTER THE PASSION AND power of the last two pathways, the next four invite us to focus on how we can embody a new life in everyday, practical ways. This one tells us that it's time to rebuild from the ground up.

According to tradition, two pillars supported the temple of Solomon in Jerusalem; their names were "justice" and "righteousness." Justice referred to the outer community: All debts were to be forgiven after seven years, all land was to revert to community ownership after forty-nine years (the "jubilee" year). According to Jewish mystics, "righteousness" in Hebrew referred to the same sort of justice applied to the inner community of the self (*nephesh* in Hebrew, *nafs* in Arabic). All voices were welcomed to the meal prepared by Holy Wisdom. In the words of David, "you spread a table before me, at which my enemies are present, you anoint my head with oil, my cup runs over."

This pathway invites us to establish this foundation of inner and outer justice in our own lives. Jesus tells the famous story about the man who built his house on sand, with predictable results. Likewise, we often need to ground our spiritual experiences in everyday life. Mullah Nasruddin elegantly demonstrates what can happen when we don't:

One day Mullah Nasruddin was riding his donkey and at the same time trying to eat a snack of very finely ground chickpea powder. Every time he raised his hand to his mouth, however, the wind blew the powder away.

"Hey, Mullah!" called a friend who saw him passing by. "What are you eating?"

"The wind!" Mullah called back to him.

You may face a situation in life in which you need to reestablish your roots at home, at work, or in your emotional life. Or, perhaps some major event has flooded your inner house. This pathway can help you establish a new, higher "basement" in your life, above flood level. In working with the inner self, this pathway can aid your highest guidance in establishing a new working relationship between the various inner selves, so that they are able to function in a more cooperative way. Uniting inner and outer means we can practice justice in a complete way, building a new temple for the divine breath to inhabit.

∽ Roots and Branches ∽

Traditional translations of this quality include "the just" and "upholder of equity." Indirectly related to *Muqit* (39), the roots of *Muqsit* show the living embodiment (*MU-*) in material form (*Q*) of a balanced, repeated movement that establishes a foundation (*-SIT*). The Qur'an uses this word in connection with *Aziz* (8), strength expressed through earth, as well as with *Hakim* (46), discriminating wisdom.

Meditation

Center again in the heart. Breathe with the feeling of this pathway, *Ya Mooq-Sit*, and allow the feeling of your breath to descend all the way from the heart to the pelvic floor. Then feel two pillars of breath supporting you, right and left, from bottom to top. Can this feeling prepare the space for a new foundation? Call a circle of your inner self and find there a new table prepared with love and respect for all the voices within you.

87. *Gathering Gems*

الجَامِعُ

Al-Jame'

When you are guided to this pathway,
take the opportunity to enjoy the process of gathering, whether of
people in your life or of the resources you need at this moment. See
the process as gathering parts of yourself that can help you better reflect
your purpose in life.

THIS PATHWAY INVITES US to a treasure hunt. On the outer level, it may be time to gather with other people, or to gather resources that we need. On the inner level, we are always gathering a wider circle of our inner selves. In both cases, we're invited to appreciate the gem-like qualities we discover in others or in ourself.

Like devotees of other traditions, Sufis sometimes use prayer beads to remember the various beautiful pathways of the heart. Since these "names" really symbolize the living activities of the One Being, the chain of beads also reminds us that all living beings in the universe are already connected, like precious stones in the necklace of the Beloved. In this sense, all gatherings are sacred. Al-Hujwiri says:

> *Devotees look for sacred space to pray,*
> *but the friends of Unity find sacred space anywhere.*
> *For them the whole world is God's meeting place.*
> *While still veiled, they find the world dark, but*
> *when the veils lift, they can see that*
> *the Beloved lives everywhere.*

Likewise, whenever we're challenged to engage more fully in life and to gather in a circle, outer or inner, we may be tempted to ask, "What's the use? Will anything really change?" A Sufi might answer, "The struggle itself reveals the light and life shining within you." As the twentieth-century Sufi Nur Hixon wrote:

The purpose of the Creation is radically spiritual. The temporal career of the eternal soul is not some lesser phenomenon in the universal drama of manifestation. The education of the soul is the central reason for the existence of the universe. . . . The soul is not an insignificant spark of life in an unknown and unknowing expanse of galaxies, as imagined by the modern scientific worldview. By truly knowing ourselves, we know directly the essence and purpose of the whole Creation. We are not groping in darkness.[45]

Perhaps life is calling you to help an outer community form a circle. Each voice is another unique gemstone through which the One Being's light can pass. Your role may be to help all the gems become aware that they are part of the Beloved's rosary. Or, you may need to gather resources to make a new start in your own life. This pathway can teach you to enjoy and learn from the gathering part of the process, rather than to simply see it as a means to an end. Or, it may be time to gather a circle of your inner self if it has been a while since you have done so.

—⟨ Roots and Branches ⟩—

A traditional translation of this quality is "the gatherer." The primary root of this name (*JM*) points to accumulating or multiplying something that has its own internal integrity in form. The same root makes up the Arabic word for a precious stone, *jaam*, related to the Latin *gemma*, from which we get the English word *gem*. What is gathered creates value. In this case, the whole Universe is Allah's gathering of selves for the sake of the gemlike quality by which each can reflect some ray of the original divine image. The Qur'an uses this word in connection with the gathering of souls on the "last day," which to the mystic can be any moment in which we consider the consequences of our life's actions and decide what to do next.

Meditation

Center again in the heart. Call a circle of the inner self and breathe the sound *Ya Jaa-Me* (with a short *e* sound) into the belly. Allow the sound and breath to create a sense of welcome for all the voices, reminding them of the home in the One Being that awaits them.

Look into your outer life through the lens of your heart and consider the opportunities to work in groups or to bring people or resources together. Ask the Beloved to show you clearly what is yours to do.

88. Tending Your Garden

الغَنِيُّ

Al-Ghani

When you are guided to this pathway,
take the opportunity to feel your heart as a garden in which everything you
need is growing. See yourself living in this garden.

AS THE HEART EXPANDS through life's experiences and spiritual practice, we may begin to feel all beings within our heart. As the American poet Walt Whitman, who had this experience, said, "In all men I see myself." Even with this vision, we still need to ask what is truly ours to do in life. We may have grand visions, or wish to save the world, but what are the practical steps that will accomplish these visions, as well as help us continue to grow in heart? As we saw in a previous pathway, *Qabid* (20), we may sometimes need to limit ourselves in order to grow.

To communicate the wisdom of containment, the ancient traditions of the Middle East used the organic image of a garden with definite boundaries, within which one cultivated everything that was needed in life. On one level, this garden is the outer province of our lives and loves. On another, it represents the heart itself. Shah Maghsoud says:

> *Do not leave the land of your heart*
> *as bare and fruitless as the desert,*
> *so that even its boundaries*
> *cannot find the way to the truth.*[46]

Perhaps life is calling you at this moment to define more clearly the boundaries of your garden. Which projects, work, or relationships will truly help you grow in your life right now? Perhaps you have been "running on automatic" due to a hectic schedule. Just as there are ecological limits to what the earth can provide, there are limits to material growth and expansion in our own lives. Another message of this pathway is that everything need not be done in the spotlight. Let the One veil you (another type of enclosure) and keep your secrets as you get on with your purpose in life.

∿ *Roots and Branches* ∿

Traditional translations of this quality include "the self-sufficient" and "free of all want." The root *GAN* means "garden" in ancient Semitic languages. For instance, the Hebrew *gan eden* in Genesis, sometimes translated as "garden of Eden," means "the living enclosure of bliss," and can be seen mystically on one level as the human being itself. In this sense, a "garden" is any enclosed, living space in which one can work, grow food, create beauty, and exist within healthy boundaries. We also find the root *GN* in the word *jinn*, as well as in the English word that comes from it, *genius*. In this sense, an enclosure can be a veil, either of delusion or protection, over divine wisdom. The Qur'an uses this word, as well as the next, *Mughni*, frequently in passages that encourage us to be generous and charitable with each other.

Meditation

Center again in the heart. Breathe the sound *Ya GhaN-ee* and feel it resonating through you, reaching the boundaries of your garden. Feel the sound of long *I* (*ee*) as the sacred Life Force activating growth within the garden. Through the eyes of the heart, view the various boundaries of your life. What lies outside? What grows within?

Then, or at another time, call a circle of your inner self, and breathe the feeling of this pathway. *Ghani* can help you close any psychic doorways that are too open, thereby enmeshing you in the atmosphere or impressions of another that do not belong to you.

BATHING IN UNITY

*T*he Sufi affirms the existence of the Real until real existence becomes her actual experience rather than merely an affirmation. We remind ourselves that "Allah" or the "One" or "Unity" only stands in for a Reality that we can't really put into words, but at some point we stop living "as if" it exists and begin living it. The names and pathways are only the map, not the journey itself. As Rumi says:

> Remember the One until you forget "two."
> After following "Namer" and "Name"
> lose your way in the Named.

Rumi also tells the story of some starving dervishes who found an empty grocery bag hanging on a wall and began to dance ecstatically around it:

> "Hey!" yelled a passerby, "Calm down. After all, it's empty!"
> "Get lost," replied the dervishes. "Love is the food of the lover.
> We're celebrating our love of bread, not bread itself."
> Real lovers don't rely on physical presence.
> They get the interest without the capital.
> Without wings they fly, and without hands
> they streak onto the field and carry off the ball.

Meditation

Just after sunset, breathe in the heart. Place your forehead on the earth, and release all impressions of the day, positive or negative, that are not your soul's concern. Allow your whole being to take a breath and feel the support from underneath as deeply as your bones. Release any thought about what you have or have not accomplished, and rest in the arms of the Beloved.

89. Life's Larger Garden

المُغْنِي

Al-Mughni

When you are guided to this pathway,
take the opportunity to see all of life as the embodiment of one garden,
with One Gardener tending it.

IN THE PREVIOUS PATHWAY, *Ghani*, we considered the boundaries of our own garden. In this one, we are encouraged to see everything and everyone we meet as an expression of some phase of Reality's greater garden. As we view life more deeply and broadly, we become very patient with others, and with ourselves. As Shabistari says:

> *Neither sober nor drunk, sometimes I feel the joy of*
> *my soul's eyes looking out through mine.*
> *Other times I feel the curl of the Beloved's hair*
> *and my life wobbles and staggers.*
> *Sometimes, the seasons of life turn and*
> *I find myself back on the compost heap.*
> *And sometimes, when her glance finds me again,*
> *I am back in the Rose Garden.*

Perhaps life is calling you right now to a wider view. You have been too focused on your own concerns and have ignored your relationships with others. There is no limit to the life energy created within the greater garden. What "compost" would activate and enrich your sphere of life? How could you see life in a larger way? Think bountiful, locally and globally. Don't just *work* in the garden, *be* the garden.

⌒ *Roots and Branches* ⌒

Traditional translations of this quality include "the enricher" and "supplier of needs to others." Just as *Muhyi* (60) more fully embodied *Hayy* (62), and as *Muqtadir* (70) embodied *Qadir* (69), so *Mughni* invites us to see all of life manifesting the activity of *Ghani*: the whole of life as a garden going through countless simultaneous cycles of growth and decay.

Meditation

Center again in the heart. Breathe the sound *Mu-GHN-ee* slowly, with one syllable on each in or out breath. Look at the wider picture of your life. Feel the sound *Mu-* at the beginning, as the One Being transforms everything you normally encounter in life into another expression of growth, in a larger garden of divine life energy. Feel the dense *-GHN-* sound in the middle, anchoring and centering you in your own part of this growth, and feel the *I* (*ee*) sound at the end, energizing everything. At the end, feel the whole substance of your body to be nothing more than the garden of the One in a continual cycle of rest and renewal.

90. The Gift of Resistance

المَانِعُ

Al-Mani`

When you are guided to this pathway,
take the opportunity to contact the part of your being that
acts to slow things down, to take away in order to give, to weaken
in order to strengthen.

IN THE TWO PREVIOUS pathways, we looked at life, inner and outer, as a garden. This pathway shows us that some plants need resistance in order to grow to their full strength. If we found everything easy in our lives, we would have nothing through which to develop our heart's garden completely. Wind and rain test us. Rumi uses another, very graphic image as he describes this process for his students:

> When those who fish hook a big one, they don't try to pull it in immediately. Instead, when the hook sets in the fish's throat, they drag it in bit by bit, so that it loses blood and becomes weaker. They let it go a little, drag some more, let it go, drag some more, until the fish gets tired.
>
> So when Love's hook sets in our throat, the One brings us in slowly, so that all our bad blood and unripe actions fade away, a bit at a time. As the Qur'an says, "God gives abundantly and draws us in again."

Perhaps life is calling you to delay, slow down, or reflect on the consequences of a proposed action, to measure yourself and put the brakes on a project or relationship. This may not be easy when the enthusiasm of the beginning proves to be intoxicating, as it often can, particularly in a group. Feel the blessing of limits. In work with the inner self, this pathway can provide the perspective that is able to listen to each self with love and respect, but not follow its desires when they may be harmful to ourself or to another.

⌒ Roots and Branches ⌒

Traditional translations of this quality include "the withholder" and "the restrainer." The roots of *Mani* show the actions of limitation and resistance (*MN*), energized by the same life force that gives everything definition and individuality (*I'*). Along with sacred diversity comes the side of life that tests and slows us down. Another meaning of this word is "protection." Just as a homeopathic medicine can introduce a weakening substance into the body in order to ultimately strengthen it, so *Mani* deprives us of something in order to ultimately give us more.

Meditation

Center again in the heart. Breathe out the open sound of *MaaN*, feeling its vibration in your bones, and breathe in with the guttural *I'* sound at the end, going backward into the body. Sit on your hands and feel your pelvic bones supported from underneath you. Allow your muscles to relax; your bones and ligaments will hold you up. Where do you feel resistance in your body, or in your life? Where is this resistance part of the One's divine image in you, keeping you strong?

Then, or at another time, breathe *Mani* into your inner circle of selves. Who are the resistant ones today? What are they trying to tell you? How does your highest guidance hear this with the ears of Allah?

91. Pain and Loss

Ad-Darr

When you are guided to this pathway,
take the opportunity to reflect on the bigger picture of any pain, loss,
or need you feel at the moment.

WE ALL EXPERIENCE PAIN and loss in the course of a lifetime: the loss of those near to us, of relationships, of work, of opportunities, or of our own self-images, which are sometimes the hardest to give up. As the Greek philosopher Heraclitus once put it, "You can't step into the same river twice."

The Sufi has been called "the child of the moment." Al-Qushayri relates this to the way a moment of truth can return us from delusion to self-honesty, sometimes with a harsh clarity:

This moment is like a sword,
gentle to the touch,
but with a very sharp edge.
Handle the moment gently
and you go unharmed.
Handle it clumsily and you
feel its cutting edge.

Rumi points out that need prompts us to both feel more deeply and to search further:

The Qur'an says, "It is We who have sent down, step by step, this Reminder, and We guard it."
*   Most commentators say this is about the revelation of the Qur'an itself. But you can also hear it this way: "We put into you, moment by moment, the capacity to yearn and search. We watch over this yearning, and don't let it go to waste, until it has found its fulfillment."*

Perhaps life is asking you: Can loss and feelings of need encourage my inner self to feel the preciousness of each moment? This pathway can also signal a wake-up call for when we have inflicted pain on ourselves through overindulgence of one sort or another. If we take away the extra *R* of the word, symbolizing the excess, *Darr* becomes *dar* in Arabic, "a door." Is there a way you can use the pain you are experiencing as a door that allows you to step into a different kind of life?

❧ *Roots and Branches* ❧

Traditional translations of this quality include "the giver of distress" and "the harmful." The root of *Darr, DRR,* shows that the divine abundance and diversity, born of division, also determine our perception of what we call time: Things in diversity seem to have a limited life, age, or cycle, at least in the realm of physical space. At the same time, loss and need, which cause all beings pain, provide a gateway for transformation. Without the extra *R,* the root *DR* forms both the word for door in Arabic (*dar*), from which our word probably derives, as well as the word for a prayer or affirmation, *darood.*

Meditation

Center again in the heart. If you are feeling distress, breathe the feeling of this pathway into it. Or, breathe *Ya DaaRR* with compassion with the circle of your inner self. Allow this feeling to remind your whole being that when you have set your feet upon the path, it is hard to go back. This means progressively giving up the attachment to previous images of yourself. Pain often results. Place this pain in the hands of Allah. Feel it as part of the loss and need that inform a universe filled with abundant diversity, of forms that die and are reborn with other faces.

92. *Immediately Useful Blessing*

An-Nafi'

When you are guided to this pathway,
take the opportunity to receive from within you whatever gift or quality
would help you right now. This is the "wild card" blessing: It can be
whatever you need to help you expand your heart and life.

THE PREVIOUS TWO PATHWAYS opened the doorways of resistance and pain, which often prepare us for this one: immediately useful blessing—whatever "suitable means" we need to
further the growth of our human personality and inner self right
now. Sometimes this blessing takes a form we may not have ex-
pected had we not been prepared for it by the two previous paths.
For this reason, when in doubt about what to ask for at any moment, it's best to use a prayer similar to that of Inayat Khan: "Use us
for the purpose that Thy wisdom chooseth."[47] Asking for more than
this—fame, wealth, or influence—can get us into trouble, as Rumi
advises his students:

> *The problem becomes that the more you cultivate the interest of rulers,*
> *the more your real interest escapes you. The further you go in that di-*
> *rection, the more the Beloved turns her back on you.*

> *Wouldn't it be a shame to reach the sea*
> *and only come back with a pitcher of water?*
> *The sea contains pearls as well as*
> *millions of other precious things.*
> *The world is just a bit of foam on that sea.*
> *Spiritual practice is the water.*
> *But where is the pearl you're looking for?*

As we have seen previously, our humanity evolves and grows as our hearts open to include more and more of the paradoxes we find within us. As our inner circle of self (*nafs* in Arabic) becomes more inclusive, we also become more compassionate toward those outside us. During this process, the feeling of our breath (in Arabic, *nafas*) centers in the heart and then expands above, beneath and around us to strengthen the feeling of interrelationship with all beings. Because our breathing can change so rapidly (for instance, becoming shorter and more shallow when we're nervous), this pathway provides whatever antidote we need right now to bring it back into harmony with ourselves and others.

Perhaps life is telling you that you need to stop and breathe in order to get your life back on track. On the outer level, perhaps you are surrounded by the means to do this, but you're not seeing the gifts of the moment. Open now to what is immediately useful and practical for taking you to the next step on your journey. This pathway also leads us to breathe with compassion and care for all of nature, which is another form of the Beloved's blessing in action.

⌒ *Roots and Branches* ⌒

Traditional translations of this quality include "benefactor" and "propitious." The root of *Nafi', NF,* shows a movement in and out, or the process of distilling some essence from a liquid. The root comes from the same source as *nafas,* the personal expression of the breath (that is, the breath we usually think of as "ours"), as well as from *nafs,* the personal self-soul, which is formed by a temporary distillation or effusion of the divine breath. We are all limited "selves" within the Self of the One Being, limited breaths connected to the One Breath. This includes not only human beings, but all beings in the universe. The Sufis often quote the sacred tradition *man `arafa nafsahu faqad `arafa rabbahu:* Whoever discovers their self (*nafs*) discovers their Sustainer.

Meditation

Center again in the heart. Breathe out and feel the sound *NaaF*-opening and forming a wider circle around your sense of self. Breathe in and feel the ending sound *-I* (very short and back into the throat and body), receiving what is needed for your next steps.

Call a circle of your inner self. Acknowledge, through the eyes of your highest guidance, that all voices of your "inner ecology" are worthy of love and respect. All are limited selves within the One Self of Allah. Listen to the needs, desires, and limiting beliefs of each as though listening with the heart of the One. What is the next practical step toward a more complete feeling of "I am" in harmony with the only "I Am"?

93. The Light of Intelligence

النُّورُ

An-Nur

When you are guided to this pathway,
take the opportunity to reflect on the divine intelligence that has illuminated
and is illuminating your life.

AN ENTIRE SCHOOL OF classical Sufis developed and worked with the inner experience of light, which in its Semitic language sense means knowing or intelligence. Light and dark don't stand for good and evil in the Sufi tradition. What is "light" represents what we know about our inner self. What is "dark" represents what is mysterious, or what we don't yet know. The "illuminationist" Sufis developed a cosmology, as well as mystical art and science, out of their Quranic interpretation that the One Being is radiating creation into existence in every moment. For instance, the twelfth-century Sufi Shihab Al-Din Suhrawardi wrote:

> *Allah's essence is the original creative Light, always illuminating existence. It constantly manifests the universe and energizes it. Allah's Essential Light radiates the whole cosmos in abundant beauty and completeness. To be illuminated by this process means nothing less than salvation.*

In this pathway, we begin to see everything as radiant, alive, and intelligent. We recognize this light because, the Sufis say, our own image in the heart of the One at the moment of creation is still radiating light to us. Light recognizes light. In this sense, the "light" or intelligence of our senses, by which we see, hear, and sense things, comes to us not only from deep within us but also from a living past ahead of us that is still radiant and active today.

Meditating on these ideas of Suhrawardi, the twentieth-century Sufi Vilayat Inayat Khan, commented:

For Shihab Al-Din Suhrawardi there is a way of looking upon the earth: rather than perceiving it through the senses, one contemplates a precognitive image inherent in one's soul. The scene on earth triggers off this image, which lays latent in one. One's mind belongs to the sphere of Hurkalya, the sphere where creative imagination moulds the archetypes of those forms which are eventually projected as objects or bodies of planets or galaxies.[48]

The light within us resembles the light of the farthest stars and galaxies, which are closest to the beginnings of the cosmos. The Sufis meditated on this radiance in all being and used the Quran's famous "verse of light" (*Sura* 24:35) to inspire them to look behind the appearances of things. The following meditation on part of this verse, the longest in the Qur'an, expresses a portion of its meaning in Arabic.

> *Light upon light upon light—*
>   *back and back we trace it to its Source,*
> *radiating light and sound—a voice, an echo*
> *guiding those who hear Love's desire*
> *unfold the universe's story,*
> *who come to this call*
> *like thirsty birds to water.*
> *Beloved, the One creates for us*
> *models, signs, symbols, parables*
> *everywhere we look to remind us*
> *of our Source.*
> *And the One behind all*
> *understands and embraces all—*
> *the past and future journey of every thing*
> *from seed to star.*[49]

Perhaps life is calling you to take some time to reflect upon your life so far. What guidance have you received? What have you learned? What would illuminate your life's path further? Take some time to contemplate the job description of a human being, according to the Sufis: to reflect the divine image and express the consciousness and heart-feeling of the entire natural cosmos that was created before humanity.

Roots and Branches

The traditional translation of this quality is "the light." The roots of *Nur* point to the constantly new (*N*) and transformational (*U*) radiance of life (*R*). It derives from the same root as the Hebrew *aor*, the primal light created at the beginning, as described in Genesis. This light illuminates in a focused beam, like a beacon lighting up a path. *Nur* also points to the archetype of the primal human being, called *Adam Qadmon* in Jewish mysticism and *Nur-i-Muhammad* in Sufism.

Meditation

Center again in the heart. Breathe the name *Ya NooR* and follow the feeling of the sound deep into your heart of hearts. Find the whole world within your heart, and your heart within the heart of the One Being.

94. Most Direct Guidance

الهَادِي

Al-Hadi

When you are guided to this pathway,
take the opportunity to check in with your highest guidance.
Open yourself to hear its clear, direct voice.

THE BIBLE RELATES THAT the prophet Elijah, when in trouble, listened for the "still, small voice" through which he heard the voice of the Holy One. We are often in need of and yearn for this simple, direct sense of guidance. In a few words, the twentieth-century Sufi Inayat Khan expressed his prayer:

Open our hearts that we may
hear Thy voice
which constantly cometh from within.[50]

If all is One, who is there to ask, and who is the asker? Admittedly, when "knower and known are one," as the Sufis say, normal prayer seems superfluous. And yet, as we have seen throughout the pathways, there is a part of us that is still growing and evolving. This voice in us needs prayer, affirmation, and practice to get us through the hard times. The best prayer reminds us that love and guidance are always present. As the eighteenth-century Persian Sufi Ahmad Hatif writes:

When you begin the journey,
Take Love along for food.
Love makes easy what Reason makes hard.
Talk about the Beloved morning and evening.
Look out for the Beloved at twilight and dawn.
Even though they tell you a hundred times:
"No one has seen the One," keep on

until its vision illuminates you.
You'll find the Beloved located
where even Gabriel can't go.
Love is the path, the rations, and the goal.

Likewise, Rumi assures us:

You thought you were dust
and now find you are breath.
Before you were ignorant—
now you know more.
The One who guided you this far
will lead you farther on as well.

Perhaps life is calling you to renew your sense of inner guidance and clear direction. The pathway invites you to breathe easily, with a feeling of devotion, and ask for clear guidance. Sometimes you can "hear" the voice by feeling your breathing becoming stronger, or your body becoming more alive. Other times, you may see an image or a color, or even hear a word. If you pick one voice within and consistently hear the voice of the One through it, the messages will continue to get stronger and clearer.

—☙ *Roots and Branches* ❧—

The traditional translation of this quality is "the guide." The roots of *Hadi* show a voice, sound, sensation, or direct message (*HAD*) that returns us to the source of life and take us further (*I*). One Arabic idiom that uses this word (*'ala hudan*) depicts guidance like a horse or camel that helps carry us to the goal of unity with Unity. The Qur'an uses this word when pointing out that prophets have always faced opposition, and yet the One Being is always there to help and guide (for instance, *Sura* 25:31).

Meditation

Center again in the heart. Breathe the sound *Ya Haa-Dee* rhythmically (for instance, in a count of four, with the final beat a rest). Feel its definition and clarity, so that the heart vibrates with the sound. Contact your sense of highest guidance, whether this be your own spirit of guidance or the reflection of it that you feel coming through a teacher, prophet, or saint. Walk in rhythm with the feeling of your heart leading you further on love's journey.

البَدِيعُ

Al-Badi`

When you are guided to this pathway,
take the opportunity to open yourself to the joy and wonder you experienced
as a child, when you looked into the night sky. The Beloved could be sending
you a message right now that will illuminate your whole life in a flash.

IF THE PREVIOUS PATHWAY, *Hadi*, reveals the reliable source of guidance always available within, *Badi`* discloses the surprising and sudden flash that places everything in a new focus. This unexpected guidance or circumstance can move our lives in an entirely new direction, yet we may miss the message if we don't take time to cultivate the qualities of joy and wonder in our lives. This is the meaning of Jesus' saying "Unless you become as children, you won't be able to enter the vision-power of the cosmos."

Could we dare to affirm that life is an adventure? Nur Hixon wrote:

This life of the Divine Love on earth, which is the perfect knowledge of
unity, is primarily an expression of true spiritual joy, arising sponta-
neously from affirming God with every cell of our body, with every
strand of our awareness.[51]

In order to cultivate wonder, the classical Sufis meditated on the soul sleeping in the heart of the divine in pre-eternity. The tenth-century Sufi Abil Khayr writes:

Resting for ages before the vault of sky arched over us,
resting for ages before the deepest blue of heaven appeared,
we slept in nonbeing timelessly, stamped with love's seal,
before we knew or felt or cared about our own existence.

Perhaps the pathway of wonder is calling you right now. You may feel hemmed in by life's circumstances, or at a dead end in work with your inner self. Allow the energy of the original wonder of creation to be reawakened in you. Be willing to return for an instant and feel the eyes of a child looking through yours in joy.

～ Roots and Branches ～

Traditional translations of this quality include "the originator" and "the unprecedented." The roots of *Badi`* show the creative power of the Holy One dividing things from the very beginning in order to make them more themselves (*BD*), and by doing so, allowing them to individuate in an entirely new way and move with their own sense of purpose (*I*). *Badi`* is related to its sister name *Mubdi* (58), which expresses the same energy more fully embodied as creativity (or, allowing us to see this creativity already embodied throughout the cosmos). The Qur'an uses this word to indicate that wonder begins the whole process of creation. According to *Sura* 2:117, creation begins when Allah says the word *kun*—Be! It uses other words of creation, such as *Khaliq* (11) and *Bari* (12), to show how the process of creative evolution continued, through definition and radiation.

Meditation

Center again in the heart. Breathe out the sound *Ba-*, opening from the heart, and breathe in the sound *-Di`* (with the final *ee* backward and guttural, into the body). Inhalation. Exhalation. Contraction. Expansion. This is the same energy the Holy One used to create the universe. "And it was evening (contraction), and it was morning (expansion)—one flash of illumination, possible every moment" (Genesis 1:5). Can you imagine yourself at this moment of creation?

The Real That Remains

البَاقِي

Al-Baqi

When you are guided to this pathway,
take the opportunity to identify with what remains in you after all
superficial appearances and masks have dissolved, when you have released
your attachment to everything you do and accomplish.

T HE PATHWAYS OF THE heart invite us down many seemingly contradictory paths that all lead to one goal—the discovery of our real self. What this means is difficult to communicate. We know that it has to do with letting go, with surrender, with learning even under the most trying conditions of life. We also know it means acting fully, with passion, courage, and sometimes even abandon, at the right times. And yet we can take none of this as a motto, moral, or philosophy of life. Where does it all leave us?

For the Sufi, the spiritual life involves gradually letting go of everything we identify with as "I." As Irina Tweedie said:

> *The spiritual life of every one of us is the drama of the soul. It's the crucifixion and the resurrection. What is crucified, of course, is the ego. The resurrection is—I hesitate to say—enlightenment, perhaps. But enlightenment of what or whom? Once you merge into oneness, there is no such thing as "I." So who is there to be enlightened?*[52]

The Sufis use the term *fana*, which means to efface oneself in the divine. When we have let go even of this letting go—that is, of effacement itself—nothing remains except the face of Allah, both seeing and being seen. This is the state or stage of *baqa*, which is related to this pathway. Rumi says:

A king once asked a dervish, "When you have received the ultimate revelation and stand in the presence of Allah, would you please remember me?"

The dervish replied, "When I'm standing in that presence, illuminated by Beauty's sun, I don't even remember myself. How can I remember you?"

And yet, something does remain, as Irina Tweedie says:

[T]here are moments of deep meditation where you and That are love and It loves you. It responds. It fulfills you absolutely. But what fulfills you? What responds? God is Nothingness. But this Nothingness loves you. You are loved and there is absolute unbelievable bliss. Mind knows nothing about it. These things cannot really be explained. They have to be experienced.[53]

Perhaps life is calling you to let go, trust, and find a deeper center within you, even as things around you seem to be falling away. Sometimes we don't have a choice about letting go. Other times, we can choose consciously. In either case, using this pathway with your inner self is another way of reminding it, with love and respect, "All is not as it once was. All is not today as it will be. Eventually, only the face of the One remains."

◦ Roots and Branches ◦

Traditional translations of this quality include "the enduring" and "the everlasting." The word *Baqi* comes from a verb that means to remain or continue. The roots show something that creates (*B*) and lives (*I*) after everything else has drained away (*AQ*). We could see this as the image of a desert landscape in which an oasis remains. The Qur'an uses this word in the passage mentioned under *Dhul-Jelal-Wal-Ikram* (85): "Everything passes away except for the Sustainer's face, full of power and bounty."

Meditation

Center again in the heart. Breathe in the open sound of *BA-*, and then breathe out the carving sound of *-QI* (with *ee* at the end). Feel the sound helping to strip away what is no longer needed in your being for this stage of the journey, each time leaving a clearer, stronger presence. As a practice, *Baqi* reminds us that after we gradually or suddenly loosen our attachment to who we think we are, the divine life remains to resurrect a different sense of "I am."

97. Reclaiming a Forgotten Inheritance

الوَارِثُ

Al-Warith

When you are guided to this pathway,
take the opportunity to remember your divine inheritance of
natural strength and healing.

LIKE THE PREVIOUS TWO pathways, *Badi* and *Baqi,* this one reminds us that what we're looking for is already ours. The embodied life we lead is not naturally "fallen" or "sinful," and we do not
need to inject ourselves with some outside force or belief in order to
save ourselves. It's as though we have simply forgotten where we
came from and the inheritance we brought with us.

An anthropologist might say that what Sufis seek to recover is an
aspect of human consciousness that we forgot or denied when we
stopped leading nomadic lives and started to believe that by settling
down and farming we could control our destinies. The old ways of
sensing and feeling, which constantly reminded our nomadic ancestors of their dependence on an unseen reality, gradually disappeared. Twenty thousand years ago, we probably lived in a state of
perpetual wonder, where the sacred and profane in life were not separate, and our inner faculties were much more advanced than they
are today. Life, however, was short and frequently ended in suffering, often due to weather, lack of food, or attack by outside forces.[54]

We cannot return to being nomads, but we can reclaim some of
this older consciousness, which links us more deeply to nature, to
each other, and to the cosmos. We can integrate it in the heart and
live more fully human lives, not only for our own development but
also to help us discover a way past the various human crises in which
we find ourselves enmeshed today. We cannot continue to live in a
world with such vast disparities of wealth and resource consump-
tion. A number of spiritual traditions, with links to this ancient wisdom, attempt to show us how to live different, more fulfilling lives.

The Sufis use the image of the divine Beloved to help balance our Western cultural penchant for the rational, which ultimately asks us to weigh every action in the context of its benefits to us. As Rumi says:

Reason is all fine and good
until it shows you the door of the Beloved.
At that point divorce reason,
which will steal from you like a bandit.

Finding what we already possess may seem like a strange goal for a spiritual path. Yet the process of finding may provide us more joy than if the universe delivered all its secrets to us without any effort on our part.

One day Mullah Nasruddin ran into the market, shouting, "I've lost my favorite donkey! Can someone find my donkey? To whoever finds it, I'll give the donkey itself, the blanket, the saddle, and the harness."

"Mullah, what are you saying?" asked a friend. "You're going to give away what you're looking for. What's the sense in that?"

"The sense is," said Mullah, "I get the joy of finding something I've lost."

Perhaps life is calling you right now to take a breath and let go of any rigidities that prevent you from receiving your natural inheritance of strength from the cosmos. You cannot possess it exclusively, but it is still yours. The only thing that can keep us from receiving this strength is our own sense of isolation and self-absorption.

—ᴑ *Roots and Branches* ᴑ—

Traditional translations of this quality include "the inheritor" and "the heir." The roots of *Warith* show a continual flow (*W-*) of strength and vigor (*AR*), which serves as both a sign of healing and the fruition of human existence (*Th*). Jesus uses a related Aramaic word, *nertun*, usually translated as "inherit," in the Aramaic version of the third Beatitude in Matthew when he says: "Ripe are those who soften what is overly rigid within; by softening they shall receive their natural inheritance of strength and healing from the cosmos."[55] The Qur'an uses this word to indicate that after the whole universe and all manifested being, seen and unseen, have vanished—along with all processes, including life and death—the One Reality will be the survivor and "inheritor."

Meditation

Center again in the heart. This quality is particularly easy to feel in nature. Breathe with the feeling of the sound *Ya Waa-Rith* in the silence. Relax, open the pores of your being, and receive.

Call a circle of your inner self. Allow your highest guidance to use this pathway to invite each self to receive what it needs—not what it thinks it needs—directly from the Source of all Life.

Illuminating the Path of Growth

الرَّشِيدُ

Ar-Rashid

When you are guided to this pathway,
take the opportunity to feel the divine light shining straight in front of you,
revealing the path of growth for you at this moment.

THE MEDIEVAL CHRISTIAN MYSTIC Hildegard of Bingen once had a vision in which she saw the whole universe constantly being nourished by divine creativity. She called this nourishing force *viriditas,* which can be roughly translated from the Latin as "greening power." Even in the processes of decay and death, the universe reveals preparation for rebirth and growth.

This pathway of the heart invites us to a similar vision, one that reveals our own best path of growth among the myriad possible ways. Attar tells the following story:

A fool once stood in the middle of the marketplace. Thousands of people were coming and going from one place to another. He yelled out, "It's clear to me that you all have a single heart, but many different desires. How can you get anywhere when you're going in all directions?"

In a similar vein, the first *sura* of the Qur'an offers the prayer *ih-dina sirat al mustaqim,* which conveys the meaning:

Show us the path that says, "stand up, get going, do it!"
which resurrects us from the slumber of the drugged
and leads to the consummation of Heart's desire,
like all the stars and galaxies in tune, in time, straight on.

In order to discover this path, we need to develop a different way of feeling and sensing our way through life. The Sufi practices can

offer this. The ninth-century Egyptian Sufi Dhu'l Nun talked about
how to benefit from the gift of each moment by developing a more
intuitive way of approaching life:

> Those who experience sacred Unity become more humble each hour and
> draw ever closer to God. They see without knowledge, sight, informa-
> tion, observation, or description, without being either veiled or un-
> veiled. They are not really themselves, but if they can be said to exist at
> all, they exist in the One.

Perhaps life is calling you right now to make a choice about your
next direction. You may be in a situation where new direction or
"greening" is needed in your life. Perhaps your "field" feels over-
worked, in need of rest or compost. From where will the next
growth come, and how? In work with the inner self, this pathway
can help your highest guidance illuminate the concerns of the inner
selves and put them in a wider, more natural context.

❧ Roots and Branches ❧

Traditional translations of this quality include "the unerring" and
"the discriminating." The roots of *Rashid* show the illumination (*Ra-*)
of all of natural existence (*ShID*), the vision of life as greening and
verdant. Viewed another way, the name *Rashid* can also remind us
that, from the divine point of view, all of life, the whole of manifested
existence, is already illuminated. Each individual particle testifies to
the fire (the root *ASh*) of the One within it. In this way, the name is
indirectly related to *Shahid* (50), the experience of One Life behind
all the diverse forms and faces we see. *Rashid* is also related to the
word *murshid*, which expresses the embodiment of the quality in a
spiritual teacher.

Meditation

Center again in the heart. Breathe the name in and out, with an emphasis on both sounds: *Ra-SheeD*. Feel your breath extending ahead of you from the heart, illuminating and lighting up the path that leads to abundance and greening. Let your heart be within the heart of Allah and ask, "Where next, and how?"

99. Perseverance

الصَّبُورُ

As-Sabur

When you are guided to this pathway,
take the opportunity to persevere on your path, containing the light and
intelligence within you until the right time to reveal them.

AT THE END OF this journey, we find a pathway of the heart that reminds us that the journey is not over. Sometimes we need to cultivate patience and allow what we have discovered to "cook" inside us, before releasing it or telling others. This pathway complements *Rashid,* the previous one. In *Rashid,* the divine light illuminates the path of our best growth. In *Sabur,* we enclose the knowing and illumination we have received within us so that it can grow brighter.

Seldom do we find ourselves in what we might consider ideal conditions for our own spiritual growth. Often we feel that we are being pulled away from our path by the necessities of life around us—for instance, by the various people or projects for whom we feel responsible. Once the prime minister of his region came to Rumi and told him that he really wanted to devote all his time to prayer and meditation, but he was always being distracted by foreign affairs (in his case, that meant making sure that the invading Mongols didn't decimate Konya, the town in present-day Turkey where he and Rumi lived). Rumi replied:

The reason you're willing to do your work with heart shows divine favor. You have sacrificed your time and your body to pacify the hearts of the Mongols, so that the rest of us can live peacefully. If God didn't send you the heart to do it, you wouldn't be able to continue. The One doesn't want this important work done by an unworthy person.

The spiritual life is like a hot bath. You start and stoke it with insignificant things: straw, firewood, dung. What seems to us cheap, nasty, or distasteful, the Beloved can use for blessing. Then we heat up, like the bath, and can serve many people.

Perhaps life is calling you to hold on a bit longer. While this pathway counsels patience, its real message is this: Now is not the time to disperse your light; that is, the deep knowing of yourself and others that you have received from the One. Don't hurry. Let things cook for a while. There is time enough in the universe of Allah. Like *Matin* (54), this pathway can also help us work with projects or relationships where progress is likely to be slow, over a long period of time. The heat of patience and discomfort may, like a cooking compost pile, produce amazing future effects, ones we couldn't dream of, as this short poem by Moineddin Jablonski expresses:

> *When your deep fear has found you.*
> *A yellow sunflower will grow*
> *beside you on the dunghill.*
> *You will be astonished*
> *as it turns to face you.*
> *It will marvel as fire*
> *comes to eat from*
> *your hand.*[56]

—ᴐ *Roots and Branches* ᴐ—

Traditional translations of this quality include "most patient" and "long-enduring." The roots of *Sabur* show a container or sack, *SaB*, which surrounds the divine light, *UR* (similar to the old Hebrew *aor*). The Qur'an uses this word in a passage that counsels people not to argue with each other and to endure adversity with patience. Another translation of the word is "avoiding agitation."

Meditation

Center again in the heart. Breathe with the feeling of the sound *Ya Saa-BooR* and call a circle of your inner selves. Who is challenged by life's call to take things slower? How can *Sabur* illuminate this challenge and build the inner fire so that it builds up more heat?

Breathe *Ya Saa-boor* as a walking meditation, feeling the whole body as a container for the divine light gradually becoming brighter within. Allow each step you take and each breath you take to reveal a universe of life and love around you.

BATHING IN UNITY

*H*ere's a famous story of Mullah Nasruddin, but I've heard many people leave out the ending. As with all these stories, you can consider everything and everyone in it as part of your inner self:

Once upon a time, Mullah was invited to speak at the mosque in a particular village at Friday community prayers. This is normally the only time when there might be a sermon or talk, since everyone would be gathered. The village that invited Mullah was widely known as the largest collection of foolish people in the region. They sent a delegation to Mullah: "O Mullah, wisest of the wise, we know that we're not worthy, but please come and give the sermon at our community prayers. Give us a chance!"

Mullah agreed and went there the next Friday. He walked to the front of the mosque after prayers and said, "Does anyone know what I'm about to tell you?"

No one dared answer, for fear of being proved foolish.

"Then," said Mullah, "you're all too foolish to tell." And he walked out.

The next day the town again sent a delegation to Mullah, begging and pleading. "We'll try to do better, Mullah! Please come again!"

The next Friday the same thing happened. Mullah walked to the front of the mosque after prayers and asked, "Does anyone know what I'm about to tell you?"

This time, as if choreographed, everyone responded at once, "Yes! We know!"

"Then there's no point in telling you," said Mullah, and he walked out again.

As you might guess, another day, another delegation, more bowing and scraping. "Just one more chance, Mullah! We promise!"

Again the following week, the same scene, the same question. This time half the crowd yelled out "Some of us know!" and the other half responded "And some of us don't!"

"So," said Mullah, "Let those who know tell those who don't!" And he walked out the third time.

Now I've heard it told that many years later, Mullah happened to be traveling again near the town of foolish people, and he noticed that it just happened to be Friday, around noon. "I think I'll go see how they're getting on," said Mullah to himself.

As he entered the mosque, prayers were over, but it looked as if everyone was waiting for something. He muttered to himself, "Oh . . . why not!" and walked to the front.

"Does anyone know what I'm about to tell you?" he asked.

At this point, everyone in the mosque stood up and walked out, leaving Mullah standing alone.

This story mirrors one view of the journey of our inner self. As we begin the spiritual path, we're in denial that we even have a voice of guidance within us. We're waiting for someone outside to illuminate us. Then we swing to the other extreme and think we know everything. When our inner life finally wakes up, the part of us that knows is able to speak to the part of us that doesn't know (Mullah's third solution). Our higher guidance is able to speak to our *nafs*, and the various voices of the inner self can gather together and work as one. Once this happens, it's just a matter of staying on the path and allowing our hearts to continue to grow. At the end, when Mullah returns, he finds that the "answer" to his question is absence. The small self, beyond affirmation and denial, has merged with the Self of the Beloved.

Meditation

Breathe a gentle yet full breath with one hand lightly over the heart. Feel the heart itself as sacred space, ready for all the questions and answers, all the paradoxes of life. For such a heart, life is an adventure, whether coming or going.

Biographies of Sufis Cited

(in roughly chronological order)

Ali and Fatima (Arabia, d. 661 and 633)

Fatima, the daughter of Prophet Muhammad, and Ali, her husband, are considered by many Sufis to have transmitted esoteric knowledge from the Prophet. This becomes, along with a mystical interpretation of various Quranic passages, the basis for a Sufi claim that Muhammad was attempting first to transmit a spiritual path of wisdom, rooted in practical morality, which later became layered over with culture and politics.

Rabia Al-Adawiyya (Iraq, d. 801)

The best known of the women Sufi mystics, Rabia continued the flowering of spiritual transmission begun by earlier women mystics such as Mu'adha, who was reputed to be a companion of the Prophet's wife, Aisha, and who transmitted an early Sufi lineage through her female disciples that lasted for almost two hundred years. Rabia was known not only for her great devotion but also for her knowledge of early Sufi practice. Rabia has sometimes been depicted as an emotional spiritual recluse, but a full picture of her life and teachings shows her mastery of spiritual states such as truthfulness, self-criticism, intoxication, love for God, and gnosis (which the Sufis call *ma'rifa*).

Fatima of Nishapur (Persia, d. 849)

Fatima of Nishapur left her native Eastern Persia, spent many years in Mecca, and traveled widely in Palestine and Syria. She was one of the main teachers of the Egyptian Sufi Dhu'l Nun, who called her "a saint among saints." Fatima was a master of both the esoteric interpretation of the Qur'an and the Sufi teachings on right guidance (*side*).

Dhu'l Nun Al Misri (Egypt, d. 861)

Dhu'l Nun, born of Nubian parents in Upper Egypt, was one of the first to develop the Sufi understanding of the mystical states of annihilation (*fana*) and resurrection (*baqa*) in the divine Unity. His prayers also show a renewed emphasis on finding the sacred in nature, which had been overlooked by some of the earlier ascetic Sufis.

Abu Yazid Bistami (Persia, d. 875)
Bistami, who for many years lived as hermit, in a state of ecstasy, once said "Glory be to me," a radical way to say that the human and divine are part of one reality. Bistami later rejected his ascetic life, considering it another veil between the seeker and divine Unity.

Mansur Al-Hallaj (Persia, d. 922)
Al-Hallaj, in a state of divine intoxication, once said, "I am the Truth." In the Baghdad of his time, he did not escape as easily as Bistami, and due to various political considerations, was crucified. Al-Hallaj also composed poetry and other writings that express an uncompromising view of divine Unity. In one, he takes the side of the fallen angel Iblis and shows him to be a tragic lover of God, who would not bow to anything other than the One, even if the One told him to do so.

Abu Sa`id Abil Khayr (Persia, d. 1048)
Among the first Sufi poets to use lyric imagery, Abil Khayr primarily taught the doctrine of the negation of self as the way to discover the authentic Self in the divine.

Abul Qasim Al-Qushayri (Persia, d. 1074)
Born in Nishapur, Al-Qushayri trained in Islamic law and Qur'an, as well as being a student of Sufism. He wrote a very popular classical treatise on Sufi practice and terminology, illustrated with quotes from other writers as Sarraj, Junayd, and Shibli.

Abul Hasan Al-Hujwiri (Afghanistan, d. 1079)
Highly revered in Pakistan today among Sufis, Al-Hujwiri wrote another early treatise on Sufism titled *Kashf-al-Mahjub*, or "The Unveiling of the Veiled." The author had the occasion to visit his tomb in Lahore in 1979, which remains a major site of prayer and pilgrimage.

Abu Hamid Al-Ghazali (Persia, d. 1111)
Al-Ghazali stands at an important cusp in the development of Sufism. As a scholar and philosopher, he attempted to reconcile the

emphasis in Sufism on personal spiritual experience with the world of orthodox religion. His success can been seen in the way that Sufism influenced mainstream Islam for many centuries after his passing. Later in life, Al-Ghazali gave up his academic career, started a Sufi community, and devoted himself to the mysticism of love.

Abul Majdud Sana'i (Persia, d. 1150)

One of the early mystical poets and collectors of Sufi stories, Sana'i became a dervish early in life, renouncing the everyday life. He wrote a collection of teachings and stories called *The Garden of Truth,* which influenced later teachers such as Rumi.

Abdul Qadir Jilani (Baghdad, Iraq, d. 1166)

Jilani represents the development of the way of concentration in classical Sufism. His writings emphasize the moral dimension of right relationship, along with powerful practices of the heart that lead to mastery through accomplishment.

Shihab Al-Din Suhrawardi (Iraq, Syria, d. 1191)

Suhrawardi counts among the initiators of the "illuminationist" school of Sufis, who formulated a doctrine of creative emanation. One of his famous books was *The Temples of Light.* He was martyred for alleged heresy.

Fariduddin Attar (Persia, d. 1229)

Attar is the first of the major classical Sufi poets. He wrote extensively about the lives of the Sufi saints before him and composed the epic poem *The Conference of the Birds.* In this poem, a group of birds go in search of their king. The stories they tell and the adventures they encounter represent stages on the path of the Sufi. The birds also represent the different aspects of our own personalities that we encounter when we begin to develop our inner nature. Attar's work influenced many later poets, and his collection of Sufi stories is still quoted today.

Moineddin Chishti (India, d. 1236)

A near contemporary of Jilani, Moineddin Chishti transmitted Sufism in India, and in a totally different culture emphasized the development of heart through music, sacred movement, and art.

Muhyi Al-Din Ibn Arabi (Andalucia, d. 1240)

Called "the great sheikh," Ibn Arabi traveled widely to Egypt, Syria, and Iraq before settling in Damascus. Along with his predecessor, Suhrawardi, he focused on a mysticism of illumination and taught through both poetry and prose a way to find the divine light in all forms and religions. His more controversial writings promote the discovery of sacred Unity in one's own deep nature, and he was fond of quoting the Quranic passage "Whoever knows one's self, knows the One Self."

Jelaluddin Rumi (Anatolia, d. 1273) and Shams-i-Tabriz (Persia, d. 1248)

Two of the most famous Sufis, Rumi and Shams met in Konya (in present-day Turkey), and their spiritual friendship resulted in an explosion of teaching and poetry that still affects the world. Shams was a wild, shamanic teacher; Rumi was a staid philosopher before meeting him. After Shams's passing, Rumi composed poetry as though in Shams's voice (a Sufi practice called *tassawuri*) and later dictated the epic work called the *Mathnawi,* which interweaves poetry, Sufi stories, and teaching in a way that still has not been equaled.

Muslihuddin Saadi (Persia, d. 1292)

Saadi represents an entirely different development of Sufi poetry and story from that of Rumi and Attar. We could usefully compare him to the American humorist Mark Twain, who teaches through satire, irony, and laughter. Saadi's many collections of stories were widely read and retold in his time. His lyric love poetry maintains a sense of humor and adds a delicate insight into the crazy highways and byways of love, passion, and relationships.

Mahmud Shabistari (Persia, d. 1320)

Like Rumi, Shabistari combines Sufi teaching and love poetry in a beautiful and unique way. His "Secret Rose Garden" contains some of the clearest expressions of mystical states in relation to everyday life experiences. Shabistari also finds the divine in every drop and particle of the natural world, and his poetry reemphasizes the primary Sufi understanding of the created Universe, not as flawed or sinful, but as a variegated window through which we can view the divine Reality.

Nizamuddin Auliya (India, d. 1325)

Nizamuddin Auliya was one of the successors of Moineddin Chishti, and the disciple of another great Indian Sufi, Farid Ganj-i-Shakar. One of his major works was *Morals of the Heart*.

Shams Al-Din Hafiz (Persia, d. 1389)

Hafiz's poetry shows us a mystic bewildered and intoxicated by love, expressing spiritual truths through images that are both humorous and profound. From many of his poems, it is difficult to say whether Hafiz is talking about passionate love between human beings or between human beings and the divine. It is perhaps enough to emphasize his insistence on love as the nexus of the universe, and the development of the heart, whether through human relationships or devotion, as the most important goal.

Fatima Jahanara (India, d. 1681)

Granddaughter of the Mogul Emperor Akbar and daughter of Shah Jehan, builder of the Taj Mahal, Fatima Jahanara inherited both a universal spiritual outlook and a love for creating beauty as a spiritual practice. Fatima prefigured many later developments in Indian Sufism, including its emphasis on art, music, and poetry.

Ahmad Hatif (Persia, d. 1794)

A Sufi from Isfahan, Ahmad Hatif wrote a famous epic poem describing the soul's journey to the Beloved, entitled *The Tarji Band*. In it, the seeker visits a Zoroastrian fire temple, a church, and a tavern and finds that everyone is really worshipping the same reality behind all the various forms.

Inayat Khan (India, d. 1927)

Born in Baroda, India, into a musical family, Inayat Khan became in his youth a virtuoso vina player. In the fulfillment of his quest for a spiritual teacher, Inayat Khan took initiation from Shaykh al-Mashaykh Sayed Muhammed Abu Hashim Madani. While he was an initiator of the four main Sufi lineages in India, Madani's primary connection was with the Chishti Order. At the end of his apprenticeship, Inayat Khan was enjoined by his teacher to travel to the West and harmonize the two cultures. He came to the West as a representative of the musical traditions of his native India, and brought with him a message of love, harmony, and beauty that was both the quintessence of Sufi teaching and a revolutionary approach to the harmonizing of Western and Eastern spirituality. During his sixteen years in the West, he created a school of spiritual training based on the traditional teachings of the Chishti Sufis and infused with a revolutionary vision of the unity of religious ideals and the awakening of humanity to the divinity within.

Samuel L. Lewis, Sufi Ahmed Murad Chishti (United States, d. 1971)

Samuel L. Lewis was a student of Pir-o-Murshid Inayat Khan (1882–1927) and was initiated as a murshid (senior teacher) in the Chishti lineage by Pir Barkat Ali of Pakistan in 1962. Samuel Lewis was a lifelong student of comparative spirituality and mysticism, in particular Zen Buddhism, Hinduism, and Kaballah, as well as a trained horticulturist and gardener. He traveled widely in Egypt, Pakistan, India, and Japan, visiting various spiritual teachers as well as sharing information about organic and other "green" farming methods. He involved himself in the early stages of what was later known as citizen diplomacy. He expressed his main peace plan as: "Eat, pray, and dance together." Toward the end of his life he started a form of group sacred movement called the Dances of Universal Peace.

Moulana Shah Maghsoud (Iran, d. 1980)

Maghsoud was among the most influential Sufis of the Oveysi Mashrab in Persia. Oveysis relate themselves to the contemporary of the Prophet Muhammad, Uways Al-Qarani, who was initiated by and received a direct inner transmission from the Prophet even though they never met in body. His father, Hazrat Mir Ghotbeddin Mohammad, was one of the great Sufis and scholars of his time; his mother was Khorshid, a descendant of one of the old Persian families. Moulana Shah Maghsoud worked for more than four decades to construct the bridge between spirituality and science. In one of his books, *Traditional Medicine,* he described the future of science from the 1960s up to the year 2000, as well as forecast many recent developments in genetic engineering and its applications to medicine.

Bawa Muhaiyaddeen (Sri Lanka, d. 1986)

Muhammad Raheem Bawa Muhaiyaddeen was a revered Sufi saint from the island of Sri Lanka who for more than fifty years selflessly shared his knowledge and experience with people of every race and religion and from all parts of the world. Little is known of his early personal history. Records of his life begin in the early 1900s, when religious pilgrims traveling through the jungles of Sri Lanka first caught a glimpse of a holy man. Some time later a pilgrim invited him to a nearby village, and with that began his public life as a teacher of wisdom. He first came to the United States in 1971 and established the Bawa Muhaiyaddeen Fellowship of North America in Philadelphia. Since then, branches have spread throughout the United States and Canada, as well as in Sri Lanka, Australia, and the UK.

Nur Al-Jerrahi, Lex Hixon (d. 1995)

The student of Shaykh Muzaffer Ashki Al-Jerrahi, Lex Hixon was a spiritual explorer in many paths. He delved particularly deeply into Hinduism, Buddhism, and Islam, and he authored nine books. His first book, *Coming Home: The Experience of Enlightenment in Sacred Traditions,* became a classic of comparative spirituality in 1978. In the Sufi tradition, his writings included a commentary and interpretation of the Qur'an titled *The Heart of the Qur'an,* as well as *101 Diamonds from the Oral Tradition of the Glorious Messenger Muhammad.* His work is continued through the Nur Ashki Jerrahi Sufi Order.

Idries Shah, Sayed Idries el-Hashimi (India-Afghanistan, d. 1996)

Born into a Sufi family, to an Afghani father and a Scottish mother, Shah was author of more than thirty-five books and over a hundred academic monographs. The books included twenty titles on Sufism, including the bestselling *The Sufis.* His public and formal work, as Director of Studies of the Institute for Cultural Research, began when Shah was in his thirties. This educational charity researched and published materials on cross-cultural patterns of human thought and behavior. He attempted to educate others to become multifaceted, high-achieving, dedicated to the service of others, and also in the best sense "ordinary."

Irina Tweedie (Russia, d. 1999)

Tweedie was born in Russia in 1907 and educated in Vienna and Paris. Eventually she moved to England, where, distraught by the premature death of her husband, she began to search for the meaning of life, especially through the Theosophical Society. When she was fifty-four, her search took her to India, where she met her Sufi Teacher Bhai Sahib (in Hindi, Elder Brother). Her years in his company, until his death in 1966, were an intense period of trial, which prepared her to contact the spiritual presence of her teacher after his death. She is well known for her spiritual autobiography *The Daughter of Fire,* and her work continues with The Golden Sufi Center.

Moineddin Jablonski (United States, d. 2000)

Spiritual successor to Samuel L. Lewis, Jablonski steadfastly held the vision to spread the message of love, harmony, and beauty through spiritual practice, healing and environmental service, and conscious community involvement. One of his great contributions was his emphasis on Soulwork, a psychospiritual counseling approach that promotes objective clarity within the individual so one may heal his or her wounds and unite the different and unique personal identities carried within. To this end he worked diligently, blending the Hawaiian way of thought with ancient and modern psychology. He was well versed in and wrote poetry, and was recognized as accomplished in the Eastern mystic traditions.

Vilayat Inayat Khan (England, d. 2004)

Son of Hazrat Inayat Khan and until his passing the spiritual director and Pir of the Sufi Order in the West. His contributions to the dialogue between Sufism, modern psychology, and science in many world colloquia remains unequaled. He sponsored international interfaith activities and promoted social action as an integral part of spiritual life, particularly with the creation of the Hope Project in Delhi, India. He developed and disseminated the spiritual teachings of his father, Pir-o-Murshid Hazrat Inayat Khan, and the ancient Sufis and traveled extensively to deliver those teachings to a broad audience. He wrote many books, notably *Introducing Spirituality into Counseling and Therapy, That Which Transpires Through That Which Appears,* and his masterful evocation of the wisdom of the greatest Sufi sages, *In Search of the Hidden Treasure: A Conference of Sufis.*

Contacts for Sufi Teachings

The Bawa Muhaiyaddeen Fellowship serves as a "pond," where individuals can gather to contemplate the truth and unity of God. Outwardly, this is done by studying the teachings and example of M. R. Bawa Muhaiyaddeen through the countless hours of audio- and videocassettes of his discourses, many of which have also been compiled into books. Inwardly, this is done by slowly cleansing oneself through prayer and by bringing these teachings into one's daily actions. Contact: 5820 Overbrook Avenue, Philadelphia, PA 19131-1221, USA. Tel.: 215-879-6300 (24-hour answering machine). Fax: 215-879-6307. e-mail: info@bmf.org. Web site: www.bmf.org.

The Golden Sufi Center is the vehicle for the work of the Naqshbandiyya-Mujaddidiyya Order of Sufism. Naqshbandi Sufis are known as silent Sufis because they practice a silent heart meditation and silent *dhikr*. The Golden Sufi Center also publishes books about Sufism, including *Daughter of Fire,* by Irina Tweedie, and several books by Llewellyn Vaughan-Lee. Contact: P.O. Box 428, Inverness, California 94937, USA. Tel.: 415 663-8773. Fax: 415-663-9128. e-mail: info@goldensufi.org. Web site: www.goldensufi.org.

The International Association of Sufism was founded by Nahid Angha, Ph.D., and Shah Nazar Seyed Ali Kianfar, Ph.D., in 1983, and through the efforts of many Sufi masters and the contributions of Sufi orders and schools, and with the help of scholars, educators, translators, and artists interested in the discipline of Sufism, the Association has come a long way toward successfully accomplishing its founding goals. The IAS is a global, nonprofit educational organization dedicated to promoting peace in the spirit of Sufism. Currently, the achievement of the International Association of Sufism has made the organization a DPI Non-Governmental Organization of the United Nations. The IAS promotes education through a variety of methods, including academic classes, lectures, conferences, and Sufi gatherings. IAS offers classes, lectures, and workshops on Sufism, Psychology, Music and Poetry, Interfaith issues, and many other subjects in the San Francisco Bay Area, the greater Seattle Area, and throughout the United States and the world. Contact: 14 Commercial Blvd., Suite 101, Novato, California 94949, USA. Tel.: 415-382-SUFI. e-mail: ias@ias.org. Web site: www.ias.org.

The Institute for Sufi Studies (ISS) is an educational department of the International Association of Sufism (IAS). The Institute for Sufi Studies offers classes directly through its centers, online through the Internet, and at other educational institutions. The faculty are practitioners of Sufism and teachers in many diverse disciplines, including religion, literature, psychology, philosophy, sociology, and physics. Contact: 14 Commercial Blvd., Suite 101, Novato, California 94949, USA. Tel.: 415-382-7834.

The Mevlevi Order of America continues the authentic Sufi tradition of the whirling dance as prayer founded by the mystic poet Jelaluddin Rumi seven centuries ago. The dervish practice is an expression of joy from the heart, a path of mystical love and union. Combining music, poetry, prayers, and songs in Arabic, Persian, Turkish, and English, the spiritual practices of the Mevlevi are a form of divine Remembrance. The Mevlevi way was brought to the West in the 1970s by Suleyman Hayati Dede. His son, Jelaluddin Loras, is the director of the Mevlevi Order of America, a tax-exempt, nonprofit religious organization. Besides traditional Mevlevi teachings and practices—Sema (the "Turning"), ritual circles for Zikr Allah (Divine Remembrance), and Sobhet (Sacred Discourse)—Postneshin Jelaluddin has instituted new expressions of the traditional dervish teachings, appropriate to North America. There are centers in the United States, Canada, Europe, and Konya, Turkey. Contact: Mevlevi Order of America, c/o P.O. Box 175, Kula, HI 96790, USA. e-mail: info@hayatidede.org. Web site: www.hayatidede.org.

The Nur Ashki Jerrahi Sufi Order is a community of dervishes within the Halveti-Jerrahi Tariqat, in the specific lineage and spirit of Sheikh Muzaffer Ashki Al-Jerrahi, Sheikh Nur Al-Jerrahi, and Sheikha Fariha Al-Jerrahi. They are based at Masjid Al-Farah in New York City, with various circles throughout the United States and Mexico. They welcome seekers and students of all religious and nonreligious paths into their gatherings. Contact: Tel.: 212-334-5212. Web site: www.nurashkijerrahi.org.

The Sufi Movement International was founded by Hazrat Inayat Khan with the following objects: 1) To realize and spread the knowledge of Unity, the religion of love and wisdom, so that the bias of faiths and beliefs may of itself fall away, the human heart may overflow with love, and all hatred caused by distinctions and differences may be rooted out; 2) to discover the light and power latent in man, the secret of all religion, the power of mysticism, and the essence of philosophy, without interfering with customs or beliefs; 3) to help to bring the world's two opposite poles, East and West, close together by the interchange of thought and idea; that the universal brotherhood may form of itself, and may meet with man beyond the narrow national and racial boundaries. The Sufi Movement is organized in five separate Activities: the Brotherhood/Sisterhood Activity, Universal Worship, The School of Inner Culture or the Esoteric Activity, Spiritual Healing, and Symbology. The work is carried out by local, regional, and national representatives. Contact: International Headquarters of the Sufi Movement, 24 Banstraat, 2517 GJ Den Haag, Netherlands. e-mail: IHQ@sufimovement.org. Web site: www.sufimovement.org.

The Sufi Order International exists to spread the message of unity and promote the awakening of humanity to the divinity in all, as taught by Pir-o-Murshid Inayat Khan and continued by Pir Vilayat Inayat Khan (d. 2004) and Pir Zia Inayat Khan; to provide a program of spiritual training to bring about a deep personal transformation, culminating in a balanced, harmonious, and creative life; to develop spiritual guides capable of giving authentic training in the inner life; to find new ways to apply the spiritual ideals of love, harmony, and beauty to the challenges and opportunities of everyday life; to serve God and humanity by helping to relieve suffering, promoting understanding and acceptance among adherents of various faiths, and encouraging the unfolding of universal loving kinship. Contact: Sufi Order International, North American Secretariat, 5 Abode Rd., New Lebanon, NY 12125, USA. Tel.: 518-794-7834. e-mail: secretariat@sufiorder.org. Web site: www.sufiorder.org.

The Sufi Ruhaniat International continues the work of Sufi Ahmed Murad Chishti (Pir-o-Murshid Samuel L. Lewis) and Pir-o-Murshid Moineddin Jablonski. *Ruhaniat* means the "way of transformation through the breath and soul." Along with the Dances of Universal Peace, the spiritual practice of the Ruhaniat includes prayer, walking meditation; sound, breath, and heart concentration and contemplation in the Chishti tradition; work with *sifat* (divine qualities) and *zat* (divine essence), and Soulwork. The path of initiation and discipleship is the central theme of the Ruhaniat, which has open study groups in North and South America, Europe, Russia, and Australia. Contact: Sufi Ruhaniat International Secretariat, P.O. Box 51118, Eugene, OR 97405, USA. Tel.: 541-345-5223. e-mail: ruhaniat@mail.com. Web site: www.ruhaniat.org.

The International Network for the Dances of Universal Peace continues the interfaith and interspiritual work in sacred movement and "peace through the arts" begun by Samuel Lewis. The Network provides contacts and resource materials, including recordings, books, and organizational guidance for the growing number of circles using the Dances. Teachers of the Dances represent many faith and spiritual traditions, including Islam, Buddhism, Christianity, Judaism, Taoism, and Hinduism. The current repertoire of the Dances celebrate an expanding number of spiritual traditions of humanity. The Dances are currently being used in therapy, education, citizen diplomacy, and worship, in clinics, halfway houses, hospitals, prisons, and schools (from primary to graduate level). Contact: www.dancesofuniversalpeace.org.

The Threshold Society, rooted within the traditions of Sufism and inspired by the life and work of Mevlana Jalaluddin Rumi, is a nonprofit educational foundation with the purpose of facilitating the experience of divine unity, love, and wisdom in the world. The Society is affiliated with the Mevlevi Order, and offers training programs, seminars, and retreats around the world. These are intended to provide a structure for practice and study within Sufism and spiritual psychology. Our programs and activities are open to people of all faiths. Contact: The Threshold Society, 151 Emerald City Way, Watsonville, CA 95076, USA. Web site: www.sufism.org.

The Halveti-Jerrahi Order of Dervishes is a traditional Muslim Sufi Order. They are a cultural, educational, and social relief organization made up of Muslims from diverse professional, ethnic, and national backgrounds. The Jerrahi Order has branches in Turkey, New York, California, Illinois, Washington, Bosnia, Germany, Greece, Italy, France, England, Spain, Canada, Mexico, Argentina, Chile, and Brazil. The way starts with knowledge. Under the protection of knowledge one grows to be a gentle, kind, and beautiful being, as all were created to be. Contact: Halveti-Jerrahi Order of America, 884 Chestnut Ridge Road, Chestnut Ridge, NY 10977 USA. Tel. (845) 352-5518. e-mail: info@jerrahi.org. Web site: www.jerrahi.org

Formal Transliterations of the Pathways of the Heart

Arabic has various *h, k, g,* and *t* sounds that cannot be spelled properly in normal English script. These formal transliterations are for those who wish to use this book as a resource along with or in comparison to other Arabic language or transliterated versions of the practice.

Allah	Al Mudhill	Ash Shahīd
Ar Raḥmān	As Samīʿ	Al Ḥaqq
Ar Raḥīm	Al Baṣīr	Al Wakīl
Al Mālik	Al Ḥakam	Al Qawī
Al Quddūs	Al ʿAdl	Al Matīn
As Salām	Al Laṭīf	Al Walī
Al Muʾmin	Al Khabīr	Al Ḥamīd
Al Muhaimin	Al Ḥalīm	Al Muḥṣī
Al ʿAziz	Al ʿAzīm	Al Mubdī
Al Jabbār	Al Ghafūr	Al Muʿīd
Al Mutakabbir	Ash Shakūr	Al Muḥyī
Al Khāliq	Al ʿAlī	Al Mumīt
Al Bāriʾ	Al Kabīr	Al Ḥayy
Al Muṣawwir	Al Ḥafiz	Al Qayyūm
Al Ghaffār	Al Muqīt	Al Wājid
Al Qahhār	Al Ḥasīb	Al Mājid
Al Wahhāb	Al Jalīl	Al Wāhid
Ar Razzāq	Al Karīm	Al Aḥad
Al Fattāḥ	Ar Raqīb	Aṣ Ṣamad
Al ʿAlim	Al Mujīb	Al Qādir
Al Qābiḍ	Al Wāsiʿ	Al Muqtadir
Al Bāsit	Al Ḥakīm	Al Muqaddim
Al Khāfiḍ	Al Wadūd	Al Muʾakhkhir
A Rāfiʿ	Al Majīd	Al Awwal
Al Muʿizz	Al Bāʿith	Al Ākhir

Aẓ Ẓāhir	Mālik ul Mulk	An Nūr
Al Bāṭin	Dhūl Jalāl wal Ikrām	Al Hādī
Al Wāli	Al Muqsiṭ	Al Bādī'
Al Muta'ālī	Al Jāme'	Al Bāqī
Al Barr	Al Ghanī	Al Wārith
At Tawwāb	Al Mughnī	Ar Rashīd
Al Muntaqim	Al Māni'	Aṣ Ṣabūr
Al 'Afūw	Aḍ Ḍārr	
Ar Ra'ūf	An Nāfi'	

Acknowledgments

To the International Association of Sufism, for permission to print excerpts from the poetry of Moulana Shah Maghsoud Sadegh Angha from Nahid, Angha, *Ecstasy: The World of Sufi Poetry and Prayer* (San Rafael: International Association of Sufism, 1998), pp. 104–105; and from Hamaseh Kianfar and Sahar Kianfar, *Sufi Stories* (San Rafael: International Association of Sufism, 1996), p. 62. Printed by permission from the International Association of Sufism (www. ias.org).

To Hohm Press, for permission to reprint an excerpt from Vraje, Abramian, *Nobody, Son of Nobody: Poems of Shaikh Abu-Saeed Abil-Kheir* (Prescott, AZ: Hohm Press, 2001), p. 44. Web site: www.hohm press.com.

To the Bawa Muhaiyaddeen Fellowship, for permission to reprint two excerpts from M. R. Bawa Muhaiyaddeen, *Islam and World Peace: Explanations of a Sufi* (The Bawa Muhaiyaddeen Fellowship, 1987), pp. 34 and 126.

To Quest Books, for permission to reprint excerpts from the words of Lex Hixon, *The Heart of the Qur'an: An Introduction to Islamic Spirituality* (Wheaton, Ill.: Quest, 1988). Web site: www.questbooks.net.

To Pir Publications, for permission to reprint excerpts from Lex Hixon and Fariha al-Jerrahi, *101 Diamonds from the Oral Tradition of the Glorious Messenger Muhammad* (New York: Pir Press, 2002). Web site: www.sufibooks.com/pirpress.html.

To the Golden Sufi Center, for permission to reprint the words of Irina Tweedie, from an interview posted at its Web site: www. goldensufi.org.

To the Sufi Movement International and the Sufi Order International, for permission to reprint excerpts from the writings of Hazrat Pir-o-Murshid Inayat Khan.

International Headquarters of the Sufi Movement
24 Banstraat
2517 GJ
Den Haag, Netherlands
email: IHQ@sufimovement.org
Web site: www.sufimovement.org

Sufi Order International
North American Secretariat
5 Abode Rd.
New Lebanon, NY 12125 USA
email: secretariat@sufiorder.org
Web site: www.sufiorder.org

To the Sufi Ruhaniat International, for permission to reprint excerpts from the writings of Murshid Samuel L. Lewis (Sufi Ahmed Murad Chishti) and Murshid Moineddin Jablonski.

Sufi Ruhaniat International Secretariat
P.O. Box 51118
Eugene, OR 97405 USA
email: ruhaniat@mail.com
Web site: www.ruhaniat.org

To Tom Grady, my literary agent, for his patient and persistent work in support of this book over a number of years, and to Janet Goldstein, Lucia Watson, and the staff of Viking Penguin for their help with and faith in this project.

To Murshid Moineddin Jablonski, whose guidance saved my life and made this book possible.

And to my partner, Kamae Amrapali Miller, for her continued and continual love and support traveling through the pathways of the heart.

Notes

1. Massud Farzan, *The Tale of the Reed Pipe* (New York: Dutton, 1974), p. xv.
2. Ibid., pp. 63–64.
3. Hazrat Inayat Khan, *Gathekas for Candidates by Pir-o-Murshid Hazrat Inayat Khan,* PDF edition 1999 (Eugene, OR: Sufi Ruhaniat International, 1926), p. 11.
4. M. R. Bawa Muhaiyadden, *Asma'Ul-Husna: The 99 Beautiful Names of Allah* (Philadelphia, PA: Fellowship Press, 1979), pp. 155, 157.
5. Gospel of Thomas, Logion 70, as translated by the author from the Coptic text and with reference to various literal translations including Grondin (1988), Guillaumont et al. (1959) and Patterson (1998). See a similar translation by the author in Douglas-Klotz, *The Genesis Meditations: A Shared Practice of Peace for Christians, Jews, and Muslims* (Wheaton, IL: Quest Books, 2003).
6. Idries Shah, *Caravan of Dreams* (Baltimore: Penguin, 1968), p. 204.
7. From a hadith transmitted by Abu Said al-Khudri. This and following versions of hadith by the author, unless otherwise annotated.
8. Hazrat Inayat Khan, *The Complete Sayings of Hazrat Inayat Khan* (New Lebanon: Omega Publications, 1978), pp. 239, 244, 245.
9. Translated in Nahid Angha, *Ecstasy: The World of Sufi Poetry and Prayer* (San Rafael, CA: International Association of Sufism, 1998), p. 100.
10. From a Hadith transmitted by Abu Hurayra.
11. Ibid.
12. Ibid.
13. Hazrat Inayat Khan (1978), op. cit., p. 49.
14. Meditation on the Arabic text of Qur'an *Sura* 2.245 by the author.
15. Version by the author, adapted from a similar one in Douglas-Klotz (1995).
16. From a hadith transmitted by Abu Hurayra. This version in L. Hixon and Al-Jerrahi, *101 Diamonds from the Oral Tradition of the Glorious Messenger Muhammad* (New York: Pir Press, 2002), p. 144.

17. Meditation on the Arabic text of the Qur'an by the author.
18. This and following versions of Rumi by the author, based on Rumi's talks in A. J. Arberry, *Discourses of Rumi* (London: John Murray, 1961).
19. From a hadith transmitted by Anas Ibn Malik, collected by Ibn Al-Arabi.
20. Hazrat Inayat Khan (1978), op. cit. p. 33.
21. Ibid., p. 164.
22. Interview with Irina Tweedie in *The Laughing Man* magazine, 1987, posted at www.goldensufi.org.
23. Vraje Abramian, trans., *Nobody, Son of Nobody: Poems of Shaikh Abu-Saeed Abil-Kheir* (Prescott, AZ: Hohm Press, 2001), p. 48.
24. Version in L. Hixon, and Al-Jerrahi (2002), op. cit., p. 141.
25. Ibid., p. 53.
26. Hazrat Inayat Khan (1999), *Commentary on "The Path of Initiation and Discipleship" with Commentary by Murshid Samuel L. Lewis (Sufi Ahmed Murad Chishti)*, PDF edition (Eugene, OR: Sufi Ruhaniat International, 1999), p. 50.
27. Ibid., p. 86.
28. Retold by the author from a story attributed by Idries Shah to the sixteenth-century Balkan Sufi Sayed Jafar, of the Gulshani order. See Shah (1968), op. cit., pp. 185–86.
29. Translated in Nahid Angha (1998), op. cit., pp. 104–105.
30. Samuel L. Lewis, *Forty Lessons on Breath*, PDF edition (Eugene, OR: Sufi Ruhaniat International, 2000), p. 6.
31. This passage from Matthew 5:12 is usually translated, "Rejoice and be exceedingly glad." For a more complete translation, see Douglas-Klotz, *Prayers of the Cosmos: Meditations on the Aramaic Words of Jesus* (San Francisco: HarperSanFrancisco, 1990), p. 72.
32. Op. cit., *Laughing Man* interview, posted at the Golden Sufi Center Web site.
33. Hazrat Inayat Khan (1978), op. cit., pp. 40, 165.
34. Samuel L. Lewis, *Gayaniat: A Commentary on the Gayan of Pir-o-Murshid Hazrat Inayat Khan*, PDF edition (Eugene, OR: Sufi Ruhaniat International, 1999), p. 36.
35. From a hadith transmitted by Anas Ibn Malik, collected by Ibn Al-Arabi.
36. Meditation on the Arabic text of the Qur'an by the author.
37. Version in Hixon and Al-Jerrahi (2002), op. cit., p. 51.

38. Samuel L. Lewis, *Sadhana: The Path of Attainment: A Commentary on the Papers of Pir-o-Murshid Hazrat Inayat Khan,* PDF edition (Eugene, OR: Sufi Ruhaniat International, 1999), pp. 33–34.

39. Samuel L. Lewis, *The Bestowing of Blessing,* PDF edition (Eugene, OR: Sufi Ruhaniat International, 1999), p. 63.

40. M. R. Bawa Muhaiyaddeen, *Islam and World Peace: Explanations of a Sufi* (Philadelphia: Fellowship Press, 1987), p. 126.

41. Moineddin Jablonski, *The Gift of Life: Sayings and Poems of a Modern Sufi* (forthcoming), (Seattle, WA: Peaceworks, 2005).

42. Samuel L. Lewis, *Shafayat: Healing: A Commentary on the Book of Health of Pir-o-Murshid Hazrat Inayat Khan,* PDF edition (Eugene, OR: Sufi Ruhaniat International, 1999), p. 48.

43. Moineddin Jablonski (2005), op. cit.

44. M. R. Bawa Muhaiyaddeen (1987), op. cit., p. 34.

45. Lex Hixon, *The Heart of the Qur'an: An Introduction to Islamic Spirituality* (Wheaton, IL: Quest Books, 2003), p. 204.

46. Translated in Hamaseh Kianfar and Sahar Kianfar, *Sufi Stories* (San Rafael, CA: International Association of Sufism, 1996), p. 62.

47. Hazrat Inayat Khan (1978), op. cit., p. 54.

48. Vilayat Inayat Khan, "Sufism and Jungian Psychology," in J. Marvin Spiegelman, et al., *Sufism, Islam and Jungian Psychology* (Scottsdale, AZ: New Falcon Publications, 1991), p. 37.

49. Meditation on the Arabic text of the Qur'an by the author.

50. Hazrat Inayat Khan (1978), op. cit., p. 56.

51. Lex Hixon (2003), op. cit., pp. 225, 226.

52. Op. cit., *Laughing Man* interview, posted at the Golden Sufi Center Web site.

53. Ibid.

54. For more on this subject, see Morris Berman, *Wandering God: A Study in Nomadic Spirituality* (Albany: State University of New York Press, 2000).

55. For more on this, see Douglas-Klotz (1990), op. cit., pp. 53–54.

56. Moineddin Jablonski (2005), op. cit.

Bibliography

Abramian, Vraje. *Nobody, Son of Nobody: Poems of Shaikh Abu-Saeed Abil-Kheir.* Prescott, AZ: Hohm Press, 2001.

Ahmad, Aftab-ud-din, trans. *Futuh Al-Ghaib: Revelation of the Unseen.* Lahore: Sh. Muhammad Ashraf, 1973.

Ali, Yusuf A., trans. *The Holy Qur'an: Text, Translation, and Commentary.* Lahore: Sh. Muhammad Ashraf, 1938.

Alim Islamic Software: Qur'an (Arabic version and translations by Asad, Malik, Pickthall, Yusuf Ali), Hadith (Abu-Dawood, Al-Bukhari, Al-Muwatta, Al-Tirmidhi, Fiq-us-Sunnah, Muslim) and other References. Silver Springs, MD: ISL Software, 2000. Web site: www.islsoftware.com.

Angha, Nahid. *Ecstasy: The World of Sufi Poetry and Prayer.* San Rafael: International Association of Sufism, 1998.

Arberry, A. J. *Discourses of Rumi.* London: John Murray, 1961.

———, ed. *The Ruhbaiyat of Omar Khayyam and Other Persian Poems.* New York: Dutton, 1975.

Arnold, Edwin. *Pearls of the Faith.* Lahore: Sh. Muhammad Ashraf, 1961.

Attar, Farid ud-Din. *The Conference of the Birds.* C. S. Nott, trans. Boulder: Shambhala, 1971.

Austin, R.W.J. *Ibn Al 'Arabi: The Bezels of Wisdom.* Mahwah, NJ: Paulist Press, 1980.

Berman, Morris. *Wandering God: A Study in Nomadic Spirituality.* Albany: State University of New York Press, 2000.

Burckhardt, Titus. *The Wisdom of the Prophets: Fusus al-Hikam.* Aldsworth: Beshara Publications, 1975.

Clarke, H. Wilberforce. *The Divan of Khwaja Shamsu-d-Din Muhammad-i-Hafiz-i-Shirazi.* (Reprint of the 1891 edition.) London: Octagon Press, 1974.

Cowan, J. Milton and Hans Wehr, eds. *Dictionary of Modern Written Arabic.* Ithaca, NY: Spoken Language Services, Inc., 1976.

D'Olivet, Fabre. *Hebraic Tongue Restored.* Nayan Louise Redfield, trans. (1921 edition republished 1991.) York Beach, ME: Samuel Weiser, 1815.

Douglas-Klotz, Neil. *Prayers of the Cosmos: Meditations on the Aramaic Words of Jesus.* San Francisco: HarperSanFrancisco, 1990.

———. *Desert Wisdom: Middle Eastern Tradition from the Goddess to the Sufis.* San Francisco: HarperSanFrancisco, 1995.

———. *The Hidden Gospel: Decoding the Spiritual Message of the Aramaic Jesus.* Wheaton, IL: Quest Books, 1999.

———. "Re-hearing Qur'an in open translation: ta'wil, postmodern inquiry and a hermeneutics of indeterminacy." Paper presented in the Arts, Literature, and Religion Section of the American Academy of Religion Annual Meeting: Toronto, Ontario, Canada, November 23, 2002, on the theme of Hermeneutics.

———. *The Genesis Meditations: A Shared Practice of Peace for Christians, Jews, and Muslims.* Wheaton, IL: Quest Books, 2003.

Elliger, K. and W. Rudolph, eds. *Biblia Hebraica Stuttgartensia.* Stuttgart: Deutsche Bibelgesellschaft, 1966/67.

Farzad, Houman. *Classic Tales of Mulla Nasreddin.* Costa Mesa, CA: Mazda Publishers, 1989.

Farzan, Massud. *The Tale of the Reed Pipe: Teachings of the Sufis.* New York: E. P. Dutton, 1974.

Fischer, Ron. *Also sprach Mulla Nasrudin: Geschichten aus der wirklichen Welt.* München: Knauer Verlag, 1993.

Feyerabend, Karl. *Langenscheidt's Hebrew-English Dictionary of the Old Testament.* Berlin and London: Methuen & Co., 1955.

Gibb, H.A.R. and J. H. Kramers. *Concise Encyclopedia of Islam.* Boston and Leidin: Brill Academic Publishers, 2001.

Hirtenstein, Stephen. *The Unlimited Mercifier: The Spiritual Life and Thought of Ibn 'Arabi.* Oxford and Ashland, OR: Anqa Publishing and White Cloud Press, 1999.

Hixon, Lex. *The Heart of the Qur'an: An Introduction to Islamic Spirituality.* Wheaton, IL: Quest Books, 2003.

Hixon, Lex and Fariha Al-Jerrahi. *101 Diamonds from the Oral Tradition of the Glorious Messenger Muhammad.* New York: Pir Press, 2002.

Jablonski, Moineddin. *The Gift of Life: Sayings and Poems of a Modern Sufi* (forthcoming). Seattle: Peaceworks Publications, 2005.

Jamshidi, Y. *Selected Poems of Hafiz: Persian Text and Translations.* Tehran, Iran, 1963.

Khalidi, Tarif. *The Muslim Jesus: Sayings and Stories in Islamic Literature.* Cambridge and London: Harvard University Press, 2001.

Khan, Hazrat Inayat. *Gathekas for Candidates*. PDF Edition, 1999. Eugene, OR: Sufi Ruhaniat International, 1926.

———. *The Complete Sayings of Hazrat Inayat Khan*. New Lebanon, NY: Omega Publications, 1978.

Khan, Hazrat Inayat and Samuel Lewis. *Commentary on "The Path of Initiation and Discipleship" by Murshid Samuel L. Lewis (Sufi Ahmed Murad Chishti)*, PDF edition. Eugene, OR: Sufi Ruhaniat International, 1999.

Khan, Vilayat Inayat. "Sufism and Jungian Psychology." In J. Marvin Spiegelman, et al., *Sufism, Islam and Jungian Psychology*. Scottsdale, AZ: New Falcon Publications, 1991.

Kianfar, Hamaseh and Sahar Kianfar. *Sufi Stories*. San Rafael, CA: International Association of Sufism, 1996.

Lane, Edward W. *An Arabic-English Dictionary in Eight Volumes*. Kesrouwan, Lebanon: Librairie du Liban, 1989.

Lane-Poole, Stanley. *Speeches and Table Talk of the Prophet Mohammad*. Lahore: Sh. Muhammad Ashraf, 1975.

Lawrence, Bruce. *Nizam Ad-Din Awliya: Morals for the Heart*. New York: Paulist Press, 1992.

Lederer, Florence, trans. *The Secret Rose Garden of Sa'd Ud Din Mahmud Shabistari*. Lahore: Sh. Muhammed Ashraf, 1920.

Lewis, Samuel L. *Gayaniat: A Commentary on the Gayan of Pir-o-Murshid Hazrat Inayat Khan*, PDF edition. Eugene, OR: Sufi Ruhaniat International, 1999.

———. *Sadhana: The Path of Attainment: A Commentary on the Papers of Pir-o-Murshid Hazrat Inayat Khan*, PDF edition. Eugene, OR: Sufi Ruhaniat International, 1999.

———. *Shafayat: Healing: A Commentary on the Book of Health of Pir-o-Murshid Hazrat Inayat Khan*. PDF edition. Eugene, OR: Sufi Ruhaniat International, 1999.

Lipinski, Edward. *Semitic Languages: Outline of a Comparative Grammar*. Leuven: Peeters, 1997.

Muhaiyaddeen, M. R. Bawa. *Asma 'ul Husna: The 99 Beautiful Names of Allah*. Philadelphia: Fellowship Press, 1979.

———. *Islam and World Peace: Explanations of a Sufi*. Philadelphia: Fellowship Press, 1987.

Nakosteen, Mehdi. *The Maxims of Sa'di*. Boulder: Este Es Press, 1977.

Nicholson, R. A. *Selected Poems from the Divani Shamsi Tabriz*. Cambridge: Cambridge University Press, 1898.

———. *Tales of Mystic Meaning: Selections from the Mathnawi of Jalal-ud-Din Rumi.* Oxford: Oneworld, 1995.

Omar, Abdul Mannan. *The Dictionary of The Holy Qur'an.* Hockessin, DE: Noor Foundation, 2003.

Renard, John, ed. *Windows on the House of Islam: Muslim Sources on Spirituality and Religious Life.* Berkeley: University of California Press, 1998.

Schimmel, Annemarie. *Mystical Dimensions of Islam.* Chapel Hill: University of North Carolina Press, 1975.

———. *Deciphering the Signs of God: A Phenomenological Approach to Islam.* Albany: State University of New York Press, 1994.

Sells, Michael. *Early Islamic Mysticism: Sufi, Qur'an, Miraj, Poetic and Theological Writings.* New York: Paulist Press, 1996.

———. *Approaching the Qur'an: The Early Revelations.* Ashland, OR: White Cloud Press, 1999.

Shah, Idries. *Caravan of Dreams.* Baltimore: Penguin, 1968.

Siddiqi, Abdul Hamid. *Sahih Muslim: Being Traditions of the Sayings and Doings of the Prophet Muhammad as Narrated by His Companions and Compiled Under the Title Al-Jami'-us-Sahih,* Vols I–IV. Lahore: Sh. Muhammad Ashraf, 1976.

Siddiqi, Muhammad Iqbal. *Ninety-Nine Names of Allah.* Delhi: Adam Publishers, 1988.

Smith, J. Payne, ed. A Compendious Syriac Dictionary. Oxford: Clarendon Press, 1903.

Smith, Margaret. Readings from the Mystics of Islam. Westport, CT: Pir Press, 1994.

Tweedie, Irina. "Both Feet Fimly on the Ground: Reflections by Irina Tweedie." First published by *Laughing Man* magazine, 1987. Posted at www.goldensufi.org. Inverness, CA: Golden Sufi Center.

The Abwoon Study Circle offers books, recordings, and information about workshops and retreats that support the work in this book. It can be contacted in the USA at P.O. Box 361655, Milpitas, CA 95036-1655. e-mail: Selim@abwoon.com. Connections with the Abwoon Study Circle internationally, as well as the small study groups that arise from it, can also be contacted via the Web site: www.abwoon.com, which posts a continually updated list of events, links, and publications.

The work of the author in Scotland, the UK, and Europe is also supported by the Edinburgh Institute for Advanced Learning, www.eial.org.

For articles, interviews, supporting information, and links to pronunciation and other sites related to the Sufi pathways of the heart and this book, see the following Web site: www.sufibookoflife.com.

Index

Abil Khayr, Abu Sa'id, 129, 195–96,
    259, 276
Abraham, 85
abundant expression, 113–15
action, embodying power in, 192–94
Ahmad Hatif, 256–57, 279
Ahmed, Shemseddin, 154
Aisha, 275
Al-Ghazali, Abu Hamid, 138, 221,
    276–77
Al-Hallaj, Mansur, 181, 276
Al-Hujwiri, Abul Hasan, 233, 238, 276
Ali, Imam, 52, 98, 113, 208, 275
Ali, Pir Barkat, 280
Al-Qarani, Uways, 280
Al-Qushayri, Abul Qasim, 84, 248, 276
Arnold, Edwin, xxi
ashes, blowing away, 226–27
assessing what is, 156–57
Attar, Fariduddin, 51, 137, 166–67,
    211, 227, 267, 277
Auliya, Nizamuddin, 39, 279

bathing in unity, 5, 34, 61–62, 89–91,
    121, 152–53, 183, 213–14, 243,
    273–74
Bawa Muhaiyaddeen, M. R., xxii, xxiii,
    216, 223–24, 280–81, 283
Bawa Muhaiyaddeen Fellowship, 283
beauty and power, overwhelming,
    233–35
beginning of the universe, 17–18,
    35–36, 100, 158
beginning the journey, 1–3
Bhai Sahib, 282
Bistami, Abu Yazid, 184, 276
Blake, William, 154
blessing, immediately useful, 250–52
blessings, flowing, 45–46, 47
blowing away the ashes, 226–27
boundaries
    contracting, 54–55
    expanding, 56–67

breath, Unity's, opening to, 49–50
burnishing, 218–20

carried away, being, 64, 89, 90–91, 145
carving and forming, 32–33
center, holding, 189–91
Chacour, Elias, 39
chains, dissolving, 84–86
challenges, meeting, 142–44
change, winds of, 145–46
charisma, 131–32, 163, 193
Chishti, Moineddin, 172, 277, 279
compassion, 8, 9, 10, 22, 192, 229
completion, 203–5
concentration, 29–31
consciousness, expanded, 215–17
contracting boundaries, 54–55
creation, 32–33
    individuated, 158–59
    of the universe, 17–18, 35–36, 100,
        158
creativity, 15
    outward, 100–102
    radiating, 35–36

David, 236
death, 134, 135, 166–67
designing and training, 37–38
details, feeling divinity in, 108–9
Dhu'l Nun Al Misri, 204, 268, 275–76
diminishment, 58–60
discriminating wisdom, 125–27
doubling back on the path, 198–200

earth, 24, 25
Eckhart, Meister, 69
ecstasy, 89, 90–91, 97
Elijah, 256
energy, life, 15, 22, 48, 126, 189
    dazzling, 131–33
    personal, 131–33, 163–65
    universal, 168–71
exaltation, 63–64

expanded consciousness, inhabiting, 215–17
expanding boundaries, 56–57
expression, abundant, 113–15
extraordinary power, channeling, 177–79
extraordinary sensing, 174–76
Ezekiel, 160

Farid Ganj-i-Shakar, 279
Farzan, Massud, xviii–xix
Fatima, 98, 275
Fatima Jahanara, 42–43, 279
Fatima of Nishapur, 204, 275
flexible strength, 87–88
forgiveness, 40–41
   of light, 92–94
form, strength of, 24–26
forming and carving, 32–33
forms and names, understanding, 51–53
foundation, new, 236–37
friendship, 150–51

garden:
   of life, 244–45
   tending, 241–42
gathering gems, 238–40
give and take, 128–30
Golden Sufi Center, 283
gratitude, giving back, 95–96
growth, illuminating path of, 267–69
guidance, most direct, 256–58

Hafiz, Shams Al-Din, xvii, 9, 147–48, 279
Hakim Sanai, 19, 128–29
Halveti-Jerrahi Order of Dervishes, 287
Hazrat Mir Ghotbeddin Mohammad, 280
healing, 27–28
   wings, 228–29
hearing, awakened, 70–71
heart:
   burnishing of, 218–20
   as garden, 241–42
   increasing capacity of, 122–24
   sweeping out, 223–25
heaven, 24
Heraclitus, 248
hidden traveler, 208–9

Hildegard of Bingen, 267
Hixon, Nur (Nur Al-Jerrahi), 238–39, 259, 281
hurt and tension, burning away, 39–41

Iblis, 276
Ibn Arabi, Muhyi Al-Din, xviii, xxii, 180–81, 195, 206, 278
"I can" power of the cosmos, 12–13, 14, 16
illuminating the path of growth, 267–69
Inayat Khan, xviii, xix, 39–40, 54, 95, 116, 119, 150, 177–78, 185, 219, 250, 256, 279–80
Inayat Khan, Hazrat, xxiv, 282, 285
Inayat Khan, Pir-o-Murshid Hazrat, 280, 282, 285
Inayat Khan, Vilayat, 253–54, 282
individuated creation, 158–59
inheritance, reclaiming, 264–66
Institute for Sufi Studies, 284
intelligence, light of, 93, 253–55
International Association of Sufism, 283–84
International Network for the Dances of Universal Peace, 286
Ismail, 85

Jablonski, Moineddin, xxiv, 58, 218, 221, 271, 282, 286
Jesus, xxiv, 2, 4, 7, 12, 13, 15, 18, 22, 30, 47, 50, 52, 60, 96, 172, 173, 195, 206, 210, 222, 223, 228, 236, 259, 265–66
Jilani, Abdul Qadir, 27, 29, 31, 277
journey, setting out on, 1–3
justice, 77, 78, 236

Kabir, 168
Khorshid, 280

Lewis, Samuel L. (Sufi Ahmed Murad Chishti), xx, xxiv, 85, 102, 137–38, 150, 168–69, 178, 210–11, 215, 219, 280, 282, 286
Leyla and Majnun, 137
life's larger garden, 244–45
light:
   forgiveness of, 92–94
   illuminating the path of growth, 267–69
   of intelligence, 93, 253–55

limits, 122–24
listening, reflective, 119–20
loss and pain, 248–49
love, xvii, xviii, xxi, xxix, 30, 36, 40, 45, 164
  as give and take, 128–30
  moon of, 8, 9–11
  sun of, 7–8

Madani, Shaykh al-Mashaykh Sayed Muhammed Abu Hashim, 279
Maghsoud, Moulana Shah, 42, 163, 241, 280
Majnun and Leyla, 137
mastering life, 210–12
Mevlevi Order of America, 284
moment:
  assessing what is in, 156–57
  truth in, 140–41
moon, 119
  of love, 8, 9–11
Moses, 34
Mu'adha, 275
Muhammad, Prophet, xxiv, xxvi, 10, 18, 20, 28, 34, 35, 47–48, 49, 51–52, 67–68, 70, 89, 92–93, 95, 98, 129, 131–32, 138, 151, 180, 183, 189–90, 206, 226, 233–34, 275, 280
Muzaffer Ashki Al-Jerrahi, Shaykh, 281
mystery, subtle, 80–81

names and forms, understanding, 51–53
Nasruddin, Mullah, 9–10, 47, 58–59, 61, 63–64, 75, 77–78, 89–90, 91, 108–9, 110–11, 125–26, 142–43, 147, 152, 156, 169, 187, 198–99, 213, 236–37, 265, 273–74
natural power, 42–44
nature, 42, 45, 264
new roots, new foundation, 236–37
no and yes of existence, 4–6, 98
Nur Ashki Jerrahi Sufi Order, 284–85

one:
  counting to, 180–82
  uniquely, 184–85
order, putting things in, 77–79

pain and loss, 248–49
passionate vision, 230–32

path of growth, illuminating, 267–69
peace at the beginning, 17–18
peak, experiencing life at its, 97–99
perseverance, 270–72
persistence, step-by-step, 147–49
potential, seed of, 82–83
power, 189–90
  in action, embodying, 192–94
  building up, 110–12
  extraordinary, channeling, 177–79
  "I can," 12–13, 14, 16
  natural, 42–44
  overwhelming, 233–35
preparing the way, 195–97
presence, watching with, 116–18
preservation, 103–5
protection, 21–23
purpose, gift of, 154–55

Rabia Al-Adawiyya, 117, 231, 275
real that remains, 261–63
rebounding, 172–73
reclaiming a forgotten inheritance, 264–66
reflective listening, 119–20
refuge for every need, 186–88
remembrance, 18, 103–5
repair and restoration, 27–28
resistance, 246–47
returning to rhythm, 221–22
return of what passes away, 134–36
reviving what is worn down, 160–62
rhythm, returning to, 221–22
roots, new, 236–37
Rumi, Jelaluddin, xvii, xviii, xxi, xxii, xxvii, 4–5, 14, 24, 30, 32, 37, 41, 47, 49–50, 54–55, 65, 67–68, 80–81, 87, 89–90, 91, 97, 100–101, 106, 113, 121, 122, 134–35, 140, 145, 174–75, 183, 201, 208, 218–19, 226–27, 230–31, 233–34, 243, 246, 248, 250, 257, 261–62, 265, 270–71, 277, 278
Ruqayya, 128, 156

Saadi, Muslihuddin, xviii, 1, 21, 45, 82, 190, 278
sacred sixth sense, 74–76
sacred space, 14–16
sacred surprise, 201–2
St. Denis, Ruth, 146

St. Paul, 21
Sana'i, Abul Majdud, 277
self, xxiii, xxviii, xxix, 49, 261
    high self-esteem, 65–66
    low self-esteem, 66, 67–69
sensing, extraordinary, 174–76
setting out on the journey, 1–3
Shabistari, Mahmud, 7–8, 56, 95–96,
    154–55, 203–4, 223, 228, 244,
    278
Shah, Idries, Sayed Idries el-Hashimi,
    29–30, 281
Shams-i-Tabriz, xviii, 183, 278
Shemsuddin Ahmed, Hazrat Haji,
    xxiv–xxv
sight, awakened, 72–73
sixth sense, sacred, 74–76
space, sacred, 14–16
star, 206–7
steady state, embodying, 106–7
step-by-step persistence, 147–49
strength, 29
    flexible, 87–88
    of form, 24–26
    pooling, 110–12
Sufi Movement International, 285
Sufi Order International, 285
Sufi Ruhaniat International, 286
Suhrawardi, Shihab Al-Din, 253–54,
    277, 278
sun, 119
    of love, 7–8
support, 19–20
surprise, sacred, 201–2
sustenance, 47–48
sweeping out, 223–25

tension and hurt, burning away, 39–41
thankfulness, 96
Threshold Society, 286
Thunder, Perfect Mind, 68
training and designing, 37–38
transition, 166–67
trust, 20, 22
truth in each moment, 140–41
Tweedie, Irina, 122–23, 174, 261, 262,
    281–82

unexpected wonder, 259–60
uniquely one, 184–85
Unity, xxii–xxiii, xxviii
    bathing in, 5, 34, 61–62, 89–91,
        121, 152–53, 183, 213–14, 243,
        273–74
    counting to one, 180–82
    experiencing universe of, 137–39
    opening to breath of, 49–50
universe:
    creation of, 17–18, 35–36, 100,
        158
    of unity, experiencing, 137–39

vision, passionate, 230–32
vision-power, 12–13, 14, 16

watching with presence, 116–18
Waterhouse, Frida, xxiv
Whitman, Walt, 154, 241
wisdom, discriminating, 125–27
wonder, 264
    unexpected, 259–60

yes and no of existence, 4–6, 98